COME
EL

The Story of the Sikeston Jaycee Bootheel Rodeo

60th Anniversary Edition

Acclaim Press
MORLEY, MISSOURI

Trick rider performing for the Jaycee Bootheel Rodeo fans.

Acclaim Press
— Your Next Great Book —

P.O. Box 238
Morley, MO 63767
(573) 472-9800
www.acclaimpress.com

Publishing Consultant: John E. Ruedrich
Authors: Daniel C. Beck and Charlie Francis
Book Design: Kimberly M. Paul
Cover Design: M. Frene Melton
Researcher: Ron Eifert

Library of Congress Cataloging-in-Publication Data

Beck, Daniel, 1979-
The story of the Jaycee Bootheel Rodeo / by Daniel Beck and Charlie Francis.
pages cm
ISBN 978-1-938905-31-5 (alk. paper)
ISBN 1-938905-31-8 (alk. paper)
1. Jaycee Bootheel Rodeo--History. I. Francis, Charlie, 1955- II. Title.
GV1834.55.M82S553 2013
791.8'4097789--dc23

2013019638

First Printing: 2013
Printed in the United States of America
10 9 8 7 6 5 4 3 2 1

This publication was produced using available information. The publisher regrets it cannot assume responsibility for errors or omissions.

CONTENTS

To the Fans....................5

Part 1: The History of the Jaycee Bootheel Rodeo....................9

Chapter One: The Sikeston Jaycees and the Birth of the Rodeo....................10

Chapter Two: The First Rodeo....................14

Chapter Three: New Traditions....................20

Chapter Four: Celebrities Come to Sikeston....................24

Chapter Five: The Rodeo Gets a New Home....................29

Chapter Six: The Rodeo Becomes a Business....................32

Chapter Seven: New Month, New Bleachers....................36

Chapter Eight: One Era Ends, Another Begins....................40

Chapter Nine: A Singer, an Organization and a Town....................42

Chapter Ten: A "Four-Star" Rodeo....................50

Chapter Eleven: Keeping the Ball Rolling....................54

Chapter Twelve: The Tradition Continues....................56

Part 2: The People Behind the Jaycee Bootheel Rodeo....................63

The Sikeston Jaycees....................64

Art Saunders....................69

The Jaycee Bootheel Rodeo and the Pro Rodeo Hall of Fame....................74

PRCA and WPRA....................76

Stock Contractors....................83

Rick Young: Serious About Being Funny....................85

The Fans....................87

Part 3: The Traditions of the Jaycee Bootheel Rodeo....................91

The Rodeo Parade....................92

Rodeo Royalty....................94

The SEMO Shrine Mounted Patrol and Scott County Sheriff's Posse....................98

Part 4: The Entertainers of the Jaycee Bootheel Rodeo....................99

Part 5: Images From 60 Years of Rodeo....................164

Index....................189

A
Coors
RODEO

TO THE FANS

The fans of the Jaycee Bootheel Rodeo–the reason for our rodeo and this book. From the Loy Baugher collection.

SIKESTON JAYCEES

Dear Reader,

On behalf of the Sikeston Jaycees, I would first like to thank you for purchasing this book, and if you have made it this far, for reading this book. Similar to every project we undertake, there has been a substantial effort by several individuals to make this project possible.

The Jaycees have made an incredible impact on the community of Sikeston and several communities in the surrounding area. Although many don't realize it, there is much more to the Jaycees than the rodeo. Throughout each year, we assist with several events in the area in addition to providing monetary donations to a number of local charitable groups. There have been countless incredible people involved with this organization that have sacrificed beyond measure to ensure the successes that we have enjoyed.

However, none of this would be possible without the support of all of the people in the community that have sacrificed their time and money to partake in and help in the production of those events. With the Sikeston Jaycee Bootheel Rodeo now in its 61st year and the Sikeston Jaycee Crawfish Boil just finishing up on a record breaking 4th year, the support of the community from sponsors to patrons has been nothing short of spectacular.

We hope that you have enjoyed reading this book and we look forward to everyone's continued support of our efforts for years to come.

Sincerely,

Ross Merideth
2013 Sikeston Jaycee President

Post Office Box 485 • Sikeston, Missouri 63801

Dear Readers,

I would like to thank the Sikeston Jaycees for allowing me the privilege of compiling and composing a written record of our rodeo over the past 60 years. I myself have been a member of the club for almost a decade and have served as the club president; rodeo board member, and current rodeo co-chairman, which made the experience of looking back in time and watching our event evolve into what has become today a real pleasure.

This, of course, would not have been possible if not for the stories and recollection of a number Jaycees from over the years as well as long time patrons, some of whom have attended almost every rodeo since its beginning. I offer my personal thanks for taking the time to sit down with us and give a first person account of your experiences with the rodeo.

On a similar note, I would like to give huge thanks to the Standard-Democrat newspaper. The Sikeston Jaycees annually turn over all of their leadership positions which makes it difficult to record on paper the goings on from year to year. Enter the Standard-Democrat. Their reporters and photographers have provided, for all intents and purposes, the only recorded history of the Sikeston Jaycee Bootheel Rodeo for the past six decades. Many of the accounts you will read about are due to articles in the Standard-Democrat. I, along with the Jaycee club, would like to extend our gratitude for your support throughout the years.

I would like to thank Doug Sikes, Charlie Francis and the rest of the staff at Acclaim Press for their patience and assistance while I tried to do justice to the story of our rodeo. Anyone can write, but it takes a publisher to edit and fine tune and I think you'll find that they did a superb job. Charlie even took the time to research every entertainer that has graced the arena and compiled biographies on them all which proves very interesting. I extend my thanks to him and numerous contributions he makes throughout the book.

It took so many people to make this book a reality that I refrain from naming individuals for fear that I'll leave someone out. However, there is one man that I must personally thank because without him I would never been exposed to the rodeo in the way that I have been. Lee Beck, my father, served as general chairman in 1981 and continued his service to the club all the way up to 2006 when he passed away. Not only did he stay involved, he also allowed me to hang around while he did it, thus making the rodeo a very large and distinct part of my childhood. Writing about him and his friends was surreal to say to the least, but growing up around them made the experience all the more special. So thank you, dad, for the opportunity to grow up at "the grounds," allowing me to one day have the opportunity to honor it in this way.

Last I would like to thank the most important part of the rodeo – the fans. YOU, the fans are the reason the first rodeo happened and you're still the reason the next one will happen. You're also the reason this book has been published and I sincerely hope that you enjoy reading it as much as I have enjoyed writing it.

Thank You,

Daniel C. Beck
Sikeston Jaycees

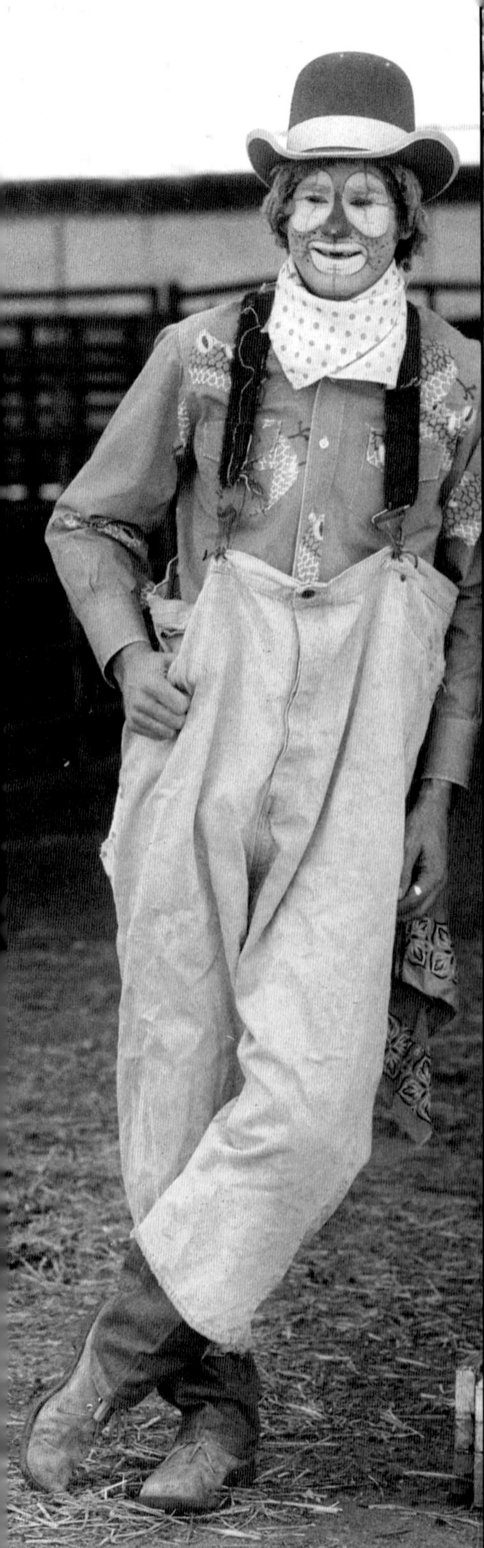

Jaycee Bootheel Rodeo Clowns entertaining the fans.

"Say ahhhh!" Clown "Dr." Jimmy Anderson gives Sarah Lasater a throat exam as other children look on during the 1992 rodeo.

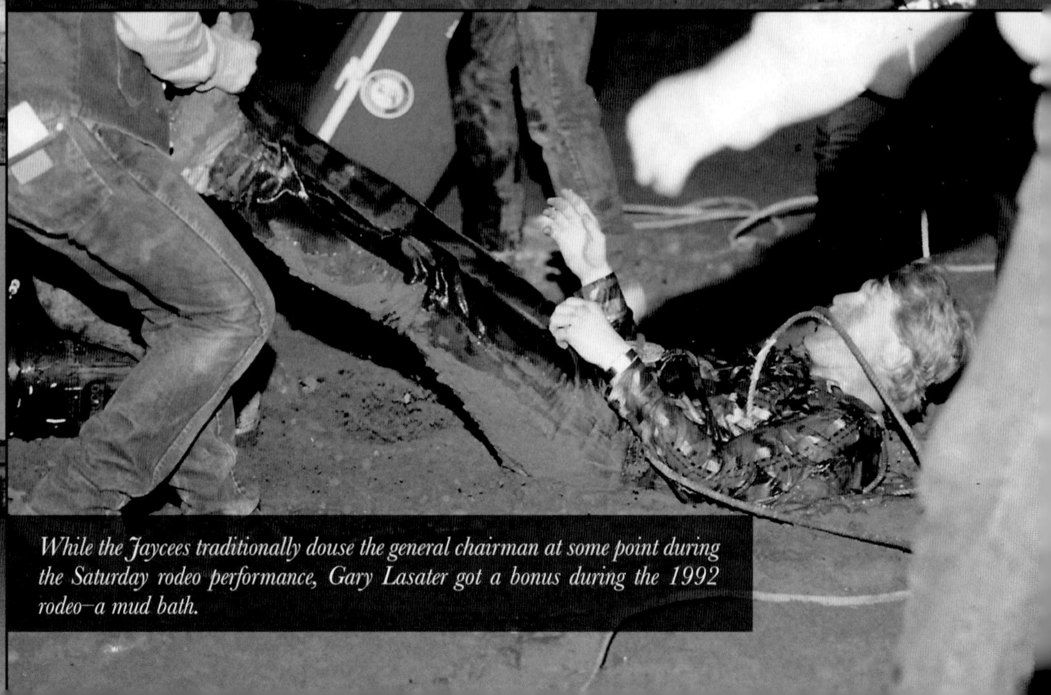

While the Jaycees traditionally douse the general chairman at some point during the Saturday rodeo performance, Gary Lasater got a bonus during the 1992 rodeo—a mud bath.

THE HISTORY OF THE JAYCEE BOOTHEEL RODEO

PART 1

CHAPTER ONE

The Sikeston Jaycees and the Birth of the Rodeo

As the sun struggled to make its final stand in the western sky, a long shadow cast itself across the diamond shaped arena. Thousands stood with their hand patriotically held over their hearts as they watched the flag ripple in the wind just above the horse and rider who majestically paraded it for the entire crowd to see. All were silent as they listened to the national anthem boom from the large speakers. Behind the red and white bucking chutes dozens of cowboys stood, hat in hand, as they silently prepared themselves for the contest they had traveled great distances to compete in. Their competition could sense this and the occasional sound of a bronc horse challenging the slide gates cut its way through the thick August air. The crowd began a slow roar as the flag made its final pass and the child sang the final notes. Excitement buzzed in the warm air as the flag girl raced out of the arena and, as if on cue, the first gladiator of the night nodded his head and chute number five exploded open to reveal a bucking mass of hooves, hair and chaps. At that moment, where the asphalt ends and the rodeo begins, everyone in the crowd felt like a cowboy and cheered wildly for both horse and rider. As the ride ended and the bronc rider slid over the rear of the pick-up horse, the crowd gave one last cheer and settled in for a night of rodeo and entertainment.

Year after year the crowd gathers in the bleachers to watch this display of animal versus rider. This is the story of the men, women and animals that have made this possible for one community over the past 60 years. This is the story of a group of individuals coming together in support of something bigger than themselves. This is the story of the Sikeston Jaycee Bootheel Rodeo and its journey from infancy to becoming a community icon.

The Sikeston Jaycees

In nearly every small town in America you can find at least one service organization or group of individuals who donate their time and services to enrich their community and make it a better place to live and work. Located at the confluence of Interstate 55 and Interstate 57 in Southeast Missouri, Sikeston has the good fortune of containing not one, but many active service organizations whose main purpose is enhancing Sikeston and the surrounding area through volunteering labor, resources, or money to various projects and charities in the region. However, one club stands out as having the most economic impact in the region, as well as having the honor of hosting one of the region's largest and well-known events.

Art Saunders, whose dream of a Sikeston rodeo came true. From the Loy Baugher collection.

The Sikeston Junior Chamber of Commerce, founded in 1934, holds this honor. It is composed primarily of young men in the community who share a common goal in making not only the community of Sikeston, but also the surrounding area a better place. A volunteer organization, the Junior Chamber of Commerce, better known as the Sikeston Jaycees, works to put on various projects throughout the year in order to raise money that is donated to various other charities and non-profit organizations in the community. One event, the Sikeston Jaycee Bootheel Rodeo, takes place every year in August. The Jaycee Bootheel Rodeo not only has the distinction of being the largest rodeo event in the region, but also has the honor of being one of the top 25 rodeos in the entire nation. Every year, the rodeo not only features the top ranked cowboys in the Professional Rodeo Cowboys Association (aka, PRCA), many of which compete in the National Finals Rodeo at the end of the season, but it also features top country music and rock and roll acts every night. This combination provides thousands of local fans and some that travel annually from across the nation with a second-to-none rodeo performance followed by an entertaining concert all in one evening. The proceeds from this event are then donated back into the community through various channels.

Not only do the Jaycees provide monetary donations to organizations within the community, the Sikeston Jaycee Bootheel Rodeo alone packs every hotel room and restaurant in town, bringing an estimated $8 million dollars in revenue to the area's businesses during rodeo week. Fans and contestants from around the country flock to the 11,000-seat arena every year to celebrate their love for cowboy culture and sing along with their favorite recording artists during the post-performance concerts. It has become an institution in the community and for the past 60 years has grown side-by-side with Sikeston to become one of Southeast Missouri's premier events.

Over the past six decades, fans of the Sikeston Jaycee Bootheel Rodeo have had the pleasure of cheering on rodeo legends such as Lane Frost, Donnie Gay and Trevor Brazil, just to name a few. Not only has the rodeo always provided top level competition, it has also played host to a number of celebrity performers ranging from actor James Arness to recording artist Garth Brooks. And while many people take for granted that the Jaycees never fail to bring a little taste of the old west to the heartland every year in August, many people are unaware that 60 years ago the Sikeston Jaycee Bootheel Rodeo came dangerously close to never happening.

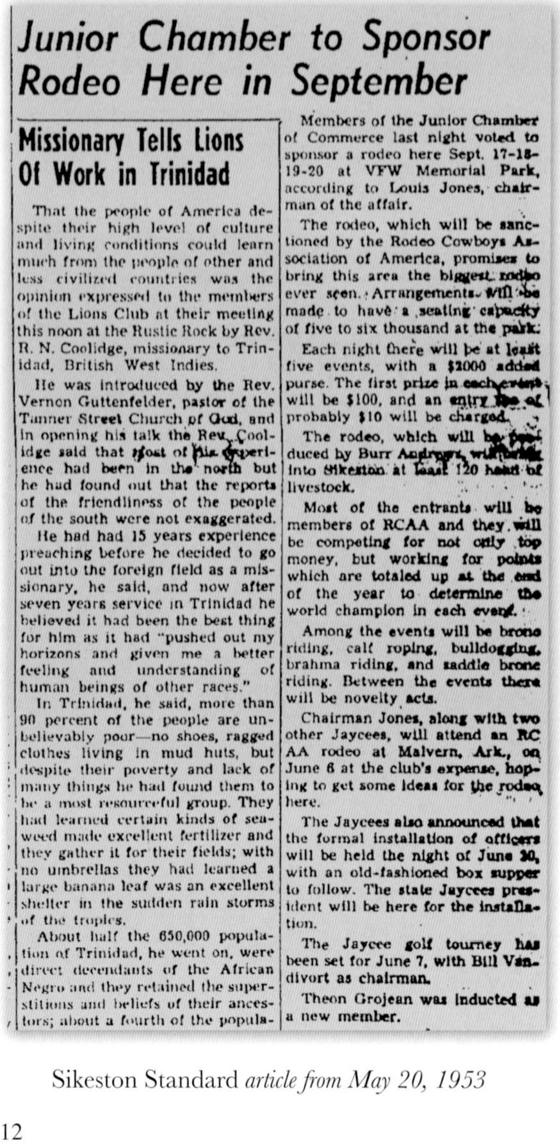

Junior Chamber to Sponsor Rodeo Here in September

Members of the Junior Chamber of Commerce last night voted to sponsor a rodeo here Sept. 17-18-19-20 at VFW Memorial Park, according to Louis Jones, chairman of the affair.

The rodeo, which will be sanctioned by the Rodeo Cowboys Association of America, promises to bring this area the biggest rodeo ever seen. Arrangements will be made to have a seating capacity of five to six thousand at the park.

Each night there will be at least five events, with a $2000 added purse. The first prize in each event will be $100, and an entry fee of probably $10 will be charged.

The rodeo, which will be produced by Burr Andrews, will bring into Sikeston at least 120 head of livestock.

Most of the entrants will be members of RCAA and they will be competing for not only top money, but working for points which are totaled up at the end of the year to determine the world champion in each event.

Among the events will be bronc riding, calf roping, bulldogging, brahma riding, and saddle bronc riding. Between the events there will be novelty acts.

Chairman Jones, along with two other Jaycees, will attend an RCAA rodeo at Malvern, Ark., on June 6 at the club's expense, hoping to get some ideas for the rodeo here.

The Jaycees also announced that the formal installation of officers will be held the night of June 30, with an old-fashioned box supper to follow. The state Jaycees president will be here for the installation.

The Jaycee golf tourney has been set for June 7, with Bill Vandivort as chairman.

Theon Grojean was inducted as a new member.

Missionary Tells Lions Of Work in Trinidad

That the people of America despite their high level of culture and living conditions could learn much from the people of other and less civilized countries was the opinion expressed to the members of the Lions Club at their meeting this noon at the Rustic Rock by Rev. R. N. Coolidge, missionary to Trinidad, British West Indies.

He was introduced by the Rev. Vernon Guttenfelder, pastor of the Tanner Street Church of God, and in opening his talk the Rev. Coolidge said that most of his experience had been in the north but he had found out that the reports of the friendliness of the people of the south were not exaggerated.

He had had 15 years experience preaching before he decided to go out into the foreign field as a missionary, he said, and now after seven years service in Trinidad he believed it had been the best thing for him as it had "pushed out my horizons and given me a better feeling and understanding of human beings of other races."

In Trinidad, he said, more than 90 percent of the people are unbelievably poor—no shoes, ragged clothes living in mud huts, but despite their poverty and lack of many things he had found them to be a most resourceful group. They had learned certain kinds of seaweed made excellent fertilizer and they gather it for their fields; with no umbrellas they had learned a large banana leaf was an excellent shelter in the sudden rain storms of the tropics.

About half the 650,000 population of Trinidad, he went on, were direct decendants of the African Negro and they retained the superstitions and beliefs of their ancestors; about a fourth of the popula-

Sikeston Standard *article from May 20, 1953*

The Rodeo That Almost Wasn't

In 1952, the Sikeston Jaycees consisted of 35 members. One of the members, Louis Jones, had an uncle named Art Saunders who sold flour for a Kansas City milling company. Over his fifteen years as a traveling salesman, the Blodgett native had attended a number of rodeos and become an ardent fan of the sport. During a visit to Sikeston in the fall of 1952, Saunders pitched the idea of having a rodeo in Sikeston to his nephew Louis. Art was certain that a rodeo would put Sikeston on the map and it didn't take long to sell the idea to Jones, who promised to bring it up at the next Jaycee meeting.

Unfortunately for Jones, the idea of bringing a rodeo to Sikeston wasn't met with a very warm reception. Most of the club members had never seen a rodeo and were very skeptical of the idea of putting on what they pictured as a "wild west show." Jones had his work cut out for him trying to erase the images of actors dressed as cowboys and Indians chasing each other around with pistols. However, in the end, Louis finally convinced his fellow members that rodeo wasn't just an exhibition, but a legitimate athletic competition.

Common misconception about the sport of rodeo at the time was only the first hurdle Louis Jones and the other supporters within the club faced. Much of the membership doubted the Sikeston market would support a rodeo. This was Southeast Missouri, not Texas or Oklahoma. People here raised cotton and beans, and horses were meant for work not pleasure. The notion of riding a bull or roping a calf instead of eating it sounded pretty farfetched to the people who had never witnessed such an event. Many members thought that there wasn't a very good chance that ten thousand people would show up and pay two dollars just to see a rodeo. However, Jones' resolve failed to waiver and over time, even though for months the issue remained in a heated debate, he began to win over support from his fellow Jaycees. By the spring of 1953, the Jaycee members seemed evenly divided over the issue and decided that the time for debating was over and the time to put the matter to a vote was at hand.

May 19, 1953 might seem like an obscure date to many, but the events of that Tuesday evening would forever change the Sikeston Jaycee organization as well the community of Sikeston. That evening, 31 Jaycee members gathered for their weekly club meeting. A vote to decide whether or not the club would put on a rodeo in the fall was the main issue on the agenda. After the many months of debating, which was described as "a hell of an argument," the motion was made and a vote was taken. When the dust was settled and the votes were counted the "ayes" had it sixteen votes to fifteen. The Sikeston Jaycees were in the rodeo business and, 60 years later, still are.

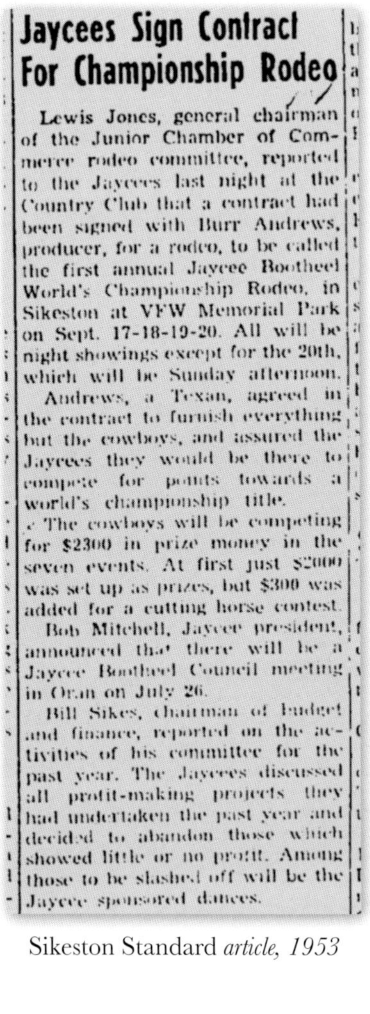

Jaycees Sign Contract For Championship Rodeo

Lewis Jones, general chairman of the Junior Chamber of Commerce rodeo committee, reported to the Jaycees last night at the Country Club that a contract had been signed with Burr Andrews, producer, for a rodeo, to be called the first annual Jaycee Bootheel World's Championship Rodeo, in Sikeston at VFW Memorial Park on Sept. 17-18-19-20. All will be night showings except for the 20th, which will be Sunday afternoon.

Andrews, a Texan, agreed in the contract to furnish everything but the cowboys, and assured the Jaycees they would be there to compete for points towards a world's championship title.

The cowboys will be competing for $2300 in prize money in the seven events. At first just $2000 was set up as prizes, but $300 was added for a cutting horse contest.

Bob Mitchell, Jaycee president, announced that there will be a Jaycee Bootheel Council meeting in Oran on July 26.

Bill Sikes, chairman of budget and finance, reported on the activities of his committee for the past year. The Jaycees discussed all profit-making projects they had undertaken the past year and decided to abandon those which showed little or no profit. Among those to be slashed off will be the Jaycee sponsored dances.

Sikeston Standard *article, 1953*

Jaycees Select Name For Championship Rodeo

The Junior Chamber of Commerce, meeting last night at the Country Club, selected a name for the rodeo they will sponsor here in September and it will be called the first annual Jaycee Bootheel World's Championship Rodeo, according to Bob Mitchell, club president.

Mitchell also announced the appointment of the following committees for the rodeo. Lewis Jones will serve as general chairman of the event and Mitchell will act as co-chairman.

Committee heads are: Publicity, Shad Old, chairman, and Don Pasaka, co-chairman; ticket and purchasing agents, Alton McCann and Milford Estes; concessions, Pat Groves and Bill Puckett; grounds, Faye Thompson and Bill Huff; program, Mark Childs and Nat Watkins; and parking, Harold Boardman and Theon Grojean.

Leslie Chandler, a high school senior sponsored by the Jaycees at Boy's State last week at Warrensburg, gave a brief talk on his experiences while in Warrensburg.

Bill Paylor was admitted as a new Jaycee member last night. Guests were Frank Tull and Tanner Dye.

Sikeston Standard *article from June 24, 1953*

CHAPTER TWO

The First Rodeo

On May 20, 1953, the day after the Sikeston Jaycees voted to put on a rodeo, the *Sikeston Standard* printed the following article on the front page:

> *"Members of the Junior Chamber of Commerce last night voted to sponsor a rodeo here September 17, 18, 19, 20 at VFW Memorial Park, according to Louis Jones, chairman of the affair. The rodeo, which will be sanctioned by the Rodeo Cowboys Association of America, promises to bring this area the biggest rodeo ever seen. Arrangements will be made to have a seating capacity of five to six thousand at the park."*

The article followed up with details of the events and noted that $2,300 in prize money was to be given out.

Even though the decision had been made to go forward with the new project, the Jaycees still had to figure out how to put on a rodeo. Since the only thing they knew of the sport had come from the stories told to them by Art Saunders, the club sent Jones and two other members to an RCAA rodeo in Malvern, AR to get some new ideas. They returned with ideas about how a rodeo should be run, but in the end decided to hire a professional rodeo producer to help them out rather than try to put on a new event themselves with little or no experience. In June, the Jaycees hired rodeo producer and stock contractor Burr Andrews, a Texan who, according to the Standard, promised to "furnish everything but the cowboys." Andrews assured the Jaycees that the prize money coupled with the world championship points they would be competing for would bring the cowboys stampeding into Sikeston.

Planning Begins

Two key things happened at the June 23rd meeting that year. First off, Louis Jones was named the first-ever general chairman of the rodeo and Bob Mitchell was named co-chairman. Next, they broke up the rodeo into separate areas or committees and appointed an area chairman to each one. Shad Old and Don Pasaka headed up the publicity committee, Alton McCann and Milford Estes would coordinate purchasing and ticket sales, Pat Groves and Bill Puckett were placed in charge of concessions while Mark Childs and Nate Watkins would handle the programs. Faye Thompson and Bill Huff took on the task of preparing the grounds and Harold Boardman and Theon Grojean were tasked with parking. To this day, the Jaycees still name a general chairman and co-chairman each year as well as assign each individual area a chair and co-chairman much in the same way as their rodeo founding fathers did that day.

Jaycee Tom Nunnelee, who failed to dress in western attire in the days before the rodeo, gets a public bath in a trough at Legion Park. Assisting with the dunking are Brad Wilson, Larry Lund, Rob Henley, Ken Walters and Jim Warf.

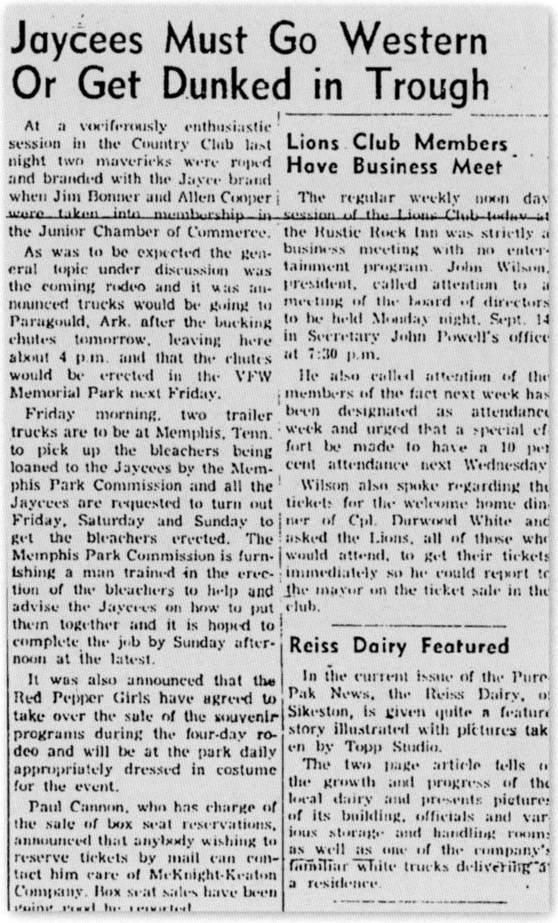

Jaycees Must Go Western Or Get Dunked in Trough

At a vociferously enthusiastic session in the Country Club last night two mavericks were roped and branded with the Jaycee brand when Jim Bonner and Allen Cooper were taken into membership in the Junior Chamber of Commerce.

As was to be expected the general topic under discussion was the coming rodeo and it was announced trucks would be going to Paragould, Ark. after the bucking chutes tomorrow, leaving here about 4 p.m. and that the chutes would be erected in the VFW Memorial Park next Friday.

Friday morning, two trailer trucks are to be at Memphis, Tenn. to pick up the bleachers being loaned to the Jaycees by the Memphis Park Commission and all the Jaycees are requested to turn out Friday, Saturday and Sunday to get the bleachers erected. The Memphis Park Commission is furnishing a man trained in the erection of the bleachers to help and advise the Jaycees on how to put them together and it is hoped to complete the job by Sunday afternoon at the latest.

It was also announced that the Red Pepper Girls have agreed to take over the sale of the souvenir programs during the four-day rodeo and will be at the park daily appropriately dressed in costume for the event.

Paul Cannon, who has charge of the sale of box seat reservations, announced that anybody wishing to reserve tickets by mail can contact him care of McKnight-Keaton Company. Box seat sales have been [illegible]

Lions Club Members Have Business Meet

The regular weekly noon day session of the Lions Club today at the Rustic Rock Inn was strictly a business meeting with no entertainment program. John Wilson, president, called attention to a meeting of the board of directors to be held Monday night, Sept. 14 in Secretary John Powell's office at 7:30 p.m.

He also called attention of the members of the fact next week has been designated as attendance week and urged that a special effort be made to have a 10 per cent attendance next Wednesday.

Wilson also spoke regarding the tickets for the welcome home dinner of Cpl. Darwood White and asked the Lions, all of those who would attend, to get their tickets immediately so he could report to the mayor on the ticket sale in the club.

Reiss Dairy Featured

In the current issue of the Pure Pak News, the Reiss Dairy, of Sikeston, is given quite a feature story illustrated with pictures taken by Topp Studio.

The two page article tells of the growth and progress of the local dairy and presents pictures of its building, officials and various storage and handling rooms as well as one of the company's familiar white trucks delivering at a residence.

Sikeston Standard *article from the summer of 1953*

With the organizational matters taken care of, the club still had one more thing to decide on that night, a name for the event. According to Bob Porter, the club had settled on "Sikeston Jaycee Rodeo" as a name for the event. Porter remembers Shad Old, an insurance agent with a gift for promotion and well known for the miniature bull mounted to the hood of his red jeep, saying, "We're going to need the support of the whole area if this thing is going to make it." Since Sikeston is located in the "Bootheel" of Missouri, Old suggested that they call it the Jaycee Bootheel Rodeo, which would encompass not only Sikeston, but the surrounding area into the name. Little did they know that in later years the actual heel of a cowboy boot would be incorporated into the rodeo logo.

According to an article printed by the *Standard*, the event would be called "The First Annual Sikeston Jaycee Bootheel World Championship Rodeo." Apparently there had been enough enthusiasm generated for the event throughout the club that they were willing to call it the "first annual," indicating that there would more rodeos to follow in the coming years.

The Work Begins

Now that the Jaycees had chosen a date, picked their leaders, hired a stock contractor and settled on a name, all that was left was to begin work preparing the grounds and the community for the event. Every Jaycee, even the ones who had been opposed to the event, came together and worked side-by-side preparing for September. The *Standard* began printing regular updates on the club's progress. One article began: "The Jaycees cowboys gather at the 'ole corral' again tonight to whoop up plans for the Jaycee rodeo." Club members were encouraged to wear western style clothing and those who didn't adhere to the new dress code were given a good dunking in a horse trough set up in Legion Park As the club's momentum for the rodeo increased, so did their membership. That summer the Sikeston Jaycees saw their membership double with new members eager to help out with the new project.

Aerial view of an early rodeo at VFW Ballpark showing the seating configuration. From the Loy Baugher collection.

Not only was the enthusiasm within the club very evident, it could also be tasted all over town and the surrounding area. Large banners were hung over the streets of Sikeston, Dexter, New Madrid and East Prairie. Soon, local residents' cars and trucks became decorated with rodeo bumper stickers. The blue jean manufacturer H.D. Lee Pants even donated 2,000 posters that found homes in the windows of area businesses. Even the Sikeston Police Department caught a bit of rodeo fever and abandoned their regular covers for cowboy hats for the three weeks leading up to the rodeo.

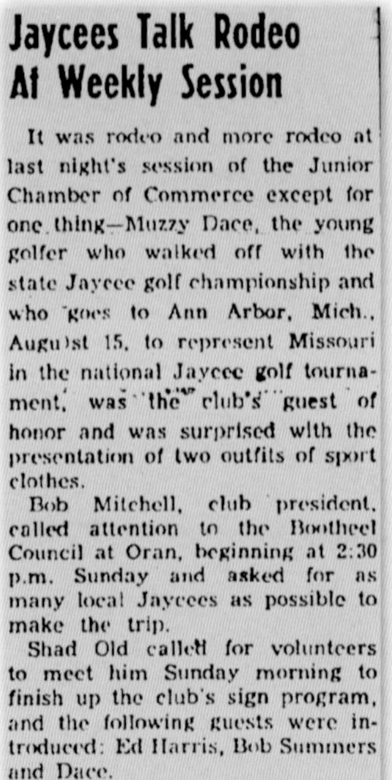

Jaycees Talk Rodeo At Weekly Session

It was rodeo and more rodeo at last night's session of the Junior Chamber of Commerce except for one thing—Muzzy Dace, the young golfer who walked off with the state Jaycee golf championship and who goes to Ann Arbor, Mich., August 15, to represent Missouri in the national Jaycee golf tournament, was the club's guest of honor and was surprised with the presentation of two outfits of sport clothes.

Bob Mitchell, club president, called attention to the Bootheel Council at Oran, beginning at 2:30 p.m. Sunday and asked for as many local Jaycees as possible to make the trip.

Shad Old called for volunteers to meet him Sunday morning to finish up the club's sign program, and the following guests were introduced: Ed Harris, Bob Summers and Dace.

The matter of bleachers for the rodeo is still bothering the club, but there are hopes this question may be settled this week.

Jean Klein and Bill Golladay were named as co-parade marshals and Jess Hamby, Jr. as chairman of a committee to arrange for holding a National Cutting Horse Contest as part of the rodeo program.

This cutting horse contest would bring to Sikeston from 20 to 40 of the top riders of the country and would provide an excellent exhibition as part of a program that promises to be an unusally good one.

The Sikeston Standard *kept readers informed about new developments regarding the rodeo on a regular basis during the spring and summer of 1953.*

Turning a Ballpark Into a Rodeo Arena

It had been decided the rodeo venue would be VFW Memorial Park, which was home to the semi-pro Sikeston Stags, the Sikeston Little League and the occasional exhibition games played by the major leaguers after the season ended. The Jaycees had to figure out a way to turn a baseball diamond into a rodeo arena with enough bleacher space to accommodate the numerous patrons that were sure to come. The park, in 1953, had three sections of permanent bleachers configured the same way they still are today – one section behind home plate and one running parallel to each baseline. The Jaycees knew that they needed several thousand more seats so they set out looking for a source of temporary bleachers. They searched for weeks until the Memphis Park Commission came through and saved the day. Not only did Memphis agree to loan several sections of portable bleacher to the Jaycees, they also upped the ante by sending a worker from the parks department to Sikeston to supervise the bleacher erecting.

On September 2, the Jaycees sent a truck donated by Scott County Milling Company to Memphis to retrieve the first set of bleachers and the next day sent one of Dale Alcorn's trucks to pick up the other set. They also sent two other trucks south to Paragould, AR to bring back the bucking chutes used by Burr Andrews in a rodeo the Jaycees had driven down to and observed just two weeks earlier.

The arrival of the bleachers and chutes brought every Jaycee out to the ball field that weekend. They work diligently under the supervision of the Memphis city worker to erect the bleachers, which were laid out parallel to each other from first and third base extending toward the outfield. In the outfield sat their newly acquired chutes that completed the rectangular arena. Just behind the temporary fence that bordered the arena, a couple of rows of folding chairs were placed just in front of the bleachers for those fans who wanted to be a little closer to the action. When it was all said and done, the Jaycees had successfully turned a baseball field into a rodeo arena with an impressive 6,000-seat capacity.

Rodeo Week Nears

As rodeo week approached, the Standard kept the public fed with continuous updates on the progress the Jaycees were making. They provided articles explaining the different events, and on September 12th, they published the purse amounts for each event, which ranged from $240 to $400. The Sikeston rodeo's purse was already larger than 90 percent of other rodeos of similar size. The entry fees paid by each contestant would combine with the added money kicked in by the Jaycees to determine the total prize money for each event. One Jaycee who had just returned from a trip to Oklahoma brought back news that there was buzz about the Sikeston rodeo and its purse all the way out in Oklahoma. The Sikeston rodeo was already attracting the top cowboys in the sport.

Due to the efforts of the Sikeston Jaycees and the *Standard*, an epidemic of rodeo fever was coursing through the town when rodeo week rolled around. Local waitresses could be seen sporting cowgirl outfits and men who had never thrown a leg over a horse were duded up in jeans, boots and hats. The Scott County Young Democrats held a western-themed dance at the National Guard Armory that drew close to 250 people. There would be a parade on Thursday afternoon, and according to the *Standard*, it was open to "anybody and everybody that can ride a horse (or a mule for that matter)." Sikeston citizens beamed with pride as contestants and rodeo fans showed up from all corners to support Sikeston's first rodeo.

Jaycees and others at the first rodeo in 1953. L-R: Shad Old, Bill Bess, Louis Jones, Paul Jones, Robert Dempster and Weber Gilmore.

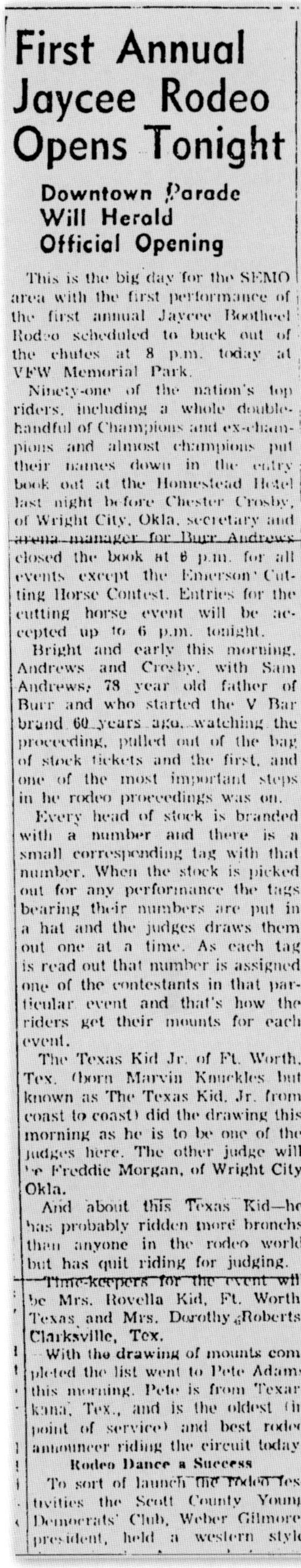

First Annual Jaycee Rodeo Opens Tonight

Downtown Parade Will Herald Official Opening

This is the big day for the SEMO area with the first performance of the first annual Jaycee Bootheel Rodeo scheduled to buck out of the chutes at 8 p.m. today at VFW Memorial Park.

Ninety-one of the nation's top riders, including a whole double-handful of Champions and ex-champions and almost champions put their names down in the entry book out at the Homestead Hotel last night before Chester Crosby, of Wright City, Okla, secretary and arena manager for Burr Andrews closed the book at 6 p.m. for all events except the Emerson Cutting Horse Contest. Entries for the cutting horse event will be accepted up to 6 p.m. tonight.

Bright and early this morning, Andrews and Crosby, with Sam Andrews, 78 year old father of Burr and who started the V Bar brand 60 years ago, watching the proceeding, pulled out of the bag of stock tickets and the first, and one of the most important steps in he rodeo proceedings was on.

Every head of stock is branded with a number and there is a small corresponding tag with that number. When the stock is picked out for any performance the tags bearing their numbers are put in a hat and the judges draws them out one at a time. As each tag is read out that number is assigned one of the contestants in that particular event and that's how the riders get their mounts for each event.

The Texas Kid Jr. of Ft. Worth, Tex. (born Marvin Knuckles but known as The Texas Kid, Jr. from coast to coast) did the drawing this morning as he is to be one of the judges here. The other judge will be Freddie Morgan, of Wright City Okla.

And about this Texas Kid—he has probably ridden more bronchs than anyone in the rodeo world but has quit riding for judging.

Time-keepers for the event will be Mrs. Rovella Kid, Ft. Worth, Texas and Mrs. Dorothy Roberts, Clarksville, Tex.

With the drawing of mounts completed the list went to Pete Adams this morning. Pete is from Texarkana, Tex., and is the oldest (in point of service) and best rodeo announcer riding the circuit today.

Rodeo Dance a Success

To sort of launch the rodeo festivities the Scott County Young Democrats' Club, Weber Gilmore, president, held a western style

Sikeston Standard *article from Sept. 17, 1953*

OFFICIAL EVENT PROGRAM THURSDAY, SEPT. 17

1ST ANNUAL JAYCEE RODEO

TIMEKEEPERS:

Rovella Kidd, Fort Worth, Tex.
Dorothy Roberts, Clarksville, Tex.

JUDGES:

Freddie Morgan, Wright City
Texas Kid, Fort Worth, Texas

ANNOUNCER:

Pete Adams, Texarcana, U.S.A.

SECRETARY:

Chester Crosby

CLOWNS:

Ike Tacker, Stilwell, Oklahoma
Pistol Holiday, Byars, Texas
Jimmy Perryman, Waco, Texas

EVENT NO. 1 GRAND ENTRY AND INTRODUCTION OF DIGNATARIES

EVENT NO. 2 BAREBACK BRONC RIDING

Contestant	No.	Name	Contestant	No.	Name
Carrol Hendricks	19	High Noon	Marcus Pierce	111	Lunatic
Jackie Roberts	14	Ole Frank	Ervin Neal	108	Pan Amm
Chuck Foster	5	High Test	Pistol Holiday	JB	John B.
Lou Lindsay	7	Seoul	Bobby Grego	17	Strawberry

EVENT NO. 3 COWGIRLS BARREL RACE

Contestant	Time	Contestant	Time
Rovella Kidd	--------	Montez Crenshaw	--------
Paulene Williams	--------	Rose Smith	--------
Jackie Thompson	--------	Shirley Smith	--------

EVENT NO. 4 IKE TACKER "DEAD EYE DICK"

EVENT NO. 5 TIE DOWN CALF ROPING

Contestant	No.	Time	Contestant	No.	Time
Dr. E. G. Bailey	--------	--------	Jack Sumpter	--------	--------
Rav Boss	--------	--------	L. N. Sykes	--------	--------
Dub Dale	--------	--------	Kenneth Allen	--------	--------
Smitty Smith	--------	--------	Sonny Bailey	--------	--------
John Johnson	--------	--------	Elvis Hopkins	--------	--------

EVENT NO. 6 IKE TACKER "SOLO"

EVENT NO. 7 SADDLE BRONC RIDING

Contestant	No.	Name	Contestant	No.	Name
Carrol Hendricks	13	I Wonder	Jackie Roberts	55	Booger Red
Bill Proctor	51	Rocky	George Bilby		Uncle Bud
Ervin Neal	30	Asthaman	George Warren	66	Headlight
Bobby Grego	54	Snake River			

EVENT NO. 8 PISTOL HOLIDAY "HIGH POCKETS"

EVENT NO. 9 BULL DOGGING or STEER WRESTLING

Contestant	No.	Time	Contestant	No.	Time
Carrol Hendricks	--------	--------	Ray Boss	--------	--------
Bill Proctor	--------	--------	George Bilby	--------	--------
Burr Andrews	--------	--------	George Liston	--------	--------
Ervin Neal	--------	--------	Smiley Talbert	--------	--------
L. N. McCarthy	--------	--------			

EVENT NO. 10 THE "JOYCE EMERSON" CUTTING HORSE CONTEST

Contestant	Name of Horse	Contestant	Name of Horse
Rendell Bell, Bloomfield, Mo.	Cheyene	Ray Carney, Jane, Mo.	Connie Mack
Dr. E. G. Bailey, Dexter, Mo.	Dawson Ema	George Killian, Portageville, Mo.	

EVENT NO. 11 BRAHMA BULL RIDING

Contestant	No.	Contestant	No.
Carrol Hendricks	10	Marcus Pierce	2
Buttons Yonnick	1	Fred Ford	44
Fred Langston	42	Chuck Foster	Xt
Ralph Robinson	0	Lou Lindsay	100

This Program Printed By The Commercial Printing Department of

Daily Sikeston Standard

A portion of the program from the first Jaycee Bootheel Rodeo in 1953

The First Jaycee Bootheel Rodeo Finally Arrives

The rodeo parade was the inaugural event that kicked the rodeo off. Onlookers flocked to the streets between the Sikeston Oil Cotton Mill and downtown. Police Chief Harold Wallace led the parade down Malone Avenue followed by restaurant owner Ted Kirby driving a car carrying waitresses from the Rustic Rock Inn all dressed in western attire. The Sikeston High School Marching Band followed Ted, providing a chorus of drums and horns. Bringing up the rear of the parade was an unknown number of horses and their riders. Although no one has the exact figures, the *Standard* reported that "There were horses of all sizes and colors."

With the rodeo parade in the bag, it was finally time to begin the rodeo that so many had come together to make happen. Opening night attendance was estimated between 3,750 and 4,000 patrons and 91 cowboys from around the country, many of them pleasantly surprised at the turnout that the Jaycees had mustered for their first-ever rodeo performance. The Sikeston Red Peppers, the high school pep squad, roamed the crowd selling souvenir programs while veteran rodeo announcer Pete Adams kept the crowd entertained. Pete kept the crowd informed with contestant introductions and round results, as well as kept them laughing with his interactions with rodeo clowns Ike Tucker, Pistol Holliday and Jimmie Perryman. Cowboys and cowgirls competed in bronc riding, barrel racing, bulldogging (steer wrestling), calf roping, bareback riding and Brahma bull riding. The rodeo even held a cutting horse event that drew a number of local contestants. Harry Sharp remembers lugging a bucket full of ice and sodas through the bleachers that he sold for 10 cents a piece, earning him a one-cent commission. Others sold beer for 20 cents.

As with any rodeo, the opening night didn't go off without a hitch. One incident involved rodeo producer Burr Andrews, who was also a contestant. Andrews suffered three broken ribs during the bulldogging event. Ever the cowboy, Burr simply taped his ribs and resumed his duties for the evening.

When Friday night rolled around the Jaycees were pleased to see a slightly larger crowd than the night before. High winds threatened to blow in a storm at the beginning performance, but the Jaycees, like so many after them, stared the storm down and the rain held off. The rest of the performance went off without a hitch and saw regional star Slim Rhodes and his Mountaineers of Memphis perform for the crowd before the grand entry and again during the performance, making him the very first professional music star to entertain the crowd at the Sikeston Jaycee Bootheel Rodeo.

Even larger numbers filled the bleachers for the weekend performances, bringing the total four-day attendance to an estimated 18,000. Profits were estimated between $5,000 and $8,000, but it looked like a million to the Sikeston Jaycees.

Skeptics Become Believers

Every Jaycee swelled with pride at what that they had accomplished as they dismantled their rodeo arena and restored it to its original purpose. They knew they had stumbled on to something great; and even the skeptics admitted that they had been wrong. *Delta Metro's 1976 rodeo h*istory quoted an unnamed Jaycee as saying, "Well, boys, I was wrong. This rodeo stuff is pretty big business."

From that weekend on, Sikeston would forever be in the rodeo business and has this original group of determined Jaycees to thank for it. This excerpt from the September 21st edition of the *Sikeston Standard* seemed to sum up the efforts of Sikeston and its Jaycees in 1953:

> *"Well, the books can be closed now on the First Annual Jaycee Bootheel Rodeo and the record shows it has been one of the most spectacular and successful presentations ever attempted by any organization in Sikeston."*

The inaugural Jaycee Bootheel Rodeo in 1953, which was successful beyond the imaginations of the Jaycee members, would be a tough act to follow. The group had its work cut out for it in dismantling the rodeo arena and getting VFW Memorial Park ready for baseball again, but once that work was completed, members were already thinking of ways to make the 1954 rodeo even better.

CHAPTER THREE

New Traditions

The silver buckle awarded to the 1954 all-around cowboy

The Jaycees began 1954 by erecting the new street signs in town that they had purchased with the proceeds of their first rodeo and were already planning ahead for the upcoming rodeo in September. It was decided to hire Burr Andrews to produce the rodeo again and, having one rodeo under their belt, the Jaycees were confident in their ability to transform VFW Memorial Park into a rodeo arena. With production and logistics already in the bag, they were left to focus on getting more fans in the bleachers for the 1954 rodeo.

"Air Time"

The advertising and publicity budget was slim, so the Jaycees were forced to find creative ways to gain more momentum for the event. The club decided to "buy some airtime" by hiring an airplane to fly a 300-mile radius around Sikeston and drop flyers advertising the rodeo. While bombarding the area with flyers, the plane also broadcast promotional messages over a loudspeaker.

The First Rodeo Queen

The 1954 rodeo also saw the first crowning of a rodeo queen. On June 24, an announcement was made that there would be a pageant to crown a queen and any female, single or married, between the ages of 16 and 24 would be eligible to compete for the crown. Not only would the pageant winner receive prizes donated by local jewelers and clothiers, the organizations sponsoring the winner and the two runners-up would receive $75. Initially, the lack of entries almost canceled the pageant but by the time the contest was held, entries had picked up. That year saw Billie Crumpecker of Morehouse crowned as the very first Sikeston Jaycee Bootheel Rodeo queen, beginning a tradition that is still ongoing today.

The rodeo queen was not the only recipient of awards that year. The Jaycees paid out over $3,000 in prize money to the cowboys and cowgirls competing in the rodeo. Along with the money, the top all-around cowboy and cowgirl also received a solid silver belt buckle with a gold bucking horse imposed on it from Mrs. L.A. Harris of Harris Drug Store.

"Kidnapping" a Family

One other very creative publicity stunt was manufactured with the help of Police Chief Harold Wallace. On Thursday morning of the rodeo, Chief Wallace, along with Jaycee president Bill Bess, took up position in a squad car on Highway 61. Their mission: pull over the first family with out-of-state plates. Their chosen "victim" turned out to be Mr. and Mrs. Lawrence Weller from Iowa, along with their son. Instead of being issued a ticket for speeding or another violation, the first ever "kidnapped family" received tickets in the Mayor's box for the opening night's performance. Along with the tickets, they were given the royal treatment in town for the day. They were treated to a tour of the city, free meals at local restaurants and a free service job on their car, complete with a full tank of gas. After spending the night in a local motel, the Wellers were back on the road and certain to spread the word about the Sikeston rodeo at their next destination.

On Friday, the Jaycees scored a big hit when they "kidnapped" Dan Bethell, his wife and three daughters. Dan was on his way from New York to Texarkana, where he was to assume a position as a new radio announcer for WSLB. No doubt, his listeners heard the story of Sikeston and its rodeo.

"Kidnapping" an out-of-state family and making them guests of the Jaycees at the rodeo is a tradition that was begun in 1954. In 1966, the unidentified kidnapped family posed with police and Jaycee officials in front of the El Capri Motel. At the left of the family are Officer Reuben Templeton, an unidentified Jaycee and Chief Arthur Bruce. At the right are Officer Gerald Howard and El Capri owner Ross Alsup. From the Loy Baugher collection.

The SEMO Shriners Mounted Patrol

The Jaycees creative publicity campaign paid off in 1954. While there are no attendance records for the year, the *Standard* reported an excellent opening night and the following three nights saw near sell-out performances. The 1953 rodeo had played to 75 percent capacity, and it was very evident that second annual rodeo well exceeded those figures.

New Producer in 1955

By 1955, the Sikeston Jaycees had two successful rodeos under their belts. However, instead of going on with business as usual, the ever-evolving rodeo decided to make a significant change in rodeo producers. Second-generation stock contractor Tommy Steiner had a reputation of putting on some of the best rodeos in the county, including a very popular rodeo in St. Louis. The decision was made to hire Steiner for the third annual rodeo – a relationship which proved to be a very long one. For the next 25 years, Steiner brought some the best stock in the nation to Sikeston, including a number of national champion bronc horses and bulls.

Having top-quality bulls and other stock attracts the best cowboys and makes for a quality rodeo. Tommy Steiner served as producer and stock contractor for the Jaycee Bootheel Rodeo for 25 years beginning in 1955. From the Loy Baugher collection.

On opening night of the third annual Sikeston Jaycee Bootheel Rodeo, the SEMO Shriners Mounted Patrol rode into the arena on their palomino horses for the first time and were met with a tremendous ovation. The *Daily Standard* reported:

> *"It has been virtually everyone who saw it says, the finest rodeo ever put on locally, and under the able direction of Tommy Steiner of Austin, Texas, set a record for performance attendance."*

Bozo – The First Rodeo National Celebrity

Bozo the Clown also made his debut in Sikeston in 1955. Bozo was tasked with entertaining the crowd before each night's performance as well as assisting in the Jaycees' publicity efforts during the week of rodeo. The dunking of the Jaycees not in western attire had become a Saturday night tradition in the weeks leading up to the rodeo and Bozo became an accomplice in this ritual as well. Since several actors were hired by Capitol records to play the part of Bozo, it's unclear who the actor was that portrayed Bozo in Sikeston. One year later, Larry Harmon bought the rights to Bozo and became the most well-known actor to wear the costume.

Jones Passes the Rodeo Reins

As the 1955 rodeo ended, so ended Louis Jones' three-year reign as rodeo general chairman. The club project he had proposed in 1953 had blossomed into a full-fledged rodeo as well as an annual community event. Content that his baby would be taken care of, Louis handed the reins to J.W. Bonner, who was to chair the next rodeo. Since then, the Sikeston Jaycees have elected a new chairman each year, making Louis Jones the only man ever to hold the title of Sikeston Jaycee Bootheel Rodeo general chairman for more than one year.

Louis Jones (left), who was general chairman of the first three Jaycee Bootheel Rodeos, poses with 1977 general chairman Ed Aldrich (center) as the Jaycees honor Art Saunders (right) for his contributions to the rodeo.

CHAPTER FOUR

Celebrities Come to Sikeston

Bull, Clown, Spectator in Big Scramble

Vanduser Man Hurt But Not Seriously In Episode at Rodeo

A Brahma bull, a clown and a spectator teamed up, unintentionally of course, to provide a thrilling and startling episode toward the close of the Brahma bull riding contest at the second night's performance of the fifth annual Jaycee Bootheel Rodeo Friday night.

The spectator was Oscar Duncan, 65-year old retired farmer who lives near Vanduser. There were a dozen conflicting stories of what happened and as many rumors as to the extent of the injuries, but, apparently, Mr. Duncan escaped with nothing more serious than a shaking up.

Onis Gilfilhan, a cowboy contestant came out of the chutes on Bull No. 2. The bull unloaded him pronto and then took off chasing the clowns. With the bull just too close for comfort, the clown went up the fence in front of the box where Mr. Duncan was sitting, assisted, some of the cowboys insist, by some nudges from the bull. As the Brahma hit the tough steel fence Mr. Duncan either fell or was knocked over and fell at the back of the box. He was removed to the Mo. Delta Community Hospital for examination and treatment of possible injuries. It was reported this morning Mr. Duncan was not seriously injured. At the hospital, last night, Mr. Duncan declared he'd be out tonight.

Sikeston Standard *article from 1957*

After three rodeos, the Jaycees were starting to get the hang of the rodeo business. However, they thought it would be a good idea to let the local citizens get a chance to compete in the arena along with the cowboys. There was a balloon race for the children and wand-waving contest for kids over the age of 16. They didn't leave the adults out though. One event featured a watch tied between the horns of a Brahma bull. Any person brave enough to snatch the watch from between the horns could claim the watch as a prize. There are no reports on who won the watch, but I'm sure they wore it proudly for many years to come.

By 1957, the Jaycees found themselves preparing for their fifth rodeo. The previous four had been successful, but Sikeston's enthusiasm for the previously brand new event was beginning to wane. This didn't go unnoticed by the Jaycees and they knew that something had to be done to create more "buzz" in town for the rodeo. Jaycee Bill Burch summed it up: "This is not rodeo country. To draw people, there had to be something added to the rodeo."

Smiley Burnette Signed for '57

The Jaycees had hired entertainers such as Onie Wheeler, Slim Rhodes and Bozo the Clown, but they felt that a more popular celebrity would give fans a bit more bang for their buck, thus drawing more of a crowd. As it turned out, Smiley Burnette, who played Gene Autry's sidekick Frog Millhouse in a number of films, lived in Springfield, Mo., where he produced a nationally-syndicated music radio show. Along with radio, Smiley was a regular on ABC's Ozark Jubilee. The club decided to send a delegation to meet with Burnette about booking him to perform all four nights of the rodeo. Smiley expressed his interest but would need an answer from the Jaycees quickly.

Smiley Burnett in Visit to Sikeston

Smiley Burnett, the famed funny man and cowboy of stage and screen fame, was in town Friday lining up some advance publicity for the Sept. 12-15 Jaycee Bootheel Rodeo, and made a tour of the city.

After looking over the town, Smiley said that he is looking forward to showing in Sikeston and predicted a good time for everyone attending the four-day rodeo, including himself.

Burnett, who is famous for his, "It's My Lazy Day," will be appearing at every showing of the rodeo this year. He plans to meet all the young cowboys and will even have some of them in his act, acting out western skits.

Sikeston Standard *article from 1957*

With no time to wait for the regular Tuesday night club meeting, the members of the delegation raced back to Sikeston and called a special Sunday meeting to decide on whether or not to hire Burnette for $1,000. According to Jaycee Harry Holsinger, a heated debate ensued due to fact that many of the members thought that a thousand dollars was entirely too much to pay for an entertainer. In the end, the motion passed and Smiley Burnette's songs and skits appeared to be a big hit that year. The decision to book him that year apparently paid off because, according to Holsinger, the rodeo made money in 1957. The rodeo was a big success, despite an incident with a bull that left a spectator from Vanduser with a slight injury. The results of the 1957 rodeo would set the wheels in motion for one of the biggest stars in the world at the time to make his appearance in Sikeston.

"Matt Dillon is Coming to Town!"

Since the rodeo coffers got a good taste of what spending a little extra money on entertainment could do for profits, the Jaycees decided to make an even larger commitment to an entertainer in 1958. At the time, nearly everyone in America tuned into the nation's top-rated show, "Gunsmoke". Marshal Matt Dillon, played by actor James Arness, was a household name at the time and since the Jaycees had such a good reception to Smiley Burnette the year before, they decided to pony up $12,000 to sign Arness to perform at the rodeo. Twelve grand was a lot of money at the time. In fact, it was 12 times more than what the club debated paying Burnette the previous year. However, with the success of hiring a big name entertainer the year before, most of the Jaycee didn't have a problem gambling $12,000 on Arness.

On June 4, the Sikeston *Standard* broke the news that Arness would be making his way to Sikeston in September. The following was printed under a picture of Arness in his Matt Dillon attire. The story began:

> ***"Marshal Matt Dillon is coming to town!***
>
> *At every performance of the sixth annual Jaycee Bootheel Rodeo, Sept. 12,13 and 14, the famous portrayer of the old time gun marshal of Dodge City – Jim Arness, all six foot of him, complete with his trusty six-gun, will stalk the arena and stage some of the fiercest man-to-man battles ever seen locally."*

Expanding the Seating at VFW Park

Now that they had booked one of the biggest celebrities in the nation, the Jaycees knew that they had to make every effort to capitalize on Arness' popularity. For starters, the Jaycees knew that ticket sales would skyrocket past the 6,000 seat bleacher set up they were currently using.

There wasn't any more real estate left to house more bleachers at the VFW Park, so it was decided to go in search for taller bleachers in order to increase seating capacity. The Jaycees found a solution in Strong City, Kan., where they were able to locate some 20-row bleachers for rent. This would increase the seating capacity to around 10,000,

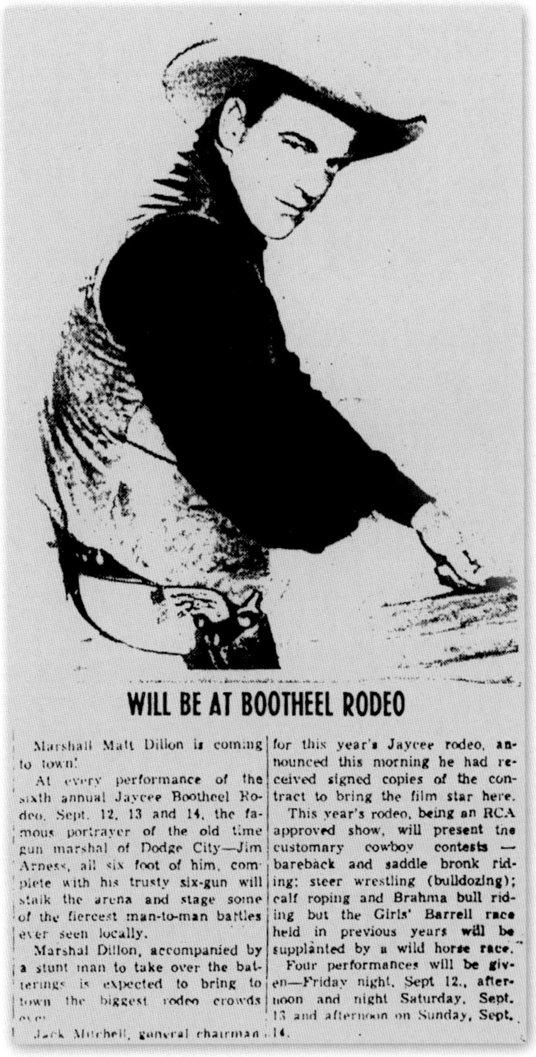

WILL BE AT BOOTHEEL RODEO

Marshall Matt Dillon is coming to town!

At every performance of the sixth annual Jaycee Bootheel Rodeo, Sept. 12, 13 and 14, the famous portrayer of the old time gun marshal of Dodge City—Jim Arness, all six foot of him, complete with his trusty six-gun will stalk the arena and stage some of the fiercest man-to-man battles ever seen locally.

Marshal Dillon, accompanied by a stunt man to take over the batterings is expected to bring to town the biggest rodeo crowds ever.

Jack Mitchell, general chairman for this year's Jaycee rodeo, announced this morning he had received signed copies of the contract to bring the film star here.

This year's rodeo, being an RCA approved show, will present the customary cowboy contests — bareback and saddle bronk riding; steer wrestling (bulldozing); calf roping and Brahma bull riding but the Girls' Barrell race held in previous years will be supplanted by a wild horse race.

Four performances will be given—Friday night, Sept 12., afternoon and night Saturday, Sept. 13 and afternoon on Sunday, Sept. 14.

Sikeston Standard *article from June 4, 1958*

enough to accommodate the large crowds that were expected to show up for Arness. Harry Holsinger remembers the construction of the bleachers being much more difficult than the 12-row bleachers they were used to. But in the end, the Jaycees did what the Jaycees do and once again converted the ballpark into a 10,000-seat rodeo arena.

Marshall Matt Dillon To Be Here Tonight For J-C Rodeo

BULLETIN

JEFFERSON CITY (AP) — The Missouri Highway Patrol's traffic death log for the 24 hours ended at midnight:

Last 24 hours—7

So far this year—606

Same time last year—662

ONLY ONE EMERGENCY

A wasp stung 9 year old Betty Jo Smith of Sikeston, and she was taken to the Missouri Delta Community Hospital for treatment, after which she was dismissed.

DREW PEARSON SAYS: GOP leaders worry about Sherman Adams as political liability; His explanation of "poor immigrant boy" doesn't hold up; Bernard Goldfine didn't consider U.S. laws

The PRAYER FOR TODAY FROM The Upper Room

Neither said any of them that aught of the things which he possessed was his own; but they had all things common. (Acts 4:32.)

PRAYER: O Father, Thou know

This Is Opening Day For Rodeo And Huge Crowd is Expected

Well, here it is again — opening day for a Jaycee sponsored rodeo. Just another opening, you say? You couldn't be more off the beam, for, in the minds of hundreds of younger fry and probably just as many adults, this year's sixth annual Jaycee Bootheel Rodeo is something super — a three day event that will be remembered long after lesser festivities have been forgotten for, by the time this is read, Marshal Matt Dillon, famed peace officer of old Dodge City, who delights and thrills audiences coast to coast in "Gunsmoke" every week, will be here in perso[n] is no doubt but what [...] ment of the area's po[...] hardly wait to get [...] glimpse of James A[...] what his name is ou[...] City.

Altogether this yea[r...] studded with unusua[l...] ing features in additio[n...] ways spine-tingling [...] tween cowboys, bron[cs,] bulls, steers and calv[es.]

The Jaycees have [...] to bring to Sikeston [...] championship rodeo, [...] trimmings. It is possib[...]

Red Feather's Fund Boosted To 25 Percent

At the regular weekly meeting of the Board of Directors of this year's Community Chest, held Thursday evening, Charles Matthews, treasurer, reported total contributions in cash and pledges to the 1958 Red Feather drive have amounted to $10,000, making the chest fund 25 percent full.

Almost the directors had to

ROUTE OF PARADE FOR SIXTH ANNUAL JAYCEE BOOTHEEL RODEO

The parade for the sixth annual Jaycee Bootheel Rodeo, tomorrow morning, will form on Stoddard street at the South Grade School and be ready to move out promptly at 10 a.m. according to Jay Sisk, in charge of this phase of the annual western show. The parade route will be—

East on Malone avenue to Kingshighway.

North on Kingshighway to Front.

West on Front to Stoddard.

North on Stoddard to Center.

East on Center to Prairie, and disband at the police sta-

Sikeston Standard *article from Sept. 12, 1958*

Dillon Proves Show Stopper

Thousands See Rodeo Parade

THE SENATOR SPEAKS

State Senator Clem McSpadden of Oklahoma, is speaking, but not in legislative terms. Clem, as he is known to hundred of rodeo cow boys, occupies his spare time as a rodeo announcer from one end of the country to the other and so well has he done the job that today he is recognized as 'top man on the totem pole' when it comes to describing the whirling action of the rodeo arena. Kind of funny, said Clem Friday night, how he came to do announcing. Seems that he was a roper and wrestler for several years and, about 10 years ago he found himself in a town, broke, and, as fate would have it, the rodeo announcer got sick or something and Clem talked himself into the job. He's been talking rodeos ever since.

Clem is a resident of Nowata, Okla., and about four years ago decided to take a whirl at politics. He did and evidently his constituents liked him for they reelected him this year to another four-year term. He's had quite a

Record Crowd Present For Rodeo Opener

Cold Fails to Cool Off Enthusiasm for A Fine Performance

In spite of a rather chilly evening that didn't get a bit warmer as the hours disappeared, the first night of the sixth annual Jaycee Bootheel Rodeo drew what officials say was a record-breaking opening night attendance and, if the weather was cool, the stock Ken Roberts, the producer brought in was plenty hot as the cowboys discovered.

Following the traditional rodeo pattern of a specified number of RCA sponsored contests spiced with entertainment features, the rodeo galloped smoothly through a lengthy program with only two incidents to mar the evening. A boy got badly shaken up and a cowboy had a shoulder dislocated or broken.

In the course of the bare-back bronc riding, Lady La Coeur, ridden by Sonny Frazier, after dumping her rider, got loose behind the bucking chutes and ran into Billy Jones, 12 year old son of Mr. and Mrs. C. J. Jones of Sikeston. The animal knocked the boy down and bruised him, but apparently not seriously although after he had been taken care of immediately after the accident by Dr. Ferguson, the boy complained of dizzy spells and the doctor had him sent home to rest.

In the last of the RCA contests, the Brahma bull riding, Bill Scott

THREE MORE THRILLING RODEO PERFORMANCES WAIT SEMO AUDIENCES

With the first nighter and the mammoth rodeo parade gone into the books, southeast Missourians have three more chances to see the most thrilling contests staged in the nation today—RCA approved contests between cowboys and animals—out at the rodeo arena on Highway 60 East. In spite of the fact the advance ticket sales broke all expectations, there are still plenty of good seats available, but they won't be long.

For the coming three performances—this afternoon, tonight at 8 o'clock and Sunday at 1:30 p.m., the Jaycees are expecting a record smashing overall attendance.

Red Artillery Drives Away Supply Ship

TAIPEI, Formosa (AP)—Communist artillery fire drove another Nationalist supply convoy off the beach at Quemoy in predawn darkness today.

Four Nationalist Chinese supply ships were forced to withdraw after unloading only a small portion of their cargo.

Within one hour the Reds poured more than 7,000 high explosive shells onto Liaolo Beach where the vessels were trying to unload badly needed supplies for the besieged Nationalist outpost

Rodeo to Have Day and Night Performances

Colorful Bands and Floats Delight Big Crowds Along Curbs

Bright and sunny, the second day for the sixth annual Jaycee Bootheel Rodeo, drew a great many spectators to town this morning to watch the customary rodeo parade and while many expressed disappointment that Marshal Matt Dillon was not included in the line of march, his absence was probably compensated for by the many smartly-uniformed and high-stepping high school bands, the interesting floats and the rear guard which was the nationally famous honor guard of the 101st Airborne Division, stationed at Fort Campbell, Ky.

A wee bit late, the rodeo parade got under way about 10:15 a.m. and moved east along Malone avenue to Kingshighway, across to Front, then to Stoddard and over to Center to go east again to Prairie, where it disbanded.

Leading the parade was the police car carrying Chief Arthur Bruce. The first riding group was the blue-shirted riders of the Circle C, Camden, Ark., who brought great applause last night with their precision riding and presentation of a square dance on horseback.

High school bands in the parade included those from Fisk, Wardell, Kewanee, Charleston, Portageville, Bell City, Campbell, Malden, East Prairie, Chas

Sikeston Standard *article from Sept. 13, 1958*

Matt Dillon Comes to the Rodeo, and So Do the Crowds

With the announcement of James Arness' upcoming visit to Sikeston, a new enthusiasm for the rodeo was palpable throughout the community. After all, Arness would be the most famous person to visit since Harry Truman. Advance tickets sales were so strong that there was concern among the Jaycees that there wouldn't be enough seating to accommodate the number of fans planning to attend the event. Friday, September 12, was opening day for that year's performance and the *Standard* printed the following:

> "Well here it is a*gain – opening day for a Jaycee sponsored rodeo. Just another opening, you say? You couldn't be more off the beam, for in the minds of hundreds of younger fry and probably just as many adults, this year's sixth annual Jaycee Bootheel Rodeo is something super – a three day event that will be remembered long after lesser festivities have been forgotten for, by the time this is read, Marshal Matt Dillon, famed peace officer of old Dodge City, who delights and thrills audiences coast to coast in "Gunsmoke"*

1958 Jaycee Bootheel Rodeo program cover

James Arness poses with Jaycee Wives before a rodeo performance. The man seated alongside Arness is unidentified. From the Loy Baugher collection.

every week, will be here in person and there is no doubt but what a larger segment of the area's population can hardly wait to get a glimpse of James Arness – that's what his name is outside of Dodge City."

While the 1958 rodeo held a record number of competitors and the best quality of stock to date, it was overshadowed by the performer that thousands had flocked to the arena to see. The crowd roared as Arness rode into the arena to put on his brief performance. He spoke to the crowd of his experiences on "Gunsmoke" and then called out stuntman Al Wyatt to demonstrate how a Hollywood fight was staged. After a brief scuffle, Marshal Matt Dillon won the brawl and then concluded his appearance by reciting "The Cowboy's Prayer."

James Arness was overwhelmed by the crowd and the hospitality offered to him in Sikeston and, in a classy move, he and Wyatt joined Jaycee president Clem Beal and paid a visit to "Gunsmoke" fan Luther Murphy, who had been bedridden for twelve years. Arness and the Jaycees even arranged for an ambulance to transport Murphy to the rodeo so he could witness the performance.

The Big Payoff

Paying Arness $12,000 to come to the rodeo was a huge gamble for the Jaycees in 1958, however, that gamble paid off big time. The total estimated attendance for all four performances was 30,000. Thanks to the increased seating capacity, the extra 6,000 tickets sold paid for Arness's appearance fee. The rodeo that year made a record profit of $27,000 that would, in time, provide the rodeo with a new and permanent home.

James Arness, better known as Matt Dillon, tips his hat to the 1958 rodeo crowd. From the Loy Baugher collection.

CHAPTER FIVE

The Rodeo Gets a New Home

As the Jaycees tore down the 20-row bleachers and shipped them back to Kansas, it became apparent that this was no long-term solution. With the success of James Arness, the rodeo planned to hire more big name stars in the future and knew that they would need another option to accommodate the large crowds. The idea of the rodeo having its own permanent home had been kicked around over past few years and according to John Harper, the hefty profit from the previous year "got the ball rolling towards the new arena."

Jaycees Agree On Permanent Site For Rodeo

At its regular weekly meeting Tuesday night at the Country Club the Junior Chamber of Commerce voted to accept the recommendations of the permanent rodeo site committee for a new permanent arena for the annual Jaycee Bootheel Rodeo. The new arena, when completed, would cost about $11,400, not including the cost of an extra 4,000 or more bleachers which would be needed, and will be located 1.7 miles north of Highway 60 on the east side of the old Harts Road, which is just east of Smith addition. The land is now city property.

In accepting the site proposal, the Jaycees were told the arena would be built in a triangular shape, the latest word in rodeo site construction, and would seat about 8,500 spectators. With the proposed shape of the arena, any seat would be about as good as another, the club was told.

The Jaycees have upward of 4,000 bleacher seats, but to seat the expected large crowds at this year's rodeo, about 4,000 or 4,500 more must either be bought or rented.

Most of the construction work on the arena will be done by the Jaycees, the club has announced, with some contracts being let for buck-out chutes and a retaining wall similar to the one at the new football field, only the arena wall will stand only about two feet high.

Sikeston Standard article from Feb. 5, 1959

PROPOSED LAYOUT FOR JAYCEES' PERMANENT ARENA FACILITIES

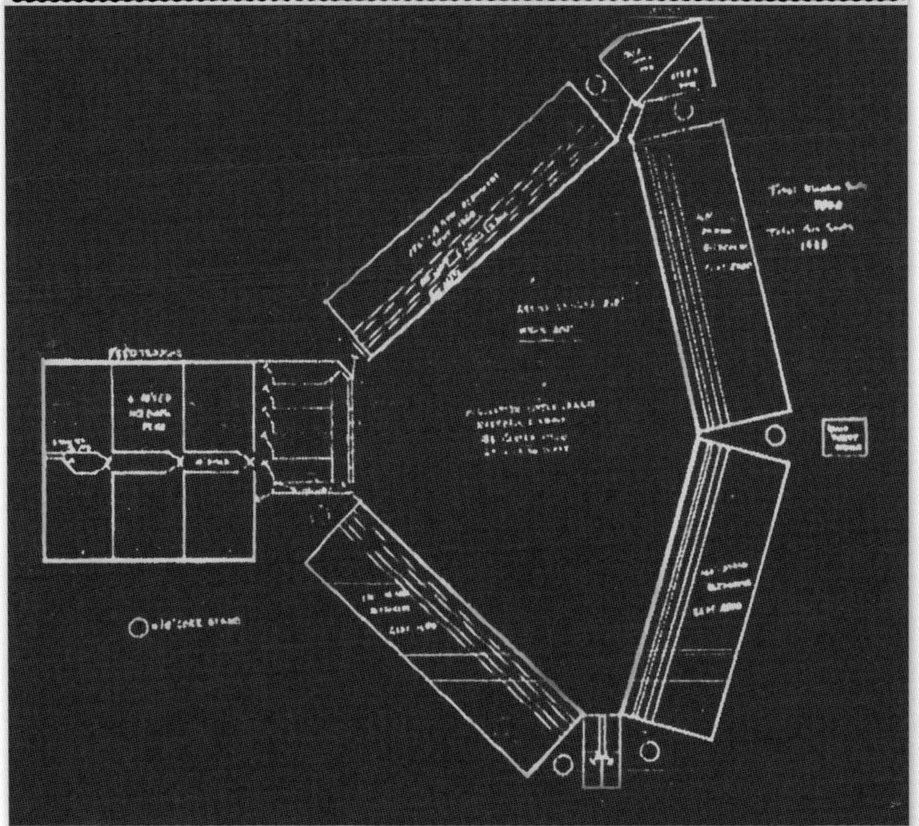

Although nothing has been definitely decided as to the purchase of a permanent site for the Junior Chamber of Commerce annual Bootheel Rodeo; it is considered quite likely that the site on the old Hart Road may be the one definitely selected.

If and when a permanent site is settled on the rodeo arena, with its seats, buck-out chutes, hold pens, etc., will probably look like the above diagram.

At the far left there would be six holding pens for broncs, steers and Brahma bulls with each pen 40 feet by 50 feet, divided by an aisle to move the stock to the five buck-out chutes immediately to the right of the holding pens.

Moving around the arena clockwise first there would be 15 rows of bleachers seating 1,650, 176 feet long, with provision for box seats in front.

At the top would be a calf catch pen and holding pen for steers.

Next another section of bleachers, 20 rows high and 160 feet long, seating 2,000.

The main ticket office separates that section of bleachers from the next bleacher section which would be the same size and seat another 2,000.

At the bottom of the diagram, the small section would be for bulldogging steers and calf roping release pens, and the last section shown and which adjoins the buck-out chutes, would be the fourth bleacher section, 15 rows high, 176 feet long, with a seating capacity of 1,650.

The public road would, of course be to the right with the main ticket office facing it.

The arena itself would have a total overall length of 318 feet and would be 200 feet wide.

It will be noted that provision is also made for space for a Little League baseball diamond.

Diagram of the proposed new rodeo grounds, published in the Sikeston Standard

40 Acres Leased From the Airport

On January 28, 1959 the *Standard* mentioned that the Jaycee club would be asked to vote on a possible new venue for the rodeo. The club would vote at the February 4 meeting to lease a 40-acre tract of Sikeston Municipal Airport property from the city. The tract was located on the east side of Hart's road, which is now known as North Ingram Street. The cost for the new venue was estimated at $11,400, plus an additional $4,000 for more bleachers. The extra bleachers would bring the total seating capacity to 8,500. The vote passed, and after obtaining special permission from the Federal Aviation Administration, required due to the fact that arena sat next to the airport and would be illuminated at night, the Jaycees began construction of the rodeo's new home.

As is tradition, much of the labor was accomplished by the Jaycees themselves, John Harper recalls. "We had some surplus army equipment available. We had guys like Joe Baker and Bill Sikes and others that operated the equipment."

Fellow Jaycee Frank Ferrell owned and operated an excavating company and did much of the dirt work required for the new arena. A diamond configuration was decided on which would accommodate play by the Sikeston Little League, which played in the arena for a couple of years before moving to Puckett Field on Pine Street. When the project was completed, the total cost came to $37,000, even with the majority of the labor being done by Jaycee volunteers. The club would assume roughly $10,000 in debt but would see it paid off in the first year of using their new facility.

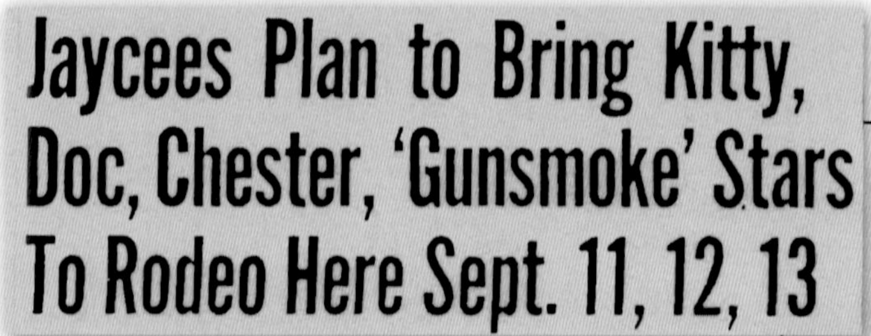
Jaycees Plan to Bring Kitty, Doc, Chester, 'Gunsmoke' Stars To Rodeo Here Sept. 11, 12, 13

Sikeston Standard *headline announcing the signing of "Gunsmoke" stars Dennis Weaver, Amanda Blake and Milburn Stone for the 1959 rodeo.*

Dennis Weaver and Amanda Blake greet the fans at the 1959 rodeo. From the Loy Baugher collection.

"Gunsmoke" stars Milburn Stone ("Doc"), Dennis Weaver and Amanda Blake at the airport. From the Loy Baugher collection.

The Jaycee Bootheel Rodeo Grounds Opens

The Jaycees had hit a homerun the previous year by booking James Arness, so it seemed only fitting that the first year in the their new facility they hired fellow "Gunsmoke" actors Dennis Weaver (Chester Goode), Amanda Blake (Kitty Russell) and Milburn Stone ("Doc" Adams). The trio had been performing together at fairs and rodeos across the country and put on a much more lengthy and creative show for the audience that included skits, songs and a three-piece orchestra.

"Chester, Kitty and Doc" helped to inaugurate the new facility on September 4, 1959. The rodeo performance was moved up a week that year to accommodate "Gunsmoke"'s filming schedule. They wowed the crowd with a 45-minute performance. Amanda Blake even made a surprise visit to Missouri Delta Medical Center's emergency room after injuring her ankle. Blake graciously visited with hospital staff and ER patients and even took a moment to visit with Mr. and Mrs. Ralph Francis, who were exiting the hospital with their newborn son, Donald.

Not only was the facility host to a PRCA rodeo, a junior championship rodeo was also held for kids 16 and under Thursday night before the performance.

The profits from the 1959 rodeo paid off the $10,000 debt incurred from building the new facility with still another $8,000 left over in profit. It seemed as though the decision to relocate had paid off, and the same 40 acres north of town is still known as the Sikeston Jaycee Bootheel Rodeo Grounds.

The 1950s could arguably be the most important and significant decade in the rodeo's 60-year history. Due to the vision of people like Art Saunders and Louis Jones, it saw the birth of the Sikeston Jaycee Bootheel Rodeo and laid a foundation for future generations of Jaycees to continue the same tradition that has now entered into its 61st year.

Jaycee Bootheel Rodeo Grounds, Sikeston, MO.

CHAPTER SIX

The Rodeo Becomes a Business

When the new decade rolled over, Sikeston and its Jaycees had managed to string together seven rodeos. The first two years moved smoothly along without incident, but in 1962 the rodeo hit its first major financial hurdle.

The First Rainout

Rain clouds invaded the Sikeston area on the first day of rodeo and opened up above the arena. The ground was completely soaked by Saturday before Mother Nature donated another inch-and-a-half of rain on the already soaked arena, causing the rodeo to have its first-ever "rain out." "It just poured all day long," Harry Holsinger recalled. "We made the decision about six o'clock that there was no way you could have a rodeo here because the arena had about three feet of water in it, so we were just going to have to postpone it." The Jaycees were forced to move Saturday's performance to Sunday afternoon and push back the Sunday matinee. Thankfully, entertainer Rex Allen agreed to hang around for both Sunday performances.

As the Jaycees were gathered at the Sikeston Country Club for the traditional Saturday night party, they were interrupted by a phone call from a panicked Jaycee working in the ticket office

No, it's not Dodge City, it's the rodeo ticket office at the Gay 90s Village in Sikeston, with a retro look.

that said, "You guys better get out here, because we're about to have a lynching." There were quite a few folks that couldn't stay in town for the postponed performance and demanded a refund for their tickets. However, no arrangements had been made for refunds. With that, a small group of Jaycees left the Country Club with a bag of cash and headed to the rodeo grounds to reimburse the angry patrons. That was the last time "rain or shine" was printed on any rodeo ticket, according to Bob Porter.

The *Sikeston Standard* reported that rodeo chairman Bill Hale was hopeful that the rodeo would break even for the year, however, the rain out proved to be too much of a strain on the financials and according to Bill Burch, "We lost our shirts."

On a more pleasant note, that same year the Jaycees crowned the very first Little Mr. and Miss Western sponsored by the Jaycee wives. Glen Bridges, age eight, from Parma and Beverly Ann Wirth, age two from Sikeston were given the honors.

Luckily the weather blessed the Jaycees the next year when over 22,000 fans filled the bleachers to see Lorne Green and Dan Blocker from "Bonanza" and Jay North, TV's "Dennis the Menace." One of the guests in attendance was Missouri Governor John Dalton, marking the first time in history the rodeo was visited by the governor. However, even though the attendance provided for a profitable rodeo, the Jaycees still remembered the years past.

Running the Rodeo as a Business

The 1962 rodeo wasn't the only rodeo to lose money. In the 1950s and '60s, some rodeos would make a profit and some wouldn't. According to John Harper, "We'd make money one year and lose money the next year. It was just a break-even overall." Since all the profits from the event were donated back into the community, there was never any money left over to start the next rodeo, especially if the previous year wasn't profitable. According to Bill Burch, much of the problem was the fact that leadership rolled over from year to year. "It was a brand spankin' new ballgame every year," said Burch. "There was no continuity. And we didn't have any reserves."

"Bonanza" stars Lorne Greene (Ben Cartwright) & Dan Blocker (Hoss Cartwright) arrive at the Sikeston Municipal Airport. From the Loy Baugher collection.

To combat this, the Jaycees formed the Sikeston Jaycee Bootheel Rodeo Corporation in 1967 in an effort to run the

Hugh O'Brian, TV's "Wyatt Earp", demonstrates some fancy gunhandling to a youngster during the 1960 rodeo. From the Loy Baugher collection.

Rex Allen gets a key to the city from Beverly Ann Wirth, the very first Little Miss Western, in 1962. From the Loy Baugher collection.

A sick boy gets a gift from Don Durant ("Johnny Ringo"), who entertained at the 1960 rodeo. From the Loy Baugher collection.

event more like a business. The rodeo board was, and still is, comprised of 11 Jaycees members representing the different areas of the rodeo who served three-year terms. The club would still elect a new general chairman annually and leadership of the different areas would still roll over. But now there would be a committee of experienced Jaycees to help guide the event from year to year and vote on financial matters and any "major" decisions. John Harper, who was the first rodeo board president, states, "The board of directors made decisions just like the board of directors of a company would make decisions." The terms were usually three years and when one would expire, another member with same area of expertise would step in to fill the new three-year term.

The Rodeo Becomes Profitable

Having a board of directors ensured accountability among the different areas of the rodeo. Even though the general chairman was still charged with budgeting and overseeing the event, he had to submit the budget to the board to be approved. Apparently the arrangement was a profitable one because according to Harper, "After we incorporated, we never lost money again."

Since one of the main goals of the board was to guarantee that the rodeo was financially able to continue in the following year, one of the first steps Harper took was to tuck a little money away for the future. Harper stated, "When I became president, we were $11,000 in debt on the rodeo. We made money that year. Not much, but we paid all our bills and had a little left over. I took $500 and gave it to our treasurer and told him to put this into a savings account and told him 'you and I are the only ones who are going to know about it. If we don't, we will not have the money to start the rodeo next year.'"

To date, the establishment of the Sikeston Jaycee Bootheel Rodeo board corporation is one of the most significant milestones in the history of the event. To put an exclamation on that, Bill Burch can be quoted as saying "I think the rodeo wouldn't be here today if the rodeo board hadn't been established."

Apathy Threatens to Kill the Rodeo

Not only did the financial issues plague the club during the '60s, but the rodeo began to run into a labor issue. The Jaycee club at the time had over 100 members on the books, but when it came time to put in the hours and days of work needed to make rodeo happen, fewer and fewer members showed up to help. That resulted in the workload falling on fewer and fewer that remained active. Part of the problem was the result of the demographics at the time.

"We had over a hundred members in my year as president," Harper said. "The ideal mix would have been to have bankers and lawyers, and then your blue collar members, because there are times when you need your blue collar people just as much as your white collar people. The white-collar people didn't want to get their hands dirty and the blue-collar people did. Between the two, when we had it pretty well meshed – excellent. When it didn't mesh, that's what you run into."

Paul Brinegar, better known as "Wishbone" from "Rawhide", takes the lead in entertaining the 1961 Jaycee Bootheel Rodeo audience while co-stars Clint Eastwood and Sheb Wooley (at the mic on the left of the stage) join in. From the Loy Baugher collection.

Charles McGill, general chairman of the 1970 rodeo, was an active member and was involved in many of the work parties during that period. "I called it the 'dirty dozen' when I was chairman," states McGill. "About 12 people you could count on out of maybe a hundred in the club to show up."

Paul Brinegar, accustomed to serving up coffee to drovers around the campfire in his role on "Rawhide," pours a cup for a local at the motel. From the Loy Baugher collection.

Bill Burch Rolls the Dice

It reached a boiling point in 1968 when the president of the board, Bill Burch, decided that some kind of action had to be taken. Burch recalls, "It got down to two weeks before the rodeo and there'd be eight guys working. So we just came to the club and said 'we can't go on this way.'" Burch then made a motion to discontinue the rodeo due to lack of participation among the club members.

According to Jaycee Tom Nunnelee, in an ironic turn of events the motion failed by one vote, thus keeping the Sikeston Jaycees in the rodeo business. It seemed for the second time the future of the rodeo came down to a single vote and the gamble paid off because, according to Burch, many of the members who had begun to take the event for granted got back to work again.

"What if it had been cancelled?" Nunnelee wonders. "Where would Sikeston have been moving through the next 43 years without the Jaycee Bootheel Rodeo? It's profound."

The question Nunnelee raised was appropriate. History shows that the best years of the Jaycee Bootheel Rodeo still lay ahead.

CHAPTER SEVEN

New Month, New Bleachers

The 1960s saw many milestones and changes, and in 1965 it saw yet another key alteration in its date that is still in effect today. For the first 12 years, the rodeo had always in been held in the month of September. The reason that it was initially scheduled in September is unclear. Some could speculate that it was because when the first rodeo was originally announced in May 1953 that the Jaycees needed four months to get ready for the big show. Or maybe it was that the Jaycees had to wait for the Sikeston Stag baseball season to close before they could transform the ballpark into an arena. Whatever the reason was, having a September rodeo held many drawbacks.

At that time there was a rodeo performance on Friday night, a matinee on Saturday followed up by an evening performance, and then a Sunday afternoon show. So, one obvious disadvantage of September was that school was in session, which all but eliminated the ability for families from out of town to come on any day other than Saturday. This also made it difficult for the possibility of moving one of the Saturday performances to Thursday.

The greased pig-catching contest was a popular feature of the rodeo in the '60s.

Robert Conrad, star of "The Wild, Wild West" and the 1967 rodeo, laughs with a stuntman in the midst of broken chairs after a demonstration of a fight scene.

Competition for Spectators

Another drawback to September rodeos was competition from high school football. The Sikeston Bulldogs were among the top teams in the state during the '50s and '60s under coaches Kenny Knox and Bill Sapp, during one stretch losing only one game in eight seasons. Therefore, most Sikeston residents understandably found themselves at the football stadium on Friday night rather than the rodeo grounds.

Not only did school and football damper attendance, but September also held other area events – the Sikeston American Legion Cotton Carnival and the Cape Girardeau SEMO District Fair. Both events were established and brought patrons from all around year after year, which meant even more competition for the rodeo.

Even though there were several reasons to move the rodeo dates up a month, the driving force behind the decision wasn't the reasons above. Mother Nature played the biggest hand in the choice.

Weather Issues

September in Southeast Missouri is generally a transition period in the weather when cold air begins to own the night and summer tries desperately to keep a firm grasp during the day. Not only did the chilly evenings make sitting through a rodeo performance difficult, often times the weather produces high winds and unpredictable rains. Those rains had proven in 1962 to be a financial disaster for the rodeo.

Bill Burch recalls the weather in 1964, which was the last year the rodeo was held in September. "In '64, the wind was so strong and it was so cold that you had problems getting the mics to work." Burch said, "We were still having problems with the rain. We finally got smart and checked with the people at the Cape fair to find out what the weather had been over the past many years."

The SEMO District Fair kept records on all things related to weather from year to year and the data they shared confirmed what

Jim Nabors, TV's Gomer Pyle, shakes hands with Jaycee Bill Lewis.

Fess Parker, better known as TV's "Daniel Boone", signs for an unidentified fan in 1969. From the Loy Baugher collection.

Buddy Ebsen, better know as Jed Clampett of "The Beverly Hillbillies" poses with a kidnapped family. From the Loy Baugher collection.

the Jaycees had known all along. September was just a terrible month for the weather and a change needed to be made. As with any event of this nature, tradition finds a firm grasp and there was much debate on the subject. However, no one could deny how the weather had treated them over the years, so a motion was made and passed to move the rodeo to August.

In 1965 the Sikeston Jaycee Bootheel Rodeo was held Thursday through Sunday August 12-15. The '65 rodeo saw Jim Nabors, TV's Gomer Pyle, entertain the crowd not only with his comedic acting, but his singing as well. No one can recall any problems with the sound equipment due to the weather. However, even though August is typically dryer than September that's not to say it doesn't rain. As always, with rain comes problems, as 1970 general chairman Charlie McGill would come to learn.

The Great Bleacher Collapse

In 1970, the rodeo booked the very popular Michael Landon from "Bonanza" as the entertainment. Landon was a household name and as such ticket sales were much higher than the previous year, especially for Saturday night. At the time, each stringer of bleachers was supported by wooden A-frames with no concrete foundation. Rain had been a problem that year and since there was concern that the soaked ground might cause problems with the bleachers, the Jaycees worked to shore up the frames but ran out of time before they got to the east section.

McGill recalls the events that unfolded just after he exited the arena after making his traditional entrance on horseback before the performance. "I had just gotten back from being out in the

"Bonanza" star Michael Landon ("Little Joe Cartwright") shows the 1970 rodeo crowd he can handle a song as well as a gun. From the Loy Baugher collection.

arena when my co-chairman came up and said 'We have a problem. Those bleachers over there are just leaning over sideways and we're afraid they're gonna fall.' We looked at the situation to see what they could do to keep them from falling."

The Jaycees came up with a new way to shame members who didn't wear western attire as the rodeo approached–a pig in the yard.

With 2,500 people in the bleachers at the time, the plan was to bring in a tractor, tie it to the bleachers via a cable and pull them back straight. Over 40 years later, McGill recalls vividly the event that unfolded.

"Before we could get anything done, all of a sudden 'Kapow!' We heard a noise. Then it was like a repeating shotgun, because as one stringer broke it put pressure on the next one. It was 'Kapow! Kapow! Kapow!' and down came the bleachers."

Luckily only one injury resulted from the collapse, resulting from a panicked woman who jumped off as they were falling and injured her back. Fans were urged to stay calm and were directed off the bleachers where they watched the rest of the performance along the arena fence. After the performance, the Jaycees made repairs for Sunday's show with no more incidents.

New Bleachers

Even though the rodeo suffered through what could have been a complete disaster, it still cleared $18,000 profit in 1970. It was a good thing, too, because the decision was finally made to do something about the bleachers that were in terrible shape. Over the next two years the Jaycees replaced the wooden frames with steel frames. Despite having a profitable rodeo in 1970, $18,000 wasn't nearly enough to cover the cost of the bleachers so the rodeo board was forced to get a loan to purchase them. However, the bank that issued the loan required personal guarantees from five Jaycees – including McGill, Harper and Burch – which made them liable for the debt should the rodeo not be able to pay the debt. Even though the personal risk was high, the five got out their ink pens and signed on the line, helping to guarantee the future of the rodeo.

"If it had not gone well, it would have devastated me," McGill said. "But I didn't think twice. I signed that sucker, and I'm proud of it, because if we hadn't done it, it was the end."

The new bleachers were erected in time for the 1972 rodeo, which starred Johnny Paycheck and Barbara Mandrell. The '72 rodeo marked a turning point in the history of the event in terms of the type of entertainment rodeo fans would enjoy.

CHAPTER EIGHT

One Era Ends, Another Begins

With the 1960s in the rearview mirror, the rodeo moved into a different era not only in the terms of rodeo, but also a different American society that forced them to rethink the way they were doing things in terms of entertainment. They still had top-notch cowboys and second-to-none rodeo stock to challenge them, but there were only so many people still interested in the rodeo competition, and ticket sales directly reflected the entertainment that was booked each year.

Up until 1970, rodeo entertainers consisted mostly of TV Western actors. This made perfect sense due to the fact that televisions had become affordable for most families and due to the high ratings that TV Westerns got in that era, many of the actors were household names. For example, in 1957-58, five of the top 10 shows in America were Westerns. The next season, the top four programs were "Gunsmoke," Wagon Train," "Have Gun Will Travel" and "The Rifleman." As a result, booking actors from this genre for entertainment to go along with a rodeo was a "no-brainer." The Jaycees were giving fans what they wanted.

Tastes in Entertainment Change

However, as the '60s trudged along things began to change culturally. No longer was our society innocent. Through television, not only did families still watch their favorite westerns, but now they watched the Cuban Missile Crisis unfold, the assassinations of President John F. Kennedy and Martin Luther King, Jr. and the coverage of the escalating war in Vietnam. This, of course, changed the way our society viewed the world. Then came the sweeping cultural changes triggered by the "British Invasion" of 1964, when young boys began asking for guitars and record players instead of guns and holster sets.

Ken Curtis, TV's Festus Haggen of "Gunsmoke", hams it up with Alice and Tom Nunnelee. From the Loy Baugher collection.

Westerns, however, were not dead. "Gunsmoke," "Bonanza" and "Rawhide" still dominated but by the end of the 60s the only two Westerns still in the top 25 were "Gunsmoke" and "Bonanza." It seemed the public had begun to crave more contemporary or modern television programs.

This cultural change wasn't lost on the Jaycees. They realized that the pool of actors that they most often chose their entertainment from was quickly drying up. When Michael Landon appeared in 1970, it marked the second time he had made his way to Sikeston. The same held true for the many other actors. According to Tom Nunnelee, "We had run the gamut."

A New Direction

Aside from actors like Jay North (aka Dennis the Menace), Jim Nabors (Gomer Pyle) and Buddy Ebsen ("The Beverly Hillbillies"), the Jaycees had almost always booked a Western TV or movie star. That was the case until 1972. The Jaycees that year decided to go in a different direction and sign on a pair of new up-and-coming country music stars named Johnny Paycheck and Barbara Mandrell. For Mandrell, this would be the first time she ever headlined a concert, according to her father and manager Irby. This was a vast difference in the type of entertainment they usually booked, but the Jaycees were betting on fans wanting to hear an hour-and-a-half of music rather than 30-45 minutes of jokes, fake gunfights and musical numbers. The bet seemed to pay off, and since it was becoming apparent that even more emphasis would need to be placed on which entertainers were booked each year, the rodeo formed the first ever "entertainment committee," chaired by Tom Nunnelee.

Out with the Old, In with the New

The 1973 rodeo marked the end of an era for the event. The Jaycees booked Roy Rogers and Dale Evans, who packed the fans in that year and set a record for over 10,000 tickets sold for Saturday night's performance. However, it would be the end of the Western-themed entertainers of the rodeo. What better way to send that era on and welcome in a new one than with the most famous singing cowboy of them all, his wife, co-star and duet partner, and with the legendary western group The Sons of the Pioneers.

The following year the rodeo continued to wow the crowd with the bulls and broncs, but instead of a TV Western star, the crown was entertained by '50's teen idol Pat Boone, who came to Sikeston with a family act that included his wife and four daughters. His daughter Debbie later went on to hit #1 on the Hot 100 for a record 10 weeks with her recording of "You Light up My Life." 1975 saw pop star Bobby Vinton entertain the crowd to be followed up in 1976 by one of the biggest stars in country music at the time, 17-year-old Tanya Tucker.

The '70s weren't over yet however, and 1977's entertainer would prove to be one of the most beneficial for the rodeo and the surrounding area. Consequently, the effects of that year are still felt here today in Sikeston.

Dennis Ziegenhorn of the Jaycees poses with Dale Evans, Roy Rogers and Dusty Rogers at the 1973 rodeo.

Pat Boone (left) poses with 1974 Rodeo Queen Teresa Scherer and entertainment committee chairman Tom Nunnelee.

CHAPTER NINE

A Singer, an Organization and a Town

In 1977, the Jaycees paid $25,000 for the entertainment and it might be one of the best investments any organization in the surrounding area has ever made.

Kenny Rogers had primarily been known as a pop singer. Some knew him as "that guy with the beard from the First Edition." The First Edition was the group he had enjoyed success with in the '60s and early '70s. The group was primarily composed of former members of the folk group the New Christy Minstrels, but the First Edition's breakthrough hit "Just Dropped In (To See What Condition My Condition Was In)" in '68 was about as far from folk music as you can get. The psychedelic hit put the group on the map, but their version of a Mel Tillis-penned song "Ruby, Don't Take Your Love to Town" the next year showed the country side of the First Edition. In 1971, the band, which was now known as Kenny Rogers and the First Edition, had its own syndicated TV show, "Rollin." But by 1975 the group had disintegrated, and Rogers had signed a solo record deal with United Artists.

Had the timing of the signing of Rogers for the rodeo been a little different, the Jaycees would probably have had to pay more or perhaps not have been able to sign him at all. His first big solo single – "Lucille" – had been released in January and was on its way to #1 on the Billboard Country charts and #6 on the Hot 100 pop charts, peaking about the time Tom Nunnelee and the rodeo entertainment committee were securing their entertainment for the August rodeo. Rogers at this point was a rising star, but not the superstar he would become in just a few months.

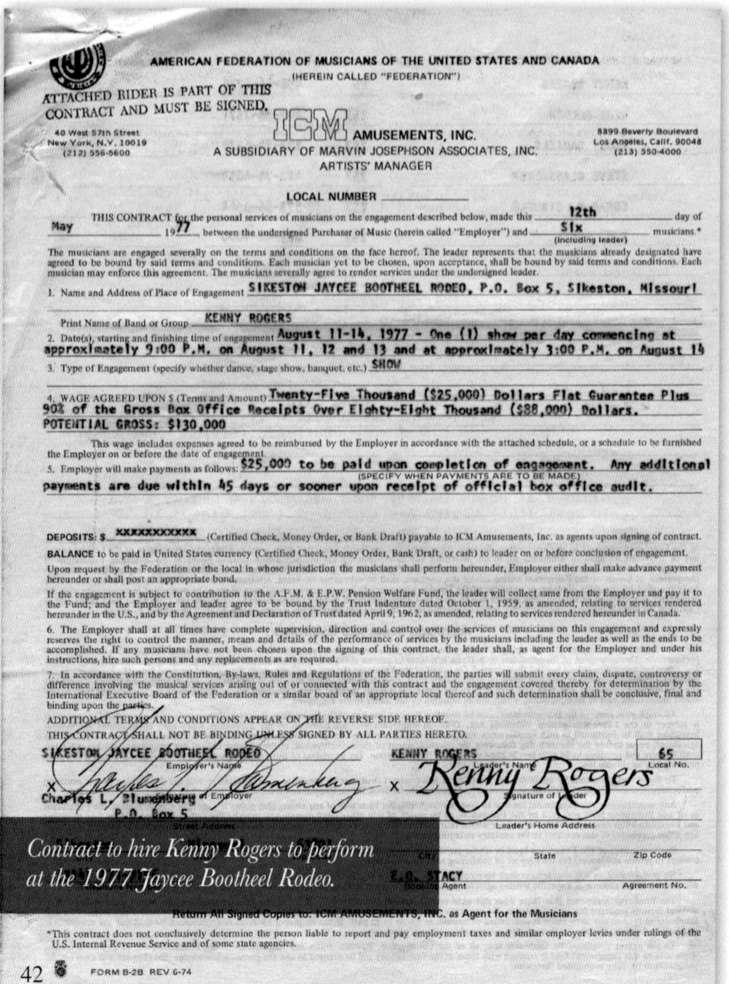

AMERICAN FEDERATION OF MUSICIANS OF THE UNITED STATES AND CANADA
(HEREIN CALLED "FEDERATION")

ATTACHED RIDER IS PART OF THIS CONTRACT AND MUST BE SIGNED.

ICM AMUSEMENTS, INC.
A SUBSIDIARY OF MARVIN JOSEPHSON ASSOCIATES, INC.
ARTISTS' MANAGER

40 West 57th Street, New York, N.Y. 10019, (212) 556-5600
8899 Beverly Boulevard, Los Angeles, Calif. 90048, (213) 550-4000

LOCAL NUMBER ______

THIS CONTRACT for the personal services of musicians on the engagement described below, made this 12th day of May 1977 between the undersigned Purchaser of Music (herein called "Employer") and Six (including leader) musicians.*

The musicians are engaged severally on the terms and conditions on the face hereof. The leader represents that the musicians already designated have agreed to be bound by said terms and conditions. Each musician yet to be chosen, upon acceptance, shall be bound by said terms and conditions. Each musician may enforce this agreement. The musicians severally agree to render services under the undersigned leader.

1. Name and Address of Place of Engagement SIKESTON JAYCEE BOOTHEEL RODEO, P.O. Box 5, Sikeston, Missouri

Print Name of Band or Group KENNY ROGERS

2. Date(s), starting and finishing time of engagement August 11-14, 1977 - One (1) show per day commencing at approximately 9:00 P.M. on August 11, 12 and 13 and at approximately 3:00 P.M. on August 14

3. Type of Engagement (specify whether dance, stage show, banquet, etc.) SHOW

4. WAGE AGREED UPON $ (Terms and Amount) Twenty-Five Thousand ($25,000) Dollars Flat Guarantee Plus 90% of the Gross Box Office Receipts Over Eighty-Eight Thousand ($88,000) Dollars. POTENTIAL GROSS: $130,000

This wage includes expenses agreed to be reimbursed by the Employer in accordance with the attached schedule, or a schedule to be furnished the Employer on or before the date of engagement.

5. Employer will make payments as follows: $25,000 to be paid upon completion of engagement. Any additional payments are due within 45 days or sooner upon receipt of official box office audit.
(SPECIFY WHEN PAYMENTS ARE TO BE MADE)

DEPOSITS: $ XXXXXXXXXXX (Certified Check, Money Order, or Bank Draft) payable to ICM Amusements, Inc. as agents upon signing of contract.

BALANCE to be paid in United States currency (Certified Check, Money Order, Bank Draft, or cash) to leader on or before conclusion of engagement.

Upon request by the Federation or the local in whose jurisdiction the musicians shall perform hereunder, Employer either shall make advance payment hereunder or shall post an appropriate bond.

If the engagement is subject to contribution to the A.F.M. & E.P.W. Pension Welfare Fund, the leader will collect same from the Employer and pay it to the Fund; and the Employer and leader agree to be bound by the Trust Indenture dated October 1, 1959, as amended, relating to services rendered hereunder in the U.S., and by the Agreement and Declaration of Trust dated April 9, 1962, as amended, relating to services rendered hereunder in Canada.

6. The Employer shall at all times have complete supervision, direction and control over the services of musicians on this engagement and expressly reserves the right to control the manner, means and details of the performance of services by the musicians including the leader as well as the ends to be accomplished. If any musicians have not been chosen upon the signing of this contract, the leader shall, as agent for the Employer and under his instructions, hire such persons and any replacements as are required.

7. In accordance with the Constitution, By-laws, Rules and Regulations of the Federation, the parties will submit every claim, dispute, controversy or difference involving the musical services arising out of or connected with this contract and the engagement covered thereby for determination by the International Executive Board of the Federation or a similar board of an appropriate local thereof and such determination shall be conclusive, final and binding upon the parties.

ADDITIONAL TERMS AND CONDITIONS APPEAR ON THE REVERSE SIDE HEREOF.

THIS CONTRACT SHALL NOT BE BINDING UNLESS SIGNED BY ALL PARTIES HERETO.

SIKESTON JAYCEE BOOTHEEL RODEO	KENNY ROGERS	65
Employer's Name	Leader's Name	Local No.
X Charles L. Blumenberg	X Kenny Rogers	
Signature of Employer	Signature of Leader	
P.O. Box 5		
Street Address	Leader's Home Address	
	City / State	Zip Code
	E.O. STACY	
	Booking Agent	Agreement No.

Return All Signed Copies to: ICM AMUSEMENTS, INC. as Agent for the Musicians

*This contract does not conclusively determine the person liable to report and pay employment taxes and similar employer levies under rulings of the U.S. Internal Revenue Service and of some state agencies.

FORM B-2B REV 6-74

Contract to hire Kenny Rogers to perform at the 1977 Jaycee Bootheel Rodeo.

Kenny's Introduction to Sikeston

Nunnelee recalls the events surrounding the announcement of Rogers' Sikeston appearance vividly, beginning with a phone conversation he had with manager Ken Kragen to tell him about the press conference at Sikeston City Hall to announce the rodeo entertainment:

"I called Ken Kragen and said 'were going to announce Kenny Rogers as our star for the rodeo' " Nunnelee relates. He also mentioned in passing to

Kragen that the Jaycees were going to announce an $8,000 donation to the city to help purchase a new fire truck. "Kragen said 'You're kidding! Kenny really likes these kinds of things. He likes charity stuff.' " Kragen told Rogers about the planned press conference, and the singer said that he wanted to be part of it.

When the morning of the press conference came, Nunnelee made a phone call to Rogers at his hotel in Las Vegas, where he was appearing, giving him the opportunity to address the media in Sikeston. "He began to talk," Nunnelee remembers. "He talked about how excited he was to come to Sikeston and what he had heard about the work of the Jaycees. 'The reason I'm on this call is because I like things like this,' Rogers said to the media. 'I think this is exciting. In fact, I'm thinking about coming (to Sikeston) in advance of the rodeo to meet with the Jaycees.'"

Although by this time Kenny Rogers was becoming a major star and had many demands on his time, he kept his word about coming to Sikeston in advance of the rodeo. "He flew in here in June," Nunnelee recalls. "We shot commercials. The Jaycees and Jaycee Wives had lunch with him." Part of the day was spent touring the rodeo grounds, and Rogers talked about the possibility of putting on a celebrity softball game as a Jaycee fundraiser at the arena. It seemed that the man who was becoming one of the biggest stars in the music industry had taken a shine to the town of Sikeston and to the Jaycees.

Kenny Rogers

A Big Announcement

By the second week in August, "Lucille" had become perhaps the most-played record on the planet, and Rogers had just released another single that would also go to #1 – "Daytime Friends." He took the time to meet with a handful of Jaycees for lunch at the Ramada Inn, where he made an announcement that caused jaws to drop around the table.

"I want you to know I've been impressed with what you've done," Rogers said. "I've seen more than enough. I've got a horse out in California – an Arabian stallion – and I was going to give it to another charity. But since I've been here I've changed my mind. I want to give this horse to the Sikeston Jaycees."

"We all looked kind of dumbfounded," Nunnelee recalls. "I said 'Kenny, what do you want us to do with a horse?' He looked at us all and said, 'Guys, I don't know what you'll do with it. But I do know one thing for sure – whatever it is, it'll be the right thing.' "

The Jaycees, Borraabby & the Cerebral Palsy Center

The 1977 Jaycee Bootheel Rodeo made $25,000 profit – ironically the same amount paid to Kenny Rogers. The Jaycees had taken an interest in the local cerebral palsy center, which had no certified therapist and only had space to treat five patients at their rented facility of Center Street in Sikeston. They had let the CP center officials know about the horse that Rogers had donated and told them that their intention was to auction the horse and donate the money to the CP center as seed money for a new facility.

On October 10, a Jaycee contingent including Nunnelee and Charles Stamp went to Nashville for the Country Music Association Awards, where Kenny Rogers was hosting and was nominated for four awards. After winning the Single of the Year award for "Lucille," Rogers spoke briefly backstage with the Jaycees, who informed him that officials from the cerebral palsy center, grateful for the donation of the stallion named Borraabby, wanted to name their potential new building after him. Rogers was flattered, but somewhat reluctant, expressing concerns about what would happen if the center failed. The conversation ended with the agreement that Rogers would give the matter some thought, and the Jaycees walked away.

At that point, Rogers' manager Ken Kragen caught up with the Sikeston delegation in the hallway and said, according to Nunnelee, "Look, he loves that organization (United Cerebral Palsy) and all you guys. He's genuinely impressed. Remember one thing. If I want him to do something, I can convince him to do it. And I want him to do this."

On the way back to Sikeston from the CMA Awards in Nashville, the Jaycee delegation determined that the $25,000 profit from the 1977 rodeo should go to the CP center to supplement the proceeds from the sale of Borraabby. On October 14, the donation of Borraabby to the Jaycees and the cerebral palsy center was announced publicly.

The Project Snowballs

Aided by the interest and promotion of *Arabian Horse Journal* editor Dixie Ryan, the auction of Borraabby and the cerebral palsy center project gained national attention. The horse had been

This article in Arabian Horse Journal *was part of a publicity campaign that resulted in the sale of Borraabby for $75,000.*

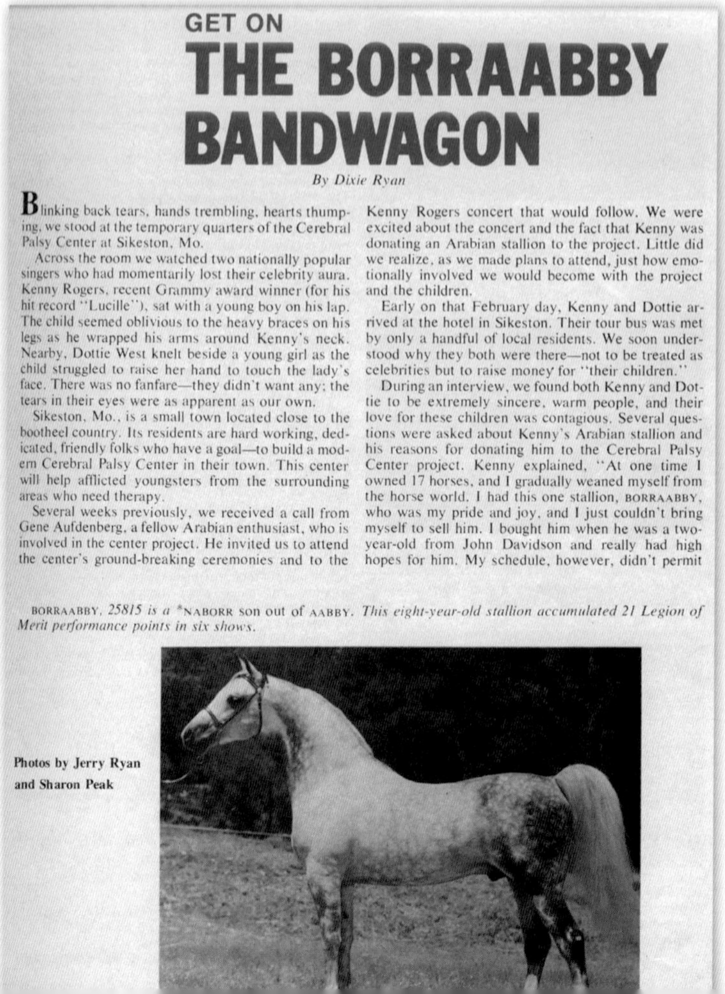

GET ON

THE BORRAABBY BANDWAGON

By Dixie Ryan

Blinking back tears, hands trembling, hearts thumping, we stood at the temporary quarters of the Cerebral Palsy Center at Sikeston, Mo.

Across the room we watched two nationally popular singers who had momentarily lost their celebrity aura. Kenny Rogers, recent Grammy award winner (for his hit record "Lucille"), sat with a young boy on his lap. The child seemed oblivious to the heavy braces on his legs as he wrapped his arms around Kenny's neck. Nearby, Dottie West knelt beside a young girl as the child struggled to raise her hand to touch the lady's face. There was no fanfare—they didn't want any; the tears in their eyes were as apparent as our own.

Sikeston, Mo., is a small town located close to the bootheel country. Its residents are hard working, dedicated, friendly folks who have a goal—to build a modern Cerebral Palsy Center in their town. This center will help afflicted youngsters from the surrounding areas who need therapy.

Several weeks previously, we received a call from Gene Aufdenberg, a fellow Arabian enthusiast, who is involved in the center project. He invited us to attend the center's ground-breaking ceremonies and to the Kenny Rogers concert that would follow. We were excited about the concert and the fact that Kenny was donating an Arabian stallion to the project. Little did we realize, as we made plans to attend, just how emotionally involved we would become with the project and the children.

Early on that February day, Kenny and Dottie arrived at the hotel in Sikeston. Their tour bus was met by only a handful of local residents. We soon understood why they both were there—not to be treated as celebrities but to raise money for "their children."

During an interview, we found both Kenny and Dottie to be extremely sincere, warm people, and their love for these children was contagious. Several questions were asked about Kenny's Arabian stallion and his reasons for donating him to the Cerebral Palsy Center project. Kenny explained, "At one time I owned 17 horses, and I gradually weaned myself from the horse world. I had this one stallion, BORRAABBY, who was my pride and joy, and I just couldn't bring myself to sell him. I bought him when he was a two-year-old from John Davidson and really had high hopes for him. My schedule, however, didn't permit

BORRAABBY, *25815 is a* *NABORR son out of AABBY. *This eight-year-old stallion accumulated 21 Legion of Merit performance points in six shows.*

Photos by Jerry Ryan and Sharon Peak

valued at $25,000, but after an article titled "Get On the Borraabby Bandwagon" was published in Ryan's magazine, bidders were now not only trying to buy a horse, but were supporting a cause. When Borraabby was sold in 1978 for $75,000, Kenny Rogers personally delivered the horse to the winning bidder at Lake Tahoe, Cal. Convinced that having his name on the new center was a pretty good idea, Rogers not only gave consent to putting his name on the building, but announced in December that he would return to Sikeston on Feb. 19 for a benefit concert at the Sikeston High School Field House.

Sunday, Feb. 19, 1978 was proclaimed "Kenny Rogers Day" across the state of Missouri. The *Daily Standard* headline that day read "Welcome back Kenny!" The singer turned the ceremonial first shovel of dirt at the groundbreaking ceremony for the Scott-Mississippi-New Madrid Counties United Cerebral Palsy Center in the afternoon, and then performed at the sold-out benefit in the evening. Appearing on "The Tonight Show" the next evening, Rogers talked about Sikeston and the cerebral palsy center and said that the benefit had raised nearly $100,000, including the $25,000 donation by the Jaycees from the 1977 rodeo.

Still More Help to Come

As news of the project spread, more celebrities wanted to help. Al Jardine of the Beach Boys, who also owned Arabian horses and had remembered appearing with the Beach Boys in Sikeston in 1969, decided to donate one of his Arabians. The Beach Boys as a group also made a cash donation of $18,000. Rogers returned for a second benefit concert, this time with frequent duet partner Dottie West, in January 1979. Mel Tillis came to Sikeston for a benefit concert in April of the same year, just after the new center opened its doors. Larry Gatlin performed at a fundraiser for the center in 1980.

All told, according to Nunnelee, Kenny Rogers' involvement with the cerebral palsy center project led to over $300,000 being raised. In 1980, the Sikeston Jaycees won the award at the national Jaycee convention for best project, beating out the Greater Greensboro Open PGA Tour golf tournament. As Nunnelee said, "it put (Sikeston) on the national map."

Not a bad return for a $25,000 investment.

A clown comes to the aid of a cowboy in trouble.

A young cowboy and cowgirl enjoy the rodeo.

Mark Miller of the band Sawyer Brown with a young cowgirl attending the rodeo as a result of the help of the Make-a-Wish Foundation

KENNY ROGERS

August 8, 2012

Congratulations to my friends with the Sikeston Jaycees on the 60th anniversary of the Sikeston Jaycee Bootheel Rodeo and my heartfelt appreciation for having been included as a performer for this ambitious event.

In 1977, I was invited to perform for the 25th Anniversary of the Sikeston Rodeo. I was so impressed with all the people I met and particularly the young Jaycee group who invited me.

After performing there, and being welcomed into your community, I felt there was more I could, and wanted to do.

I was told of the Jaycee's dream to build a children's therapy center in the city. At the time I was raising Arabian horses, so with their permission I donated an Arabian Stallion for an auction just to help them get started. Once started, I felt I could continue to participate on a lot of different levels.

I returned to Sikeston with my friend Dottie West a few times to perform and to visit. Each time I watched their little dream grow into something life-changing for a lot of people.

I'm so thankful for the opportunity to have been a part of this great event and this facility that has helped so many children, and their families.

It is a dream come true for all of us.

My thanks again to the Jaycees and the city of Sikeston.

Sincerely,

Kenny Rogers

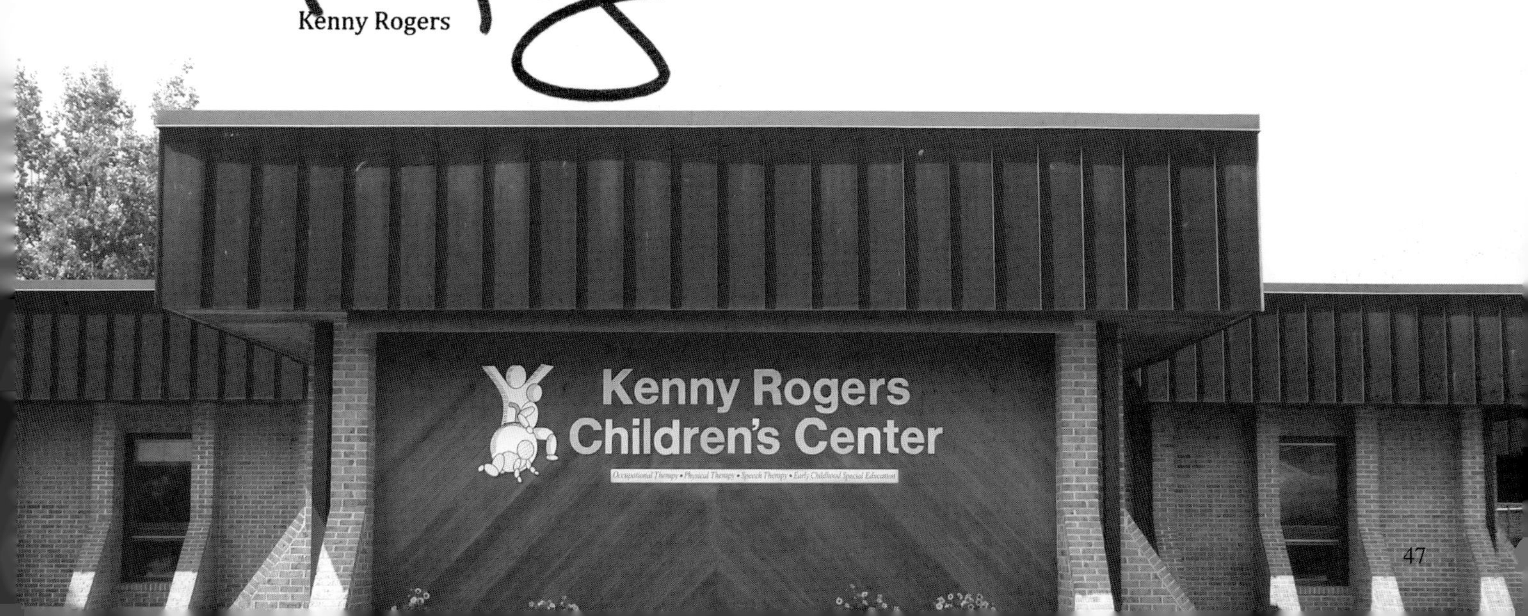

THE HISTORY OF THE KENNY Rogers CHILDREN'S CENTER

The following information is provided by the Kenny Rogers Children's Center:

The Kenny Rogers Children's Center is rich in history. It is a one-of-a-kind, state-of-the-art facility – the envy of therapists who visit the Center and often ask, "How do you have all of this in the middle of no where?" We just tell them, "No one ever told us we couldn't." It all started once upon a time. . .

1973

When the Center opened, it was primarily due to the efforts of Helen Shelton and Tom Richey. Helen was the mother of a child with cerebral palsy who needed physical therapy and there wasn't a facility that provided pediatric therapy locally. So she took it upon herself to attend seminars, read pertinent information and talk with others to learn the basics needed to provide such services. As word spread, other families contacted her about services for their children with special needs as well. Tom Richey, PT, was then employed at Missouri Delta Medical Center and was also doing some work at the Regional Center, located behind the hospital, when he noticed a file cabinet with a few files in it. He was told those were kids with severe disabilities and if he wanted to do anything with them he could, on his own time. Tom began doing evaluations on one Saturday morning per month. Before long it became all day long on Saturday and eventually he was doing evaluations every Saturday – all day long for the volunteers to follow through with therapy. Out of that effort, the Scott-Mississippi-New Madrid Counties United Cerebral Palsy Center opened in September of 1974 at the Sikeston Regional Center for the Developmentally Disabled at One Plaza Drive in Sikeston. It opened with five clients, one paid employee, two foster grandparents and several other volunteers.

1974

The Center's first fundraising effort was a Charity Walk – which continues today. The Sikeston Eagles were responsible for this event and for most of the funds that were raised in the early days. Due largely to their support, by 1976, the Center had grown considerably and was serving 23 children. This growth warranted a move. The Sikeston Eagles assisted with the first year's rent and the Center moved to a 30 by 60 foot building located at 510 East Center Street which is the old Moll Printing Building.

1977

In 1977, country music legend Kenny Rogers was the featured performer at the 25th annual Jaycee Bootheel Rodeo. He was so impressed with the Jaycees and what they were doing for the community that he donated an Arabian stallion valued at $25,000 to the Jaycees to benefit the community as they saw fit. The Jaycees decided to donate the proceeds to building a new Center and the stallion was ultimately auctioned for $75,000, seed money for more to come.

1978

Kenny teamed up with Dottie West for two benefit concerts in 1978 – first, A "Dream Come True" theme netting $74,000 and again in 1979 - A "Dream to Reality" theme netting $72,000.

1979

Mel Tillis followed in April of 1979 with a "Prayer Answered" theme, and the Gatlin Brothers in April of 1980, both with very successful concerts, which also benefited the Center.

Through the efforts of the Sikeston Jaycees in sponsoring these benefit concerts, and the support of numerous other interested parties from throughout the area, construction of the Kenny Rogers United Cerebral Palsy Center of Southeast Missouri was completed in June of 1979 at a total cost of $325,000.

1980

In 1980 Nick Zaharopolis and Kenny Bridger decided an annual telethon should be held to raise funds annually to meet operating expenses. This is a tradition that continues today and is the Center's primary fund-raising event.

1990

Over the years, the Center continued to grow, not only in size, but in scope as well. In 1994 a 3,000 square foot expansion was added to the existing building. Kenny returned to welcome everyone to the newly expanded space.

2000

In 2000, the Center officially changed its name to The Kenny Rogers Children's Center recognizing the fact that we treat children with dozens of different diagnoses, not just cerebral palsy.

2001

In April of 2001, Kenny Rogers returned to Sikeston and performed a greatest hits benefit concert. This event raised more than $75,000. The Center also received a matching grant from Lions International, which enabled us to update our sensory room, vision room, indoor tree house and make other needed repairs.

2009

In the summer of 2009 Kenny returned to town for his fourth benefit concert and teamed up with Sikeston native Neal E. Boyd, winner of the popular "America's Got Talent" contest. Kenny & Neal spent some time in the Center getting to know the therapists and some of the children that benefit from the amazing services offered at the Center. A reception was held at the home of Richard & Christy Montgomery and Governor Jay Nixon was on hand to introduce Kenny and Neal at the reception and at the concert. At that time, it was announced that plans were underway for a 7,000 square foot expansion providing the Center with additional treatment space, office space for the therapists and education / meeting room. The project is budgeted at $750,000 and the concert got us started with $117,000, which was held in a CD until construction began.

Recently expanded playground area located inside the Kenny Rogers Children's Center.

2010

Our 27th Annual Telethon scheduled in March each year was our most successful to date! When all was said and done, we raised $513,067 – the most ever!!! That's more than half a million dollars! A lot of our success came from our "Lend A Hand" campaign where we asked for 500 - $1,000 donors. We got almost 100 donors, which was fantastic. We immediately began on the remodel of our original building, which was pretty outdated. We cut down the gym size and created office cubicles where we can now house up to 20 therapists. We currently have 14 and counting! The more therapists we have, the more children we can treat. In October, 2010 the Center officially broke ground on it's new expansion project. Plans for the new expansion included a state-of-the-art, fully accessible sensory-motor learning center, a motion analysis laboratory, three new therapy rooms including our vision and suit therapy rooms as well as a conference/meeting room. The expansion was completed in 2011. As a result of the overwhelming generosity of this community, the Kenny Rogers Children's Center continues to provide superior therapy services to the children throughout Southeast Missouri at no charge to the families served. Currently we serve more than 350 children with special needs from birth through 21 years of age.

Dottie West performs at a fundraiser for the Kenny Rogers Children's Center.

CHAPTER TEN

A "Four-Star" Rodeo

Rain struck again on opening night of 1978 when over 3,500 people were forced to leave the arena due to rain. While Dottie West wasn't able to go on stage that night, she still performed the other nights and even mounted up and participated in the rodeo parade. Having Dottie perform the other nights gave fans that were rained out another chance to see her. However, 1978 would be the last year that the rodeo would see the same performer on multiple nights.

Since the Jaycees began hiring entertainers in the 1950s, booking actors and musicians for multiple nights had been common practice. Usually, when more than one entertainer was booked for the week it was due mostly to the celebrities' schedule more than anything. This was advantageous due to the fact that they could choose what night they wanted to get dolled up and come watch the rodeo and see their favorite celebrity. This format made it easier on the Jaycees as well, since they only had deal with hiring a couple of entertainers at the most, which made things smoother logistically as well as kept the financial cost down.

Rodeo general chairman Geary Yant, 1983.

The drawback to this format was that once a spectator had watched one rodeo then he or she had seen them all. This was not lost on the rodeo board. Also, the Jaycees began to realize that, while plenty of folks would still buy a ticket to watch a quality rodeo many people would attend primarily for the entertainer. To capitalize on this, the rodeo board decided to take yet another gamble and book four different acts, thus having a different entertainer for every performance. While this wasn't the first time multiple acts had been hired, it was the first time a different one was booked for each night.

The Jaycees were understandably apprehensive since the cost of entertainment would dramatically increase but were betting that ticket sales would increase as fans would purchase more than one ticket every year to see different performers. After some debate, the decision was made and during a press conference in April of '79 scheduled by the Jaycees for Mel Tillis, which he showed up too late to attend, rodeo chairman Ed Pike announced to the press that rodeo board had decided to experiment with the idea of having four different entertainers at the rodeo.

Thankfully, the experiment paid off. The Jaycees began to see bigger crowds at the rodeo, which increased revenue and ultimately offset the higher cost of entertainment. To this day, 35 years later, the general chairman still gets together with his entertainment chairman in the fall and books four entertainers for the upcoming year.

Things Heat Up During the '80s

Over the previous decade the Jaycees had made leaps and bounds in the way they facilitated their rodeo. Many changes had been made in the way the rodeo was run financially, how and what entertainment was booked as well as a number of changes and upgrades to the infrastructure. They would need all of this in the years to come because the world of rodeo was about to heat up in more ways than one.

The 1980s saw one of the hottest performances on record. During Sunday's sold out performance the temperature soared over 100 degrees and general chairman Dan Lape had to contend with some 250-plus heat-related ailments in the crowd during the performance. However, battling through the heat that year paid off with a very prestigious award given by the National Junior Chamber of Commerce (National Jaycees). Jaycee president Bud Werner accepted the "Project of the Year Award" on behalf of the Sikeston Jaycees, beating out every other Jaycee project in the nation. This was a good start to the decade, and things would only get better.

Change in Stock Contractor

It's important to note that while the Jaycees had been focused on making changes in the entertainment department, the actual rodeo went on from year to year with little alteration because it didn't need changing. Tommy Steiner had been providing stock and producing a top-notch rodeo year after year and there wasn't much need to change things up. That is, until 1981.

Stock contractor Dell Hall, who has provided livestock to the Jaycee Bootheel Rodeo since 1981.

Steiner produced a number of large rodeos, so often times he would hire out subcontractors to provide the stock at Sikeston. One such contractor was Dell Hall from Oklahoma, who often worked for Steiner and had a relationship with the Sikeston Jaycees. In 1980, the Jaycees decided that if they were going to pay someone to provide stock, they would rather pay the person that was actually there, so Dell was approached and asked to be the primary stock contractor for the rodeo. Hall replied that he liked the idea but didn't want to burn any bridges with Steiner and would get back to them. He contacted Steiner and told them what the Jaycees had proposed and luckily Steiner didn't have a problem with it. The rest is history.

In September of 1980, a group of Jaycees led by 1981 general chairman Lee Beck headed to a rodeo in Springdale, AR to meet up with Hall to negotiate a contract. Once the details were hammered out, both Beck and Hall signed a contract agreeing that the Rafter H Rodeo Company would become the primary stock contractor for the Sikeston Jaycee Bootheel Rodeo.

The next August saw Dell Hall lead the grand entry, followed up by his 11-year-old daughter Shelly carrying the American flag on horseback during the National Anthem. Since that day, the Rafter H Rodeo Company, still led by Dell and Shelly, has provided the stock for Sikeston's rodeo. That relationship has continued for over 30 years.

The Popularity of Rodeo Escalates

The rodeo paid over $17,000 in '81 for their new stock contractor, and if there were any reservations, they quickly vanished. The opening night featuring Merle Haggard saw a sold out crowd, followed up by three more sold out performances, marking the only time in history the rodeo saw every seat filled during all four performances.

The 1980s, referred to by 1983 general chairman Geary Yant as the "Golden Years" of rodeo, saw a massive increase in the popularity in the sport of rodeo. After the 1980 movie "Urban Cowboy" it seemed everyone owned a hat and a pair of boots. In the case of Sikeston, it seemed everyone was eager to get duded up and come out to the rodeo to watch cowboys do what cowboys do. This, of course, benefited rodeos across the nation, and it also benefited individual cowboys as they began to see national companies and corporations sponsoring individual cowboys and rodeos. During this time national sponsors such Dodge, Coors and Winston came on board with the Jaycees as sponsors and partners. Some such relationships still exist today.

Bullfighting, a competition of skill pitting clown against bull, was a popular rodeo event until 2002. From the Loy Baugher collection.

The installation of the Cattle Baron seats over the bucking chutes was one of the upgrades to the rodeo grounds during the 1990s and 2000s. From the Loy Baugher collection.

The increase in revenue to rodeo directly increased the amount of money they were able to donate to the community as well as allowed for improvement to the rodeo grounds itself. Some such improvements include the addition of the entertainment barn and the cattle baron seats over the bucking chutes. A new event was added to line up as well, known as American bullfighting, which lasted until 2002.

No More Matinees

Another format change took place during the '80s. Since the rodeo had been moved to August in 1965, the Sunday performances had become known for their sweltering heat and stifling humidity since they were during the day. Due to this, often times ticket sales would suffer for the Sunday matinee, so the Jaycees finally decided that something had to be done. Their solution was to move the Sunday performance to Wednesday. This idea was met with apprehension, since there were also difficulties selling tickets on Thursday as well. According to Bill Burch, they even went as far as offering a free Kentucky Fried Chicken dinner one year and still didn't draw a crowd. The only exception to this was the 1981 sellout.

After much debate it was decided that the Sunday performance would be moved to Wednesday. It seemed the argument that won out was that if they were going to have trouble selling tickets, then the rodeo might as well do it in the evening instead of the middle of the day.

The announcement by the *Daily Standard* on March 24, 1989 that Willie Nelson would be performing on the first ever Wednesday night came as welcome news to rodeo fans. The article reported:

Nelson headlines Rodeo entertainment

Willie Nelson

SIKESTON — Willie Nelson.

His name, and little else, is necessary to draw the picture for Wednesday, Aug. 9, opening night of the 37th Annual Jaycee Bootheel Rodeo.

Nelson's familiar face and and sound will highlight the rodeo, but fans will also see something new about this year's program. Making the hot, steamy summer in Sikeston a little easier for rodeo fans, the executive board, headed by Rik LaPlant, decided this year's entertainment would run only in the evenings.

"Anything we can do to make our fans comfortable — including more shade and better seating and concessions — will be in the works for this year," said LaPlant during a press conference and gathering of supporters on Thursday.

The schedule calls for Wednesday through Saturday evenings, with no Sunday afternoon session as in previous years.

Other stars on the roster are the Charlie Daniels Band, on Thursday, Aug. 10; Tanya Tucker, Friday, Aug. 11; and Earl Thomas Conley, Saturday, Aug. 12. All shows begin at 7:30 p.m.

"This is probably the strongest entertainment package we have brought to the rodeo," said Mike Marshall, entertainment chairman.

The rodeo committee urged area merchants to contribute ideas for rodeo week, which is still in the planning phase. Gary Lasater said he would welcome any suggestions to enhance the project.

This year's arena program features top cowboys competing for $60,000 in prizes and American-style bullfighting.

Livestock will be provided by Dell Hall, owner of the Rafter H Rodeo Livestock Company of Tahlequah, Okla.

Hall, known primarily for the bucking stock, has won a number of national awards and his stock has been chosen to participate in the last 12 National Finals Rodeos.

Clowns for this year's arena performances will be Rick Young and Quail Dobbs. Young will be returning for his 28th season at the Jaycee event. Competing as barrel man, Dobbs was voted the Coors "Man in the Can" for 1985 through 1987 and won the Clown of the Year

See page 2: Jaycees

Rik LaPlant

Daily Standard *article from March 24, 1989, announcing the elimination of the Sunday matinee rodeo performance*

"Nelson's familiar face and sound will highlight the rodeo, but fans will also see something new about this year's program. Making the hot, steamy summer in Sikeston a little easier for rodeo fans, the executive board, headed by Rik LaPlant, decided this year's entertainment would run only in the evenings."

"Anything we can do to make our fans more comfortable, including more shade and better seating and concessions, will be in the in the works for this year," said LaPlant.

A four-night rodeo beginning on Wednesday is the format still used today by the Sikeston Jaycee Bootheel Rodeo.

In 1990, fans were once again entertained by Willie Nelson during his Wednesday night performance. While they were watching one of country music's biggest stars, they had no idea that four days later a little-known country music singer by the name of Garth Brooks would be making his debut as a headlining act in the same arena. Brooks had been on tour with Kenny Rogers that year and was relatively unknown. Saturday night's crowd had the privilege of watching the very first concert Brooks headlined. Little did the fans know they were watching the birth of one of most popular performers in country music.

By the 1990's the Jaycees had, for the most part, ironed out the kinks that came with putting on a top-notch rodeo. They finally had a working format and business model which is still used today. This left the Jaycees with more time and money to concentrate more on improving the rodeo and less on fixing it.

CHAPTER ELEVEN

KEEPING THE BALL ROLLING

In 1991, the Jaycees replaced the old bucking chutes with chutes used previously at the National Finals Rodeo.

Driver Jeff Sutton pulls a scratcher around the arena. The hard work of Jaycees and the grounds crew have helped the Jaycee Bootheel Rodeo win awards such as the 1995 "Justin Boots Firm Footing Award."

The Sikeston Jaycees started in 1991 by getting rid of the old bucking chutes and replacing them with chutes previously used by the National Finals Rodeo. Between 1994 and 1995 general chairman Tom Green and Jimmy Gipson oversaw the addition of new aluminum bleachers and box seats, along with a brand-new concrete footing for support. This ended the days of the "bleacher crew" spending weeks replacing wooden bleachers that were worn out. According to various Jaycees who worked the bleacher crew, the $45,000-dollar improvement was well worth it.

The '90s not only saw improvements to the arena fence, it also saw the addition of a new stage, a pole barn to house the stage and a number of new buildings, including the main concession stand. The hard work of Jaycees didn't go unnoticed by the fans, and the world of rodeo was taking notice as well.

Recognition from the Rodeo World

Over the years, the Sikeston Jaycees had received a number of awards from the state Jaycees for their "project" but they also began receiving accolades from the rodeo contestants as well. In 1992 the rodeo was awarded "Great Lakes Circuit Rodeo of The Year" by the Professional Rodeo Cowboys Association, followed up in 1993 by "Great Lakes Circuit Best Ground" award. The rodeo would go on to win "best footing" awards in 1999 and 2000 as well. Even in 1995 when three inches of rain canceled the grand entry, a group of Jaycees spent the entire night working on the arena and were awarded with the "Justin Boots Firm Footing Award."

The entire PRCA took notice of Sikeston also when in 1998 the rodeo was given the "Top Five Outdoor Rodeo of the Year" award. This was quite an accomplishment, since rain decided to set in during all four performances that year. Even the WPRA (Women's Professional Rodeo Association) recognized the Jaycees by awarding them "Committee of the Year" in 2000.

Workers install the new video board at the Rodeo grounds. Photo by Keith Hente.

More Facility Upgrades

In the year 2000, the Jaycees charged ahead into the new millennium with the construction of their brand new "sponsors building" to accommodate the growing number of sponsors. The new building included a dining area, kitchen and even a "cowboy room" where weary cowboys and cowgirls could stop in a grab a much needed shower or even a nap. This marked one of the latest major improvements to grounds. As a result of the hard work put in during the previous decade, most of the infrastructure that still stands in 2013 was in place and ready for the new century.

In 2002, the rodeo fans showed up on Wednesday night to see Alabama perform one last time during their stop in Sikeston on their farewell tour. They packed out the arena, marking the only time the rodeo has sold out on Wednesday night.

The next year saw two more changes in the format. Team roping was added to the roster of events, and instead of having the entertainer perform in the middle of the rodeo, the entertainment portion was moved to the end of the performance.

A Million Dollar Honor

Over the next few years it was business as usual with Jaycees always tweaking and making improvements to their event. Their standings in the PRCA began to grow to the point where in 2009 general chairman Matt Matthews was contacted by the PRCA and asked to become one of only 14 rodeos on the Wrangler Million Dollar Silver Tour, where cowboys and cowgirls compete to go to the Tour finals for a chance to win a million dollars. It was a "no-brainer" for Matthews, and since 2009 the Jaycee Bootheel Rodeo has become an annual stop for most of the elite cowboys and cowgirls hoping to compete in the tour finals as well as the National Finals Rodeo. In a circuit dominated by rodeos in western states, Sikeston has the distinction of being the easternmost stop on the Wrangler Million Dollar Silver Tour.

As usual though, the 2009 rodeo didn't go off without a hitch. On Monday of rodeo week the Jaycees received news that Billy Currington, Thursday night's performer, was injured in a stage accident and wouldn't be able to perform on Thursday. Matthews and entertainment chairman Cal Crader immediately got the wheels spinning to try and find a replacement and by that evening had Blake Shelton lined up to perform in place of Currington. All that was left to do was have the board of directors vote to approve the change so an impromptu meeting of the board was held in a small camper located at the grounds. The change was approved and in less than 48 hours after finding out they lost their entertainer, the Jaycees already had another one on the way from Nashville.

CHAPTER TWELVE

The Tradition Continues

The year 2013, which is the 60th anniversary of the first Jaycee Bootheel Rodeo in 1953,will mark the 61st time the Jaycees have gathered to put on their project. Today, the Sikeston Jaycee Bootheel Rodeo hosts a four-night performance every second week of August. While the cost and liabilities of producing the rodeo have been exponentially inflated since the first rodeo in 1953, the Jaycees still face some of the same issues the very first rodeo Jaycees faced and, therefore, still organize the rodeo in the same fashion that it was organized in the '50s.

The Organization

For example, every year a new rodeo co-chairman is elected. The co-chairman will work with rodeo general chairman for the next year and then take his place at the bow of the ship. The individual areas of the rodeo are also run in a similar manner. Rotating leadership every year has served to ensure new and fresh ideas are always being introduced, as well ensuring that anyone who wants to step up to a leadership role has ample opportunity. Like the leaders of the past, they still face the familiar challenges of publicity, cost of production and the weather. Thankfully, the Jaycees who were instrumental in producing the rodeo in past years are always around to help guide the younger generation by offering them support and advice. These "older" members are called "Exhausted Roosters," an honor given to a Jaycee past the age of 40 who has given his time and efforts to the club over the years.

Every year in January the club general membership votes to approve a budget brought forth by that year's general chairman. At over three-quarters of a million dollars, this budget far surpasses that of the first rodeo, but just like the first time, it has to pass a majority vote before the club can move forward with the project. During that same meeting, the club votes to elect new rodeo board members to replace those board members whose three-year term has come to an end. Then, with the housekeeping in order, the general chairman and co-chairman begin the process of getting the club, the community and the grounds ready for the rodeo while the board of directors keeps a watchful eye to the future. Ron Payne, the rodeo general chair-

2011 Jaycee Bootheel Rodeo Board of Directors. Bottom row left to right: Bart Ziegenhorn, Sam Thomas, Barry Johnson, Nathan Cox. Top row: Daniel Beck, Matt Drake, Cal Crader, Chris Deen, Ryan Merideth, Justin Wibbenmeyer.

man in 2008 can be quoted as saying, "The chairman's job is to put on the rodeo. The rodeo board's job is to make sure we have another one."

The Work

Once tickets go on sale in March, the club members come together to begin preparing for the August event that always seems to creep up on them before they know it. The "grounds crew" gets busy repairing any water lines, electric lines, buildings or bleachers that may be out of order as well as keeping the rodeo grounds mowed and free from weeds and trash. "Pens and chutes" spends the summer repairing any broken fences and gates that house the stock during the rodeo along with replacing or building new pens and alleys as they are needed. While the "stage crew" finalizes the contracts with that year's entertainers and prepares the stage and other equipment for the four-night performance, the ticket office is busy keeping up with ticket pre-orders. The members tasked with selling food, novelties and beer use the time to get their perspective buildings and stands ready and work with the appropriate vendors to ensure they will have enough product for the throngs of fans sure to pay them a visit during the rodeo. Other areas, such as sponsors, stay active selling sponsorship packages and arrange the catering and other activities offered to the sponsors during the event. "Advertising and publicity" stay in constant contact with local radio and television stations as well as provide community events to generate publicity for the rodeo. Other members are tasked with overseeing the rodeo pageants and parades as well as organizing the ushers that assist patrons to their seats during the performance.

All of this takes place under the watchful eyes of the rodeo chairman and co-chairman, who have the daunting task of moving the whole project along and "putting out fires" when they emerge. They work with the Jaycee president and the area chairmen to coordinate work parties and a couple of fun parties such as the rodeo picnic that takes place every year just before rodeo week. They stay in constant contact with the PRCA event directors and stock contractors and are the first point of contact for anything involving the production.

David Teachout at a rodeo work day

A group of "Exhausted Roosters" takes a break from work. L-R: Danny Lape, Larry Miller, Tom Nunnelee, Charlie McGill, Buddy Werner and Ben Werner.

Jim Cox at work on a concession area project.

The stage crew prepares the stage for the night's entertainers.

Rodeo Week Excitement

The first Monday of the second week of August kicks off rodeo week with the first "slack" (i.e., competition held with no paid spectators) performance followed by the second installment of slack on Tuesday night. The big show begins on Wednesday with the first rodeo performance, followed by the night's entertainer. The process is repeated for the next three nights. Jaycee club members come together and keep the show moving along, while an army of fans pour through gates every night. At the end of the performance on Saturday, the general chairman hands "the phone" over to his co-chairman officially ending his reign as chairman for the year and beginning the term of the next general chairman. Shortly after, the Jaycee club begins the 12-month preparation for the next year's performance.

The Big Payoff

In September, the club elects a new rodeo co-chairman and sends him, along with the chairman and a small delegation, to various PRCA meetings, rodeos and conventions to network with rodeo officials and sponsors. Late in the year, after the bills are paid and the books have been closed, the board gathers for one last time in December to determine the monetary success of the rodeo. They decide how much of the profits to re-invest back into the rodeo and then hand the rest over to the Jaycee president. During the last, and most important, Jaycee meeting of the year the club membership debates on how best to distribute the profits from the rodeo back into the community through charitable donations. They then close up shop for the holidays and begin the whole process over again on the first Tuesday of the New Year.

Thanks to the hard work and dedication of the Sikeston Jaycees and the community over the past 61 years, the rodeo has now become an institution in Sikeston that has provided not only entertainment for the community, but also given the Jaycees the privilege of being able to donate millions of dollars in donations to organizations and charities throughout the area. It's doubtful that the first group of Jaycees knew what their experiment would one day turn into as they were erecting the bleachers for the first rodeo in 1953, but they can be sure that they have the undying gratitude of today's members and can rest easily knowing that their efforts helped to put their town on the map and have benefitted countless individuals throughout the community.

This quote from an anonymous Jaycee seems to sum it up:

> "Words can't describe how thankful and honored we are to be handed down such an amazing responsibility. We owe everything that we do today to the men and women throughout the years that made this event what it is now and we will certainly do everything in our power to honor their sacrifice by keeping the rodeo a successful event for the next 60 years."

Photo courtesy of Lynda Warren.

Jaycees enjoy a break from their hard work during the 1992 rodeo. In the foreground is Mike Bohannon. In the background are Doug Lambert (sunglasses) and Tim Merideth.

Novelties chairman Jeff Long and Mamie Hamra at the rodeo novelty stand, 1992.

Barrel man Rick Young, world champion bullfighter Jerry Norton and Mike Johnson during the 1992 rodeo.

Secretary Shelly Hall and timer Betty Hall, daughter and wife of Rafter H Rodeo's Dell Hall, post the day's rodeo lineup.

Front, L-R: Gary Lasater, Larry Littleton, Danny Bridger, Jeff Wagner, Steve Ferrell, Joe Heckemeyer. Middle: Brian Bedell, Dan Beussink, Steve Johnston, Geary Yant, Dan Lape, George Hawthorne, Ed Pike, Larry Miller, N. J. "Bud" Werner, Charlie Walls, David Vaughn. Top: Todd Pierce, ?,?, Kevin Ward, Lee Beck, Charlie McGill, David Hough, Bruce Taylor, Rik LaPlant.

General Chairman Gary Lasater and sound coordinator Gary Smith discuss music for the 1992 rodeo.

Chick Elms accepting the B/B Champion Buckle for Sandy Kirby and John McDonald from General Chairman Lee Beck at the 1981 rodeo.

Morgan Hough and Chase Ferrell at the Jaycee family picnic before the 1992 rodeo.

THE PEOPLE BEHIND THE JAYCEE BOOTHEEL RODEO

Jaycees Charlie DeRoush, Bud Bradley, Larry Miller and Jack Vinson. From the Loy Baugher collection.

PART 2

The Sikeston Jaycees

The Sikeston Junior Chamber of Commerce (Sikeston Jaycees) was formed in 1934 and since has been dedicated to improving Sikeston. Today the club is comprised of over 100 men in the community who share the same desire and commitment to serve their community by volunteering their time to help out where needed. Not only do the Sikeston Jaycees facilitate their rodeo every year, but they also run the Sikeston little league football program, put on the annual "Haunted Hayride" and in the spring have an annual "Crawfish Boil." Throughout the years the club has put on countless other projects outside of the rodeo and also helped out with other organizations that provide community events and fundraisers. These events, coupled with the rodeo, have given the club the ability to donate to hundreds of charities over the years. Some recent donations include the Kenny Rogers Children's Center, Missouri Delta Medical Center, Three Rivers Community College and the local YMCA, just to name a few.

According to the Standard-Democrat in a 2008 article, the Jaycees had donated over $3 million to Sikeston area charities over the years. Among the major beneficiaries of Jaycee donations have been the Sikeston YMCA (over $700,000 donated and pledged to date), the Kenny Rogers Children's Center (see article on page 48 and 49).

2012 Jaycee Bootheel Rodeo Board of Directors: Front, L-R: Cal Crader, Nathan Cox (President), Chris Deen (General Chairman), Barry Johnson (General Co-Chairman), Ryan Lindsey (Jaycee President), Craig Templeton. Back row: Matt Drake, Daniel Beck, Bart Ziegenhorn, Sam Thomas, Kris Eastwood.

Another major recipient of Jaycee donations has been the Missouri Delta Medical Center Foundation, with donations totaling $181,000 from 1991-2008. These include:

The Missouri Delta Regional Dialysis Center—$55,000
Machine for the dialysis unit—$18,000
O'Bannon Family Care Center (obstetrics services)—$45,000
Computer system for Cardiology department—$36,000
Monitors for Intensive Care Unit—$11,000
Radiology department—$5,000

Other donations in recent years have gone to Sikeston Jaycee Little League Football, Justin Cowboy Crisis Fund, American Red Cross, Wrangler National Patriot Program, Three Rivers Community College, Southeast Missouri State University, Girl Scouts, Boy Scouts, Sikeston Area Youth Baseball, Sikeston United Way, House of Refuge, Sikeston Nutrition Center/Heritage House, Sikeston Department of Public Safety, Kelly Schools, Sikeston Senior High School, 4-H Club, Sikeston Swim Team, Community Counseling Center and Matt Barnes Memorial Scholarship.

Jaycees Tom Nunnelee (left) and 1977 president Charlie Stamp present a check at an early Kenny Rogers United Cerebral Palsy Center telethon.

N.J. "Bud" Werner, past President of Sikeston Jaycees, accepting project of the year award for 1980 Sikeston Jaycee Bootheel Rodeo, Dan Lape, General Chairman, at the 1981 National Jaycee convention. San Antonio, Texas. Among the other contenders for the project of the year was the Creater Greensboro Open Golf Tournament.

2012 Sikeston Jaycees. Standing, L-R: Joey Heckert, Jeff Hall, Paul Myers, Chris Deen, Barry Johnson, Marshall McTigue, Andrew Irvin, Lance Myer, Heath McGill, Blake Walker. Seated: Dennis Snider, Jason Grojean, David Teachout, Andrew Lawson, Blake Wethington, Ryan Thomure, Doug Glenn, Bart Ziegenhorn, Marc Leible. Kneeling on stage: Dale Mock, Nathan Eftink, Jerome Henson. Standing: Kenny Graham, Jayson Snider, Nathan Cox, Brad Dockins, Lad Neal, Brandon Kuehn, Jonathan Hall, John Heuring, Greg Copeland, Ross Merideth, A.J. Horn, Terry Jones, Zach Fayette, Matt Drake, Jason Pounds, Zac Black, Kris Eastwood, Patrick Shelton, Matt Johnson, Britt Taylor, Ralphie Pobst, Brian Dover, Andrew Kerby, Shayn Mabury, Walt Moody, Justin Littleton, Dave Klueppel, Craig Cox, Mark Grimes, Bryn Ledbetter, Dustin Knight. Highly-active Jaycees not pictured were Ryan Merideth, Ryan Lindsey, Daniel Beck, Justin Wibbenmeyer, Cal Crader, Sam Thomas, Craig Templeton, Shawn Towe, Jeff Hay, Jay Cox, Bryce Wibbenmeyer, Mike Adams and J.T. Morton.

THE 2012 SIKESTON JAYCEES

Jaycee Bootheel Rodeo Leadership

Ross Merideth
2013 Jaycee President

Barry Johnson
2013 Rodeo General Chairman

Photos courtesy of Lynda Warren

Year	Jaycee President	Rodeo General Chairman
1953	Bob Mitchell	Louis Jones
1954	Bill Bess	Louis Jones
1955	Mark Childs	Louis Jones
1956	John Marshall	J.W. Bonner
1957	Bob Porter	Bruce Hampton
1958	Clem Beal	Jack Mitchell
1959	Jack Mitchell	Alton McCann
1960	Alton McCann	Buddy Cox
1961	Bruce Hampton	Bob Porter
1962	Keith Ziegenhorn	Bill Hale
1963	Don Bohannon	Claude Benny
1964	Dan Norton	Bill Burch
1965	Paul Slinkard	J.D. Schaffer
1966	John Sides	Jay Sisk
1967	John Harper	Jim Cox
1968	Bill Burch	Joe Marsh
1969	Stan Eudy	Jack Sides
1970	Gene Yokley	Charles McGill
1971	Don Newton	Charles Walls
1972	Richard Adams	Ken Bridger
1973	Dennis Ziegenhorn	Larry Miller
1974	Steve Sikes	Dan Wagner
1975	Steve Taylor	Lloyd F. Stoner
1976	Rob Mitchell	Charles Blumenberg
1977	Charles Stamp, Jr.	Ed Aldrich
1978	Dan Lape	Ken Walters
1979	Bob Fuchs	Ed Pike
1980	Bud Werner	Dan Lape
1981	Rich Wrather	Lee Beck
1982	G. David Bird	Bob Fuchs
1983	Phil Black	Geary Yant
1984	David Dolan	Alan Keenan
1985	Mike Marshall	David Hough
1986	Terry Freeland	Doug Griffin
1987	Lew Polivick	Kevin Ward
1988	Chris Matthews	David Dolan
1989	Joe Blanton	Rik LaPlant
1990	Tim Merideth	Ken Lape
1991	Steven H. Burch	Lew Polivick
1992	David Teachout	Gary Lasater
1993	Jeff Sutton	David Vaughn
1994	Matt Vowels	Tom Green
1995	Matt Puchbauer	Jim Gipson
1996	Brian Menz	Tim Gilmore
1997	Greg Turnbow	Todd Pierce
1998	Dennis Fraser	Dan Beussink
1999	Jeff Miles	Greg Turnbow
2000	John Rowland	Jimmy Cox
2001	Mike Conway	Shannon Garrett
2002	Deke Lape	Randy Tuttle
2003	Corey McNew	Rob Clay
2004	Chad Crow	Lloyd F. Stoner, II
2005	Brian Bradley	Marshall Conway
2006	Jason Pounds	Chris Harper
2007	Patrick Douglas	Nathan Hawkins
2008	Matt Drake	Ron Payne
2009	Daniel Beck	Matt Matthews
2010	Ryan Merideth	Justin Wibbenmeyer
2011	Bart Ziegenhorn	Cal Crader
2012	Ryan Lindsey	Chris Deen
2013	Ross Merideth	Barry Johnson

Art Saunders

When Blodgett native and traveling flour salesman Art Saunders approached his nephew Louis Jones of the Sikeston Jaycees in 1952 with the notion that the Jaycees should put on a rodeo, some may have thought Saunders was off his rocker. But Saunders convinced Jones that the idea was a good one. Not only could a rodeo be a success, but also it could put Sikeston on the national map.

It took a lot of arm twisting and politicking by Saunders and Jones, but a slim majority of Jaycees were convinced enough of the merits of the rodeo that in May of 1953 the club voted to put on its first rodeo that September. The rest, as they say, is history.

Art Saunders not only helped get the rodeo off the ground, but also was there every year as an adviser to the club. He was a familiar presence during rodeo performances, seated by the main gates and chatting it up with the cowboys. He never missed a rodeo performance from the first rodeo in 1953 until his sudden death in 1981. Even years before his death, Saunders was already known as "the Granddaddy of the Jaycee Bootheel Rodeo."

The annual rodeo program carries the following brief statement at the end of Saunders' tribute page:

> "It was Art Saunders' insight, guidance and invaluable assistance to the Sikeston Jaycees that the Rodeo is the success it is today. His vision continues to live on in the hearts of all those who enjoy this Rodeo. Thanks, Art."

In 1981, the year of Saunders' death, the Sikeston Jaycees instituted a new tribute to the "Granddaddy." The Art Saunders Founders Award is given each year to an "Exhausted Rooster" of the Jaycees in appreciation and recognition of their service to the Jaycee Bootheel Rodeo. As of 2013, 32 Jaycees have been honored with the award. The following winners of the Art Saunders Founders Award through 2012 have played a large role in helping the rodeo become the major event that it is today.

Art Saunders acknowledges the applause of the rodeo crowd. From the Loy Baugher collection.

ART SAUNDERS FOUNDERS AWARD

Bill Hale - 1981

Bruce Hampton - 1982

Jim Cox - 1983

John Harper - 1984

Bill Burch - 1985

Larry Miller - 1986

Charles McGill - 1987

Ed Pike, Jr. -1988

Dan Lape - 1989

Geary Yant - 1990

Lee Beck - 1991

Tom Nunnelee - 1992

Rob Henley - 1993

N.J. "Bud" Werner - 1994

Rich Wrather - 1995

Terry Lape - 1996

Alan Keenan - 1997

Doug Griffin - 1998

= Deceased

ART SAUNDERS FOUNDERS AWARD

Rik LaPlant - 1999

Steve Lomax - 2000

Steve Lambert - 2001

Ken Lape - 2002

Lew Polivick - 2003

David Vaughn - 2004

Tom Green - 2005

David Hough - 2006

David Teachout - 2007

Kevin Wade - 2008

David Dolan - 2009

Michael Bohannon - 2010

Jimmy Gipson - 2011

Phil Black - 2012

THE ART SAUNDERS FOUNDERS AWARD is presented annually to an Exhausted Rooster of the Sikeston Jaycees in recognition of their years of service, time, labor, dedication and support toward the advancement and betterment of the Sikeston Bootheel Rodeo. It is the highest award that can be given to any member of the Jaycees from the Rodeo Corporation. With the true dedication of these men, the rodeo as you see it today, has grown to become one of the top rodeos in North America. These men, now no longer active in the day-to-day operation of the Sikeston Jaycees Club, are still very much a part of the rodeo and will forever be a part of the history of this event.

Loy Baugher

Many of the photographs in this book are the work of Loy Baugher, a Sikeston native and professional photographer serving the area from 1946 through 1974. He owned and operated The Baugher Studio on South Main Street in Sikeston. After his death, his files were shown to contain over 31,000 completed jobs and upwards of 280,000 photographic images. Loy was dedicated to community and service. He sought to constantly photograph the area he loved, in essence, becoming Sikeston's and Southeast Missouri's "visual biographer".

Each year, Loy looked forward to the Sikeston Jaycee Bootheel Rodeo, always attending every performance. Most times he could be found moving around inside the arena with contestants, clowns and animals, camera in hand, ready to capture great rodeo action shots such as you'll find in this book.

All photographs taken by Loy Baugher are protected under copyright of The Baugher Studio, Myra Baugher Gilliland and Dawn Baugher Kobiske.

Loy Baugher

"Wyatt Earp" star Hugh O'Brian mixes with fans at the buffet table, 1960. From the Loy Baugher collection.

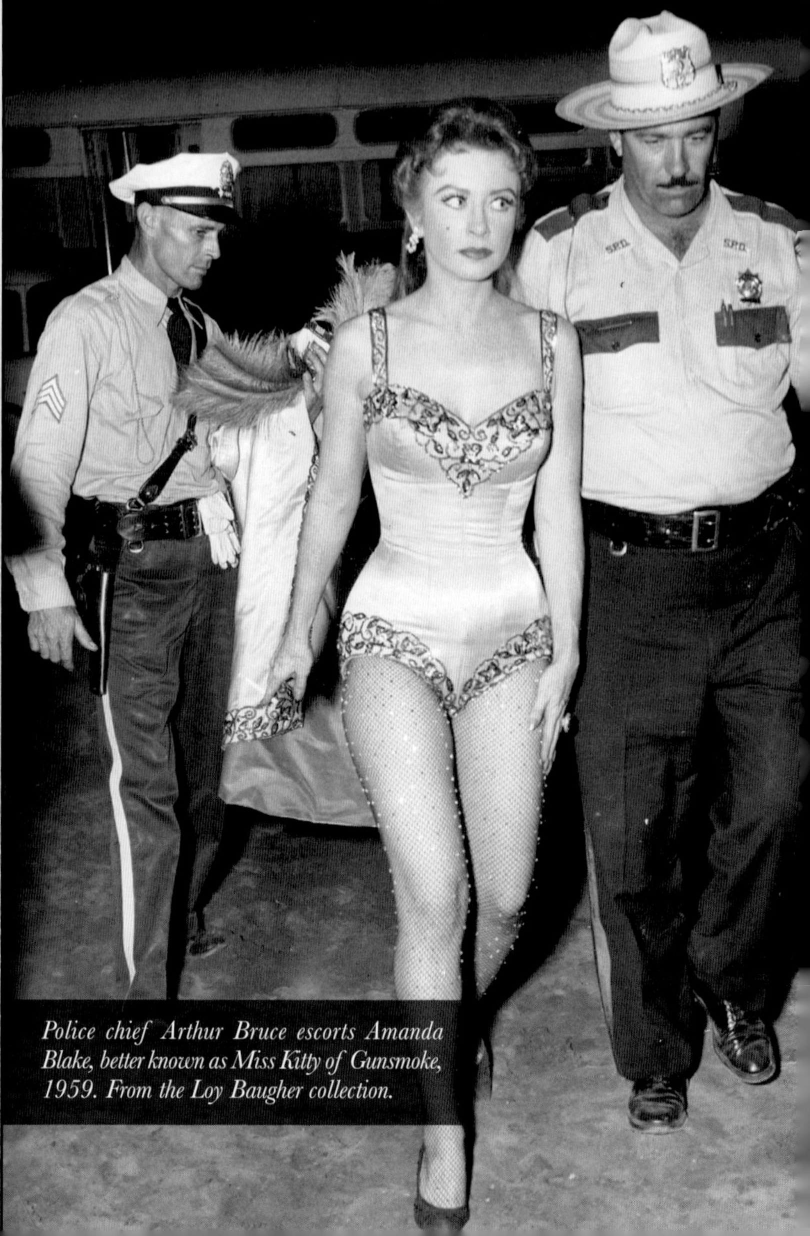

Police chief Arthur Bruce escorts Amanda Blake, better known as Miss Kitty of Gunsmoke, 1959. From the Loy Baugher collection.

Sign inside the arena at the rodeo grounds. Photo courtesy of Lynda Warren.

General Co-Chairman David Vaughn (center), gives direction to Matt Vowels, Greg Turnbow and Steve Johnson during work on the main arena gate, 1992.

Past General Chairmen Kevin Ward (left, 1987) and David Hough (right, 1985) pose with clown Jimmy Anderson during the 1992 rodeo.

THE JAYCEE BOOTHEEL RODEO and the PRO RODEO HALL OF FAME

Beginning with the very first Jaycee Bootheel Rodeo in 1953, when future Pro Rodeo Hall of Famers Jim Shoulders and Casey Tibbs competed, the very best rodeo athletes and personalities in the sport have made Sikeston a stopping-place on their itineraries.

A comprehensive list of every person who has ever been involved in the Jaycee Bootheel Rodeo isn't available. But through newspaper archives, old rodeo programs and the personal recollections of Jaycees, we can confirm that a number of people in the Pro Rodeo Hall of Fame have been here. These pages contain career highlights of some of these personalities.

JIM SHOULDERS
Cowboy – Inducted 1979
- 16-time world champion
- All-around 1949, 1956-59
- Bull riding 1951, 1954-59
- Bareback riding 1950, 1956-58

CASEY TIBBS
Cowboy – Inducted 1979
- Nine-time world champion
- Saddle-bronc riding 1949, 1951-54, 1959
- Bareback riding 1951
- All-around 1951, 1955

DON GAY
Cowboy – Inducted 1979
- Eight-time world champion
- Bull riding 1974-77, 1979-81, 1984

LARRY MAHAN
Cowboy – Inducted 1979
- Eight-time world champion
- All-around 1966-70, 1973
- Bull riding 1965, 1967

CLINT COREY
Cowboy – Inducted 2004
- World champion
- Bareback riding 1991

CHRIS LEDOUX
Cowboy & Musician – Inducted 2005
- World champion
- Bareback riding 1976
- Wrote and recorded hundreds songs about rodeo life that helped popularize sport

TOMMY STEINER
Stock Contractor – Inducted 1996
- Stock has included three Bull of the Year and one Bareback Horse of the Year winners
- Over 400 animals selected for National Finals Rodeo

TOM HADLEY
Announcer – Inducted 2001
- 40-year career as announcer
- Announcer for National Finals Rodeo in 1971, 1973 and 1982

PETE LOGAN
Announcer – Inducted 1996
- Announced National Finals Rodeo eight times, including first in 1959
- Announced first-ever live telecast of a rodeo
- Appeared in movies "Junior Bonner" and "The Misfits"

Hall of Fame announcer Clem McSpadden was a frequent announcer at the Jaycee Bootheel Rodeo.

Pro Rodeo Hall of Fame member Chris LeDoux not only competed at the Jaycee Bootheel Rodeo as a cowboy, but also was entertainer during the 1996 and 2003 rodeos.

Hall of Fame clown Quail Dobbs demonstrates the sport of mud skiing for the fans at the 1977 rodeo.

1961 Rodeo program touting the appearance of Jim Shoulders, "the Babe Ruth of Rodeo."

CLEM McSPADDEN

Announcer – Inducted 1990

- Announced National Finals Steer Roping 27 times
- 1986 PRCA Announcer of the Year
- PRCA President 1970
- General Manager of National Finals Rodeo for 18 years

QUAIL DOBBS

Clown & Bullfighter – Inducted 2002

- Twice PRCA Clown of the Year
- Four-time Coors "Man in the Can" winner
- One of only three clowns to work National Finals Rodeo as both a clown and barrelman

JOE BEAVER

Team roper & Tie Down Roper – Inducted 2000

- Eight-time world champion
- All around world champion 1995-96, 2000
- Tie down world champion 1985, 1987-88, 1992-93

TUFF HEDEMEN

Bullrider – Inducted 1997

- Three-time world champion
- Bullriding world champion 1986, 1989,1991
- Featured in the movie "Eight Seconds"

LANE FROST

Bullrider – inducted 1990

- World champion
- Bullriding world champion 1987
- First cowboy ever to ride the infamous bull "Red Rock"
- Featured in the movie "Eight Seconds"

TY MURRAY

Multiple Events – inducted 2000

- Nine-time world champion
- All around world champion 1989-94, 1998
- Bullriding world champion 1993, 1998

FRED WHITFIELD

Tie Down Roper – inducted 2004

- Six-time world champion
- Tie down world champion 1991, 1995-96, 1999, 2000
- All around world champion 1999

CLAY O'BRIEN COOPER

Team Roper – inducted 1997

- Seven-time world champion
- Team roping world champion 1985-89, 1992, 1994
- Starred as "Hardy Fimps" the youngest and smallest cowboy in the 1972 John Wayne film "The Cowboys"

CHARMAYNE JAMES

Barrel Racer

- Eleven-time WPRA world champion
- Barrel Racing world champion 1984-93, 2002

SHERRY CERVI

Barrel Racer

- Two-time WPRA world champion
- Barrel racing world champion 1995, 1999, 2010

PRCA

The Professional Rodeo Cowboys Association (PRCA), headquartered in Colorado Springs, Colo., is the largest and oldest rodeo-sanctioning body in the world. The recognized leader in professional rodeo, the PRCA is committed to maintaining the highest standards in the industry in every area, from improving working conditions for contestants and monitoring livestock welfare to boosting entertainment value and promoting sponsors. The PRCA also proudly supports youth rodeo with educational camps and financial assistance to young standouts preparing to enter the professional ranks, as well as supporting allied organizations such as Tough Enough to Wear Pink, Miss Rodeo America, the American Quarter Horse Association and the ProRodeo Hall of Fame.

Annually, the PRCA sanctions about 600 of the most elite multiple-event rodeos on the continent, in 37 states and three Canadian provinces – the cream of the crop among thousands of rodeo-related events that take place each year in North America. As a membership-driven organization, the PRCA works to ensure that every event it sanctions is managed with fairness and competence and that the livestock used is healthy and cared for to the highest standard.

Following are descriptions of the different competitions held at the Jaycee Bootheel Rodeo:

Bull Riding

Rodeo competition, in the beginning, was a natural extension of the daily challenges cowboys confronted on the ranch - roping calves and breaking broncs into saddle horses.

Bull riding, which is intentionally climbing on the back of a 2,000-pound bull, emerged from the fearless and possibly foolhardy nature of the cowboy. The risks are obvious. Serious injury is always a possibility for those fearless enough to sit astride an animal that literally weighs a ton and is usually equipped with dangerous horns.

Bull riding is dangerous and predictably exciting, demanding intense physical prowess, supreme mental toughness and courage. Like bareback and saddle bronc riders, the bull rider may use only one hand to stay aboard during the eight-second ride. If he touches the bull or himself with his free hand, he receives no score. But unlike the other roughstock contestants, bull riders are not required to mark out their animals.

While spurring a bull can add to the cowboy's score, riders are commonly judged solely on their ability to stay aboard the twisting, bucking mass of muscle.

To stay aboard the bull, a rider grasps a flat braided rope, which is wrapped around the bull's chest just behind the front legs and over its withers. One end of the bull rope, called the tail, is threaded through a loop on the other end and tightened around the bull. The rider then wraps the tail around his hand, sometimes weaving it through his fingers to further secure his grip.

Then he nods his head, the chute gate swings open, and he and the bull explode into the arena.

Every bull is unique in its bucking habits. A bull may dart to the left, then to the right, then rear back. Some spin or continuously circle in one spot in the arena. Others add jumps or kicks to their spins, while others might jump and kick in a straight line or move side to side while bucking.

Bareback Riding

Bareback riders endure more abuse, suffer more injuries and carry away more long-term damage than all other rodeo cowboys.

To stay aboard the horse, a bareback rider uses a rigging made of leather and constructed to meet PRCA safety specifications. The rigging, which resembles a suitcase handle on a strap, is placed atop the horse's withers and secured with a cinch.

Bareback riding has been compared to riding a jackhammer with one hand. Jason Jeter can probably attest to that definition. As the bronc and rider burst from the chute, the rider must have both spurs touching the horse's shoulders until the horse's feet hit the ground after the initial move from the chute. This is called "marking out." If the cowboy fails to do this, he is disqualified.

As the bronc bucks, the rider pulls his knees up, rolling his spurs up the horse's shoulders. As the horse descends, the cowboy straightens his legs, returning his spurs over the point of the horse's shoulders in anticipation of the next jump.

Making a qualified ride and earning a money-winning score requires more than just strength. A bareback rider is judged on his spurring technique, the degree to which his toes remain turned out while he is spurring and his willingness to take whatever might come during his ride.

It's a tough way to make a living, all right. But, according to bareback riders, it's the cowboy way.

Steer Wrestling

The objective of the steer wrestler, who is also known as a "bulldogger," is to use strength and technique to wrestle a steer to the ground as quickly as possible.

A perfect combination of strength, timing and technique are necessary for success in the lightning-quick event of steer wrestling. In addition to strength, two other skills critical to success in steer wrestling are timing and balance.

When the cowboy reaches the steer, he slides down and off the right side of his galloping horse, hooks his right arm around the steer's right horn, grasps the left horn with his left hand and, using strength and leverage, slows the animal and wrestles it to the ground. His work isn't complete until the steer is on its side with all four feet pointing the same direction. That's still not all there is to it.

Linus Thornton has his steer by the horns, with the help of hazer J.W. Farrington during the Steer Wrestling competition at the 1977 rodeo.

To catch the sprinting steer, the cowboy uses a "hazer," who is another mounted cowboy who gallops his horse along the right side of the steer and keeps it from veering away from the bulldogger.

The efforts of the hazer can be nearly as important as those of the steer wrestler. For that reason, and the fact that he sometimes supplies the bulldogger with a horse, the hazer often receives a fourth of the payoff.

Team Roping

Team roping, the only true team event in Pro Rodeo, requires close cooperation and timing between two highly skilled ropers - a header and a heeler - and their horses. The event originated on ranches when cowboys needed to treat or brand large steers and the task proved too difficult for one man.

Similar to tie-down ropers and steer wrestlers, team ropers start from the boxes on each side of the chute from which the steer enters the arena. The steer gets a head start determined by the length of the arena.

The header ropes first and must make one of three legal catches on the steer; around both horns, around one horn and the head or around the neck. Any other catch by the header is considered illegal and the team is disqualified. After the header makes his catch, he turns the steer to the left and exposes the steer's hind legs to thc heeler. The heeler then attempts to rope both hind legs. If he catches only one foot, the team is assessed a five-second penalty. After the cowboys catch the steer, the clock is stopped when there is no slack in their ropes and their horses face one another.

Another important aspect to the event is the type of horses used by the ropers. The American quarter horse is the most popular among all timed-event competitors, particularly team ropers. Heading horses generally are taller and heavier because they need the power to turn the steer after it is roped. Heeling horses are quick and agile, enabling them to better follow the steer and react to it moves.

Saddle Bronc

Saddle bronc riding is rodeo's classic event, both a complement and contrast to the wilder spectacles of bareback riding and bull riding. This event requires strength to be sure, but the event also demands style, grace and precise timing.

Saddle bronc riding evolved from the task of breaking and training horses to work the cattle ranches of the Old West. Many cowboys claim riding saddle broncs is the toughest rodeo event to master because of the technical skills necessary for success.

Every move the bronc rider makes must be synchronized with the movement of the horse. The cowboy's objective is a fluid ride, somewhat in contrast to the wilder and less-controlled rides of bareback riders.

One of the similarities shared by saddle bronc and bareback riding is the rule that riders in both events must mark out their horses on the first jump from the chute. To properly mark out his horse, the saddle bronc rider must have both heels touching the animal above the point of its shoulders when it makes its first jump from the chute. If the rider misses his mark, he receives no score.

While a bareback rider has a rigging to hold onto, the saddle bronc rider has only a thick rein attached to his horse's halter. Using one hand, the cowboy tries to stay securely seated in his saddle. If he touches any part of the horse or his own body with his free hand, he is disqualified.

Judges score the horse's bucking action, the cowboy's control of the horse and the cowboy's spurring action. While striving to keep his toes turned outward, the rider spurs from the points of the horse's shoulders to the back of the saddle. To score well, the rider must maintain that action throughout the eight-second ride. While the bucking ability of the horse is quite naturally built into the scoring system, a smooth, rhythmic ride is sure to score better than a wild, uncontrolled effort.

Tie-Down Roping

As with saddle bronc riding and team roping, the roots of tie-down roping can be traced back to the working ranches of the Old West. When calves were sick or injured, cowboys had to rope and immobilize them quickly for veterinary treatment. Ranch hands prided themselves on the speed with which they could rope and tie calves, and they soon turned their work into informal contests.

As the event matured, being a good horseman and a fast sprinter became as important to the competitive tie-down roper as being quick and accurate with a rope.

Today, the mounted cowboy starts from a box, a three-sided fenced area adjacent to the chute holding the calf. The fourth side of the box opens into the arena.

A cowboy's success in tie-down roping depends in large part on the precise teamwork between him and his horse. The calf receives a head start that is determined by the length of the arena. One end of a breakaway rope barrier is looped around the calf's neck and stretched across the open end of the box. When the calf reaches its advantage point, the barrier is released. If the roper breaks the barrier before the calf reaches its head start, the cowboy is assessed a 10-second penalty.

The horse is trained to come to a stop as soon as the cowboy throws his loop and catches the calf. The cowboy then dismounts, sprints to the calf and throws it by hand, a maneuver called flanking. If the calf is not standing when the cowboy reaches it, he must allow the calf to get back on its feet before flanking it. After the calf is flanked, the roper ties any three legs together with a pigging string - a short, looped rope he clenches in his teeth during the run.

While the contestant is accomplishing all of that, his horse must pull back hard enough to eliminate any slack in the rope, but not so hard as to drag the calf.

When the roper finishes tying the calf, he throws his hands in the air as a signal that the run is completed. The roper then remounts his horse, rides forward to create slack in the rope and waits six seconds to see if the calf remains tied. If the calf kicks free, the roper receives no time.

All Around

The PRCA world all-around champion is considered by many the most talented and versatile cowboy in the sport. The PRCA Cowboy who wins the most prize money in a year while competing in at least two events, earning a minimum of $3,000 in each event, wins the world all-around championship.

As General Chairman Ken Walters (middle) looks on, Jim Robison presents Charles Lowry with the saddle in recognition of winning the All-Around award in 1978.

WPRA

The Women's Professional Rodeo Association was formed in 1948 when thirty-eight cowgirls came together in San Angelo, Texas to create an organization dedicated to the promotion and advancement of women in the sport of rodeo. The earliest pioneers of the Girl's Rodeo Association (GRA) were ropers, bronc riders, and barrel racers. They were fed up with a system which did not grant them competitive opportunities in the arena and, when it did, operated under unfair conditions. The GRA began with 74 original members with 60 approved contests and total payout of $29,000. In 1981 the GRA changed its name to the Women's Professional Rodeo Association. It is the oldest women's sports association in the country and the only one governed entirely by women.

Today, the fast paced event of barrel racing dominates the activities of most WPRA members. WPRA barrel racers compete for millions of dollars each year, culminating in twelve circuit finals rodeos held throughout the country, the Dodge National Circuit Finals Rodeo held in Pocatello, Idaho in April, and the Wrangler National Finals Rodeo held in Las Vegas each December.

The WPRA still honors its roots by hosting the WPRA World Finals Rodeo in Tulsa, Oklahoma each November. The World Finals Rodeo is the largest all-women's rodeo event in the world. At the World Finals, the WPRA crowns world champions in ten events, including original events, bareback riding, bull riding, tie-down roping, team roping, and breakaway roping.

In 2008 the WPRA celebrated sixty years of women in rodeo and are looking forward to the next sixty as the future of women in the sport of rodeo has never looked better.

The WPRA . . . the past, present, and future of women in rodeo!

From the Loy Baugher collection.

Barrel Racing

Barrel racing is a timed rodeo event, where the fastest time is what matters most. Cowgirls compete in the arena against each other and the clock.

Barrel racing is about cooperation between horse and rider. Because of the competition and money involved, finding a good horse is very important to the competitors. A top of the line barrel horse can cost up to $50,000.

For the barrel racing event, the arena is cleared and three barrels are set up at different marked locations. The riders then enter the arena at full speed, quickly rounding each barrel in a cloverleaf pattern and then exiting where they entered. A stopwatch or timer is used registering down to a hundredth of a second.

Speed is what it is all about in this event. The riders steer their horses as close as they can to the barrels trying to shave precious seconds off the clock. For each barrel they knock over (which happens sometimes) a 5 second penalty is assessed to their total time. Leaving the barrels standing and ripping through the course is every barrel racers goal.

Stock Contractors

For casual rodeo fans, the most important parts of a rodeo performance are the things that are at the forefront of the event – the cowboys and cowgirls, the clowns, the organist and the announcer.

But for hard-core rodeo fans, they will tell you that without good stock, there can't be a good performance. And it's the job of the stock contractor to provide the best animals that can test the skills and talents of the athletes. The Sikeston Jaycee Bootheel Rodeo has partnered with some of the best producers and stock contractors in rodeo.

Ken Roberts produced several Sikeston rodeos in the '50s. He was inducted into the Pro Rodeo Hall of Fame as a bull rider in 1979. It can't be verified that he also competed at the Jaycee Bootheel Rodeo, although he was still winning money as an athlete at age 50. But his vantage point from the backs of Brahma bulls and bucking horses gave him a good eye for first-class stock.

The Steiner Rodeo Company, led by Tommy Steiner, produced a number of Jaycee Bootheel Rodeos over a period of over a quarter-century. As a regional rodeo company, Steiner produced the fledgling Sikeston rodeo twice in the '50s. After striking a deal with Hollywood's Wild Bill Elliott during that decade, doors opened to bigger events for Steiner, and he became a major player among producers and contractors. As the Jaycee Bootheel Rodeo became a major event on the PRCA circuit, Steiner provided livestock

Stock contractor Dell Hall (left) and Jaycee Geary Yant

again for several years during the '70s. That period saw Steiner's stock win three Bull of the Year awards and one Bareback Horse of the Year award from the PRCA. Over 400 of his animals were picked for the National Finals Rodeo. He was inducted into the Pro Rodeo Hall of Fame in 1996.

Kinney Brothers Rodeo, operated by Edward and Cotton Kinney, were in high demand for their livestock during the '50s and '60s. The number of Kinney Brothers bulls chosen for the National Finals Rodeo was unmatched by any other contractor for over 40 years. They provided stock for a number of Jaycee Bootheel Rodeos in the '60s.

Tommy Steiner provided stock to the Jaycee Bootheel Rodeo for over 25 years, such as #68, ridden by Butch Kirby during the 1977 rodeo.

Dell Hall's Rafter H Ranch has been providing the stock for the Jaycee Bootheel Rodeo for over 30 years, after previously serving as a stock subcontractor for the Steiner Rodeo Company. Three of Rafter H's animals have won PRCA awards, including the legendary bull King Kong. In 1998, no cowboy stayed on King Kong for the required eight seconds during a PRCA sanctioned rodeo. King Kong won the PRCA Bucking Bull of the Year award that year, and another bull, named No. 105, won the award twice – in '81 and '84. Since his debut as the rodeo's stock contractor in 1981, Dell Hall, his daughter Shelly and the rest of the Rafter H Rodeo Company have become like family to the Sikeston Jaycees and for over 30 years have provided the Jaycees with top quality stock for their rodeo.

Brahma bulls relax in the bullpen before their turn in the rodeo spotlight

Rick Young: Serious About Being Funny

As a high school athlete in Louisiana, Rick Young was an all-stater in baseball, football and basketball. He passed up an athletic scholarship to focus on the sport he loved most – rodeo.

So what was it about horses and bulls that made Young leave the other sports behind? Maybe it was because as an outfielder, a quarterback or a guard he wouldn't have any opportunities to make people laugh.

Rick Young is one of rodeo's most famous clowns and a member of the National Cowboy Hall of Fame. As of 2012, he has performed in every Sikeston Jaycee Bootheel Rodeo but one since his first appearance in 1960. His love affair with Sikeston and the fans of the rodeo has lasted over a half-century. He makes no secret about his love of the Sikeston rodeo and is an unofficial ambassador for the event and for the city as he travels the rodeo circuit performing. "Everybody knows that Sikeston is my favorite rodeo," Young says.

Rick Young during a lighter moment in the barrel. In 1991 he was awarded the Coors "Man in the Can" award, presented to the best barrel man in rodeo.

L-R: Rick Young, Mike Johnson and Jimmy Anderson take a break from protecting the cowboys to entertain the fans.

In the modern era of rodeo where many rodeo bullfighters have little or no desire to do comedy, the man once known as the "Ragin' Cajun" and now as the "Agin' Cajun" is an anachronism. Rick Young still sees comedy as an important part of the fans' rodeo experience.

"People love to laugh," Young said. "I don't care where they go – they want to laugh."

Having passed the 70-year mark awhile back, Young doesn't have the agility to distract the bulls from fallen cowboys anymore, or even to work in the barrel. He'll leave that to the younger clowns and bullfighters and focus on what he does best – making the fans laugh.

"Now the guys are specialized. They just want to be called bullfighters," Young said about the new generation of clowns. But when he himself was younger, he was doing it all. He started in rodeo out of Southeast Louisiana State as a bull rider himself before trying his hand at clowning. After a few years of doing both, he had settled on being a full-time clown by the time he made his first appearance at the Jaycee Bootheel Rodeo in 1960. Sure, he got the laughs, but he was also so good at protecting the bull riders that he was voted by the cowboys to work the 1974 PRCA National Finals in Oklahoma City, a.k.a., the "World Series of Rodeo." He was PRCA Clown of the Year in 1980, and in '91 was awarded the Coors "Man in the Can" award, emblematic of rodeo's best barrel man. Young was inducted into the National Cowboy Hall of Fame in 2004.

While the cowboys appreciated Young's skills in protecting them, it was his comedic antics that helped keep the fans coming back. They've been coming back to see Rick Young at the Jaycee Bootheel Rodeo year after year, and he keeps coming back to see the fans.

And according to Rick Young, it's all about the fans. He's cut back to working about 16 rodeos a year and concedes that someday he'll have to retire. But he's in no hurry.

"When it's time to quit, I'm not gonna miss the rodeo as much as I'll miss the fans."

The Fans

There's no doubt that it takes a dedicated organization, good livestock and skilled cowboys and cowgirls to put on a great rodeo. But all their efforts would be for naught if people didn't lay down their hard-earned money for tickets and go through the turnstiles.

Over 2 million fans have attended the Jaycee Bootheel Rodeo since its inception in 1953. Many of these fans are repeat customers. Some have made attending the rodeo a family tradition, coming back year-after-year. What keeps these loyal supporters of the rodeo coming back for more? Let them tell you in their own words.

Dixie & Bill Wilson

Dixie and Bill Wilson have been attending rodeos for 40 years and have seen 120+ performances. The couple attended the Sikeston Jaycee Bootheel Rodeo for the first time in 1972, traveling 125 miles from Mt. Vernon, Illinois.

"We first attended the Jaycee Bootheel Rodeo in 1972 at the invitation of my brother and his wife. We have not missed a year since then, although it was 1991 before we started attending all four sessions. This will be our 22nd year for that.

"A few years go the last event, which we liked, was the bullfighters competing in fighting bulls. Dangerous, but exciting. Also, we like Rick Young with his jokes and tricks.

"One rodeo we remember was in 2000 when bullrider Jessie Bail scored 95 points when he rode King Kong.

"We like both the rodeo competition and the entertainment. Together it makes a complete evening for a good time.

"Even though the rodeo is in always in August, we have experienced nearly all kinds of weather and conditions in our 40 years. It has been extra hot, cold enough for coats, storms, rain and a wet, sloppy arena. Regardless of conditions, we always look forward to attending the rodeo."

Lloyd & Sharon Adams

Lloyd and Sharon Adams first attended the Jaycee Bootheel Rodeo in 1975 when they traveled 105 miles from Bonnie, Illinois. They have returned 38 times to Sikeston for Rodeo week.

"We enjoy the rodeo very much. I don't think there is one that stands out above the others.

"We come mainly for the rodeo and are not that interested in the music. We would like to see more rodeoing.

"We really did like the group of riders that came in to perform in between the rodeoing. That was great.

"Since we don't travel a lot, we like to make a vacation out of going to Sikeston for the Rodeo. We attend all four peformances every year.

"The Jaycees do an awesome job."

Jim & Brenda LaBrot

Front, L-R: Ethan Ross, Jake Melton, Hannah Melton. Behind the children is mother Paula Melton. Back: Vikki Ross holding Langston LaBrot, Devin Miller, Mike LaBrot, Brenda LaBrot and Jim LaBrot.

Jim and Brenda LaBrot first attended the 1968 Jaycee Bootheel Rodeo. Since that first visit, they have enjoyed sharing the Rodeo festivities every year with their growing family. The LaBrot family lives 22 miles from Sikeston in Dexter, Missouri.

"Rodeo started for our family of two in 1968; 45 years later, we still look forward to the rodeo with our expanded family of three children and six grandchildren.

"I would have to say our favorite event has always been the bullriding, but visiting with family and friends at the trailer starting the week prior has been the most enjoyed. There are truly no strangers at the rodeo!

"Special memories include our daughters, Vicki and Paul, as rodeo queens. And who can forget when Dad and daughter Paula each missed a Saturday night performance due to separate trips to the ER? I guess our palomino "Missy" thought they looked better on the ground than in the saddle! Thank goodness there were no major injuries, just "hurt pride" and some soreness that lasted well pas August! "Missy," "Dixie" and "Red" have now gone on to "horse heaven" and along with our blue heeler, "Jill," are greatly missed.

"It is fun to remember back to the early years of the rodeo when Jim was a Jaycee member and I was Jaycee Wives president. Jim recalls the tradition of the "Kidnap Family." He was on the committee the year "Daniel Boone" (Fess Parker) was one of the stars. A family was "kidnapped" off the Interstate each day by the local police and treated to a free night at the rodeo.

"Also, at that time, the rodeo was held Thursday through Sunday. Saturday night was party night just for the Jaycees and the cowboys at the country club. That was always fun, and another reason to wear sunglasses to the Sunday afternoon peformance!

"Each rodeo is special and our family is looking forward to another 45 years of great rodeo memories!"

Kenny Bridger

Kenny Bridger is a Sikeston, Missouri resident and has been to every Jaycee Bootheel Rodeo since its beginning in 1953.

"I had the honor of being a Sikeston Jaycee and was the Rodeo Chairman for a year. It was an honor to be a Sikeston Jaycee and I enjoyed every aspect of the rodeo and the other projects that the Jaycees sponsored.

"The rodeo has been something that my family and I have looked forward to every year. It is not only enjoyable to attend, but it also helps out the city of Sikeston. The donations that they have given to so many organizations have been outstanding year after year. For myself the Kenny Rogers Children Center has been especially special to me. I served on the board there for many years and

without the Sikeston Jaycee donations, it would not be the center that it is today.

"The entertainment has always been something that draws the crowds at the rodeo, but the rodeo itself has always been first class. "

Joe R. Acord

"My Dad and Mom, Ralph and Mildred Acord, started taking me to the rodeo every year starting in 1958. I have only had to miss the rodeo only a very few years. So far, I have attended the rodeo 50 different years.

"I competed in the rodeo in 1976, '77 and '78. I competed in calf roping all three years, saddle bronc riding one year and steer wrestling one year.

"Once I was married I started taking my wife, June Ellen. After we had our son, Cliffton, we continued taking him. June Ellen has been a total of 30 years and my son Cliff has attended a total of 23 years.

"My Mom and Dad attended the very first rodeo at Sikeston, so as you can see, in our family it has been a family tradition since the beginning. My Dad and Mom have passed away, but I still think of them and all the good times we had at the rodeo every time that I attend it. It is one of my favorite things to do, and always will be.

"My son says that he is going to continue the tradition when he gets married some day. We all love your rodeo. It has been a big part of our lives and will continue to be for the rest of our lives."

L-R: Cliff Acord, June Ellen Acord and J.R. Acord at the 2012 rodeo, which marked the 50th year for Joe to attend. It was June's 34th year and Cliff's 24th year.

From the Loy Baugher collection.

Led by drum majorette and twirlers, the Sikeston High School Band marches in the rodeo parade.

Speck Rhodes (in the checked suit) and other members of The Rhodes Show band ride in the rodeo parade.

Young Rodeo fan, Duncan Paul watches as the horses pass on Salcedo Road during the 2012 Sikeston Jaycee Bootheel Rodeo Parade.

THE TRADITIONS OF THE JAYCEE BOOTHEEL RODEO

From the Loy Baugher collection.

PART 3

Rodeo Traditions

While the competition and activities in the rodeo arena account for much of the story of the Jaycee Bootheel Rodeo, the annual rodeo parade and pageants have been a part of the colorful tradition of the event.

In the early days of the rodeo, the celebrities often rode in the rodeo parade to greet the town. Rex Allen tips his hat to the parade viewers in 1962. From the Loy Baugher collection.

The Rodeo Parade

While rodeo fans today know the rodeo parade as a Saturday event, that wasn't always the case.

In the early years of the rodeo, the parade was held the afternoon of the first performance. The first rodeo parade, held on Sept. 17, 1953, started at 4 p.m. and consisted largely of a processional of assorted vehicles and horses. The route had the parade going west on Malone St. from the old Sikeston Cotton Oil Mill to the old South Grade School, then detouring through a portion of downtown Sikeston before making it back to the end of the route at the corner of Malone and Kingshighway.

Not your typical mount. Jaycees ride in Shad Old's tricked-out Jeepster in the rodeo parade.

In the years that followed, area high school bands joined in the parade, a tradition that continued until the rodeo was moved to August in 1965, which was before area schools were in session. Businesses and organizations entered floats in the parade. In some cases, the celebrity entertainers rode in the parade, giving even fans who didn't buy a ticket to the rodeo an opportunity to see some of their favorite television and movie personalities up close.

Interest in the rodeo parade waned through the years, and the event was discontinued in the mid-90s before being revived again after an absence of about five years. The new rodeo parade was held the Saturday before the rodeo,

Crowds line front street to get a good view of the rodeo parade in the '60s. From the Loy Baugher collection.

The Sikeston Freshman Band performs at the rodeo parade, early 1960s. From the Loy Baugher collection.

Residents of Shuffit's Nursing Home and Gray Ladies view the rodeo parade from Malone Park, 1958.

but in 2010, the parade was switched to the Saturday morning of rodeo week. The change, said the Jaycees, was to allow many of the rodeo participants, including the athletes, clowns and other rodeo personnel, to participate in the parade.

Tammy Clark and Michael Snider, Little Miss and Little Mr. Western of 1965, pose with Rodeo Queen Linda Rowland. From the Loy Baugher collection.

Rodeo Royalty

While the Jaycee Bootheel Rodeo Queen pageant has been an annual part of the rodeo since 1961, it was a tradition that was slow to get off the ground.

The first queen pageant was announced in the summer of 1954. The contest would be open to both single and married women between the ages of 16 and 24, who would compete in both swimsuit and western wear. As the pageant approached there was talk that it might be canceled due to lack of interest, but enough entries were received to go ahead with the contest. Billie Crumpecker of Morehouse became the first rodeo queen, winning the pageant and the $40 first prize. It would be 1961 before Virginia Bridges of Sikeston became the second rodeo queen.

In 1962, the Jaycee Wives organization sponsored a Little Mr. and Miss Rodeo pageant for children between the ages of one and eight. Glen Bridges, 8, of Parma and Beverly Ann Wirth, 2, of Sikeston were the first winners. The following year the title of the winners was changed to Little Mr. and Miss Western, which continues to be the case.

In 1982, Sherry Melton of Sikeston, age 15, became the first Junior Miss Rodeo pageant winner.

Tom Baker crowns Vivian Huff 1962 Rodeo Queen. From the Loy Baugher collection.

Little Mr. Western 1971, Mike Keasler

Little Miss Western 1971, Karen Cain

1974 Rodeo Queen Teresa Scherer with Little Mr. Western Joey Causey and Little Miss Western Stacey Wescoat.

Rodeo Royalty

Through the Years

Year	Rodeo Queen	Jr. Miss Rodeo	Little Miss Western	Little Mr. Western
1954	Billie Crumpecker	None	None	None
1961	Virginia Bridges	None	None	None
1962	Vivian Hough	None	Beverly Ann Wirth	Glen Bridges
1963	Sandy Smith	None	Jalonda Kay Bird	Jay Fitzsimmons
1964	Deene Ann Whitten	None	Melinda Ann Ivey	Bill Roberts IV
1965	Linda Rowland	None	Tammy Clark	Michael Snider
1966	Jan Engram	None	Tommie Ray Love	Christopher Vinson
1967	Patti McMullin	None	Jill Ann Humphries	Lee Van Marshall
1968	Kathy Matthews	None	Ronda Jaynes	Craig Smith
1969	Charline Freeman	None	Shori Lynn Hagy	Bradley DeWitt
1970	Sharon Spitzmiller	None	Robin Denise Linzenbee	Todd Mitchell
1971	Cynthia Hamm	None	Karen Leigh Cain	Mike Keasler
1972	Mary Shuffitt	None	Tina Edwards	Bradley McDonald
1973	Jana Moyers	None	Amanda Barnett	Douglas Johnson
1974	Teresa Scherer	None	Stacey Wescoat	Joey Causey
1975	Wendy Litzelfelner	None	Kristi Lewis	Matthew Garner
1976	Susan Wilson	None	Laura Lester	Eric Hutchison
1977	Tamara Fister	None	Audra Sherman	Chad Borders
1978	Carla Thomason	None	Jennifer Denise Mims	Cory Lee Kelso
1979	Gail Schell	None	Chantelle Crider	Michael Porter
1980	Judy Brock	None	Farrah Matthews	Mikell Kilgore, Jr.
1981	Mary Shuffitt	None	Amy Yount	Christopher Dye

Sherry Melton, who in 1982 was chosen as the first Junior Miss Rodeo.

Rodeo queen candidates. From the Loy Baugher collection.

1982	Jodi Harris	Sherry Melton	Allison Nowell	Ronald Self
1983	Jeanne Aufdenberg	Lori Little	Samantha Star Adams	Charles Wade Lawrence
1984	Kim Nester	Ann Marie Cook	Patricia Trickey	Greg Copeland
1985	Deanne Pate	Amanda Barnett	Stephanie Todd	Christopher Porter
1986	Melinda Dame	Sherry Vanover	Bridgett Danielle Toton	Joshua Allan Adkisson
1987	Alice Aufdenberg	Debbie Jackson	Whitney Lyn Wade	John Tyler Myrick
1988	Leah Belvin	Audra Sherman	Lindsey Renee Cook	Jordan Tyler Lucy
1989	Vikki LaBrot	Heather Bloemer	Jordan Myrick	Mark Adam Wade
1990	Leigh Ann Wilkins	Heather Thornbrough	Amanda Shelton	Justin James
1992	Jamie Satterfield	Frannie Trum	Jessica Blair	Robby Throop
1993	Julie Stone	Jessica Parris	Micah Bryan	Chase Ferrell
1994	Elena McCall	Lindsey Thornbrough	Jordi Ferrell	Preston Newell
1995	Jenny Keller	Brittany McDonald	Brooke Smith	Ben Brown
1996	Tami Criss	Brandy Wolfenkoehler	Kristen Pratt	Corey Hanselmar
1997	Mattie McCall	Brooke McDonald	Mallory Cowger	Tanner Williams
1998	Amanda Jordan	Rebecca Throop	Taylor Davis	Spence Vaughn
1999	Leslie Hanschen	Misty Menz	Sydney Lambert	Christopher Shelby
2000	Jessica Hampton	Crystal Stokes	Morgan Cashmer	Zach Stinett
2001	Rebecca Throop	Kyleigh Cowger	Courtney Todt	Kyle Fetters
2002	Crystal Stokes	Lauri Lewis	Paige Chasteen	Kevin Jobe
2003	Samantha Kluesner	Kaci Menz	Kelsey Thompson	Austin Stafford
2004	Jillian Lee Dittmer	Catherine Presson	Bailey Branum	Jacob Fetters
2005	Katie Palmer	Mamie Williams	Ashtyn Rains	Nelson Shadwick
2006	Andrea Duncan	Kaitlin Ray	Emma Drury	Joseph Kendell
2007	Marty Berry	Shaye Bouckaert	Kylyn Newton	Wyatt Greenfield
2008	Erin Watts	Kirstie Anderson	Leah Lambert	Conner Wallace
2009	Catherine Presson	Mallory Cowger	Abbigayle Siler	Ashton Faris
2010	Lindsey Riley	Rachel Lowe	Landy Easton	Joshua McClendon
2011	Katie Patterson	Micayla Gray	Avery Newton	Maverick James
2012	Micayla Gray	Kelsy Patterson	Katie Staples	Luke Gadberry

Tom Nunnelee poses with new and outgoing rodeo royalty in 1984. L-R: New Junior Miss Rodeo Ann Marie Cook, New Rodeo Queen Kim Nester, 1983 Rodeo Queen Jeanne Aufdenberg and outgoing and 1993 Junior Miss Lori Little.

Little Miss Western Landy Easton and Little Mr. Western Joshua McClendon, 2010

The SEMO Shrine Mounted Patrol and the Scott County Sheriff's Posse

Beginning in 1955, a local organization of horsemen made their first appearance in the Jaycee Bootheel Rodeo parade and rodeo. The SEMO Shrine Mounted Patrol would be a fixture in the annual rodeo lineup for over 20 years to come.

The SEMO Shrine Mounted Patrol was made up of members of the SEMO Shrine Club. Led by captain Melvin Dace, the team of 15-20 riders had been formed in the early 1950s primarily to represent the Shriners in parades. The patrol rode dazzling white palominos, with matching saddles, tack and outfits.

While the patrol looked great in parades, they enjoyed showing off in the rodeo arena as well. The team worked up a precision riding routine that they performed each year prior to the Grand Entry. The SEMO Shrine Mounted Patrol performances were a tradition at the Jaycee Bootheel Rodeo until the mid-1970s when they disbanded due to the advancing age or passing of many of their members.

Scott County Sheriff Bill Ferrell, whose father Frank had been a member of the patrol, looked for a way to continue the tradition of precision riding exhibitions at the rodeo. In 1980, Ferrell formed the Scott County Sheriff's Posse, which rode in the rodeo parade and also performed the same riding show the Shrine Patrol had made famous. The Sheriff's Posse didn't ride palominos – in fact, their horses didn't match at all, except for the tack and the matching shirts worn by the riders. But they perfected the precision routine of the Shriners and entertained rodeo fans for nearly 20 years before disbanding themselves.

Ferrell saw the Sheriff's Posse as a way of honoring the legacy established by the Shrine Patrol and his father Frank Ferrell, who never missed a performance of the Jaycee Bootheel Rodeo from its inception in 1953 until his death in 2007.

Interestingly, the Scott County Sheriff's Posse wasn't only about showing off in parades and rodeos. The group, which included law enforcement personnel as well as volunteers, was called into service on occasion to help search for missing persons.

The Scott County Sheriff's Posse continued the tradition of precision riding exhibitions that was begun years earlier by the SEMO Shrine Mounted Patrol.

THE ENTERTAINERS OF THE JAYCEE BOOTHEEL RODEO

"Gunsmoke" stars Dennis Weaver (Chester), Milburn Stone (Doc) and Amanda Blake (Kitty) entertain at the 1959 rodeo. From the Loy Baugher collection.

BOOTHEEL RODEO Sikeston SIKESTON, MO.

PART 4

Rodeo Entertainment

While the Jaycee Bootheel Rodeo has been closely identified with the high-profile entertainers it has brought to the event, the early years of the rodeo were carried almost completely by the barrel racing, calf roping, bull riding and other rodeo athletic events. Rodeo purists came from miles around to watch this western athletic tradition brought to Missouri, along with strong support from locals who wanted to see this thing called rodeo that they had previously only heard and read about.

There were no celebrity performers at the first four years' worth of Jaycee Bootheel Rodeos. However, it should be noted that a couple of regional stars of note did entertain the audience before the performances – Slim Rhodes and his Mountaineers ('53) and Onie Wheeler and his Ozark Cowboys ('54).

Rhodes had area roots and had a regular show on stations in Poplar Bluff and Memphis before getting a daily TV show in Pine Bluff, AR He went on to record a few singles on the legendary Sun Records label in the early days of rockabilly and traveled with the likes of Elvis Presley, Jerry Lee Lewis and Johnny Cash. Sikeston area viewers likely remember Rhodes best from "The Rhodes Show," a syndicated TV show that aired locally on KFVS-TV in the '60s.

Wheeler had a recording contract with Columbia Records at that time, and although didn't have any hits of his own when he performed at the rodeo, he had co-written a top-10 single – "Run 'Em Off" – for country star Lefty Frizzell. Wheeler was a local boy who had made good, but his career didn't really take off until later in the decade when he, like Slim Rhodes, signed with Sam Phillips' legendary Sun Records label in Memphis in 1957. Onie toured as a solo performer with Presley, Carl Perkins, Cash and Lewis while with the Sun label, then spent most of the rest of his career performing in the bands of legends such as George Jones and Roy Acuff. He did finally have a minor hit of his own in 1973 with "John's Been Shucking My Corn," but his greatest claim to fame was his association with Acuff and his appearances on the Grand Ole Opry as a member of the Smoky Mountain Boys.

The year 1957 marked a turning point in the history of the Jaycee Bootheel Rodeo as the Sikeston Jaycees brought in nationally-known entertainment for the first time. This section of the book presents brief biographies for each headline performer that has entertained at the Jaycee Bootheel Rodeo.

(Editor's note – Unless otherwise indicated, all references to television ratings refer to the A. C. Nielsen ratings. All references to music charts refer to Billboard Magazine's charts.)

Acronyms:

ACM ....Academy of Country Music
CMA.................Country Music Association
RIAA ....Recording Industry Association of America
ASCAP ....American Society of Composers, Authors and Publishers

SMILEY BURNETTE – 1957

Smiley Burnette

Burnette was a versatile performer who was best known as a prolific actor in Hollywood Westerns, most memorably as Gene Autry's comical sidekick Frog Millhouse in 54 films. Often called "Old Frog" in the movies, Burnette sported a checkered shirt, baggy pants, bandana and a trademark black Stetson hat with a turned-up brim. While providing comic relief, Burnette also teamed with Autry on countless duets and wrote many of the songs that were an obligatory part of Westerns. Smiley was such an accomplished musician that he played over 100 instruments during his career – most notably guitar, accordion and piano. As a result, he was able to put on an entertaining rodeo performance that blended western music with comedy.

Smiley Burnette was also a prolific songwriter who penned hundreds of western songs, including the classic ballad "Ridin' Down the Canyon." He gained a new audience in the '60s in the role of Hooterville Cannonball train engineer Charley Pratt on the popular TV sitcom "Petticoat Junction."

JAMES ARNESS – 1958

As the lead actor on TV's top-rated program – "Gunsmoke" – James Arness was one of America's most-popular and most-recognized stars when he performed at the Jaycee Bootheel Rodeo for three days in 1958. An estimated 30,000 packed the stands at VFW Stadium to get a glimpse of the man who played Marshall Matt Dillon. The 1958 rodeo marked the last time the rodeo was held there before moving to the new rodeo grounds on North Ingram St.

Arness enjoyed a moderately successful film career, appearing in 33 low-budget films before landing the lead role on "Gunsmoke." Many of his films were non-Westerns, including science fiction classics "The Thing" in 1951 and "Them" in 1954. But once "Gunsmoke" hit the air in '55, Arness would be forever associated with the series and the Dillon role. "Gunsmoke" ran until 1975, making it the longest-running drama in TV history to that point.

After "Gunsmoke" completed its run, Arness kept working, starring in the popular mini-series "How the West was Won" from 1976-'79 as well as the early-'80s crime drama "Big Jim McLain." He also did four "Gunsmoke" made-for-TV movies.

DENNIS WEAVER, AMANDA BLAKE & MILBURN STONE – 1959

Since "Gunsmoke remained the highest-rated program on television, and since James Arness was such a big draw the previous year, the Sikeston Jaycees brought in the three most-prominent supporting cast members of the show to help christen the new rodeo arena on North Ingram Street in 1959.

Gunsmoke stars Dennis Weaver (Chester), Milburn Stone (Doc) and Amanda Blake (Kitty) entertain at the 1959 rodeo. From the Loy Baugher collection.

Dennis Weaver, Amanda Blake and Milburn Stone shared a similar career path in that they had enjoyed modest success in films – though remaining relatively unknown to most fans – before landing the roles that would make them household names.

Blake portrayed Kitty Russell, proprietor of the Long Branch Saloon and Marshall Matt Dillon's implied romantic interest. Referred to as "Miss Kitty" by most of Dodge City's residents, Kitty was a kindhearted woman who had a soft spot for the downtrodden. But Miss Kitty was also a shrewd businesswoman and not afraid to stand up to the troublemakers who inevitably wound up in her saloon.

Stone played Galen "Doc" Adams, Dodge's resident physician. Doc was a crotchety-but-kind soul who could always be relied on to buy Matt a beer when he was having a bad day. In fact, Doc seemed to spend more time at the Long Branch that he did his office. Stone would be honored with an Emmy award in 1968 for best supporting actor in a drama series.

But of the three "Gunsmoke" stars who entertained at the 1959 rodeo, Dennis Weaver would go on to have the most successful career.

On "Gunsmoke," Weaver played Chester Goode, the simple-but-conscientious deputy of Matt Dillon. Chester toted a shotgun instead of a sidearm and always referred to Matt as "Mister Dillon." The character had a stiff leg and walked with an awkward gate that would make him the subject of many impressionists, but in real life Weaver was a track star at the University of Oklahoma and narrowly missed making the 1948 Olympic team as a decathlete. Weaver won an Emmy for his "Gunsmoke" role before leaving the series in 1964. He went on to play in eight other TV series, including starring roles in "Gentle Ben" as Florida Everglades game warden Tom Wedloe and "McCloud" as a New Mexico sheriff-turned-New York lawman Sam McCloud.

In addition to his accomplishments in front of the camera, Weaver was president of the Screen Actors Guild from 1973-75 and was also well-known for his humanitarian and environmentalist work.

DON DURANT – 1960

Rodeo fans in 1960 knew Don Durant from his role in "Johnny Ringo," playing a gunslinger-turned lawman. By the time Durant played the Friday night session Jaycee Bootheel Rodeo the series had been canceled after one season of 38 episodes. Durant continued to make occasional personal appearances as Ringo into 1964. Durant guest starred in a number of popular shows over the next decade before walking away from show business to focus on his business interests.

Don Durant

HUGH O'BRIAN – 1960

Hugh O'Brian

Appearing at the rodeo Saturday and Sunday was Hugh O'Brian, star of the popular Western "The Life and Legend of Wyatt Earp" – a show that had considerably more staying power than "Johnny Ringo." O'Brian played the legendary lawman who kept peace in Tombstone, Arizona with the help of his Buntline Special – a pistol with a 12-inch barrel. The show ran from 1955-61 and made O'Brian, who had enjoyed a modest career in film and theater before the role, a star. After "Wyatt Earp" ended its run O'Brian continued his film and stage career and also was in high demand for guest roles on popular television series. O'Brien reprised his signature role three times in the '90s – first in the Western series "Guns of Paradise" (1990). He played Wyatt Earp again in 1992 in the TV movie "The Gambler: Luck of the Draw" and finally in another small-screen flick, "Wyatt Earp: Return to Tombstone."

PAUL BRINEGAR, SHEB WOOLEY & CLINT EASTWOOD – 1961

Sheb Wooley, Clint Eastwood, Jaycee Charles Mitchell and Paul Brinegar.

The 1961 Jaycee Bootheel Rodeo brought three more familiar Western TV stars to Sikeston – one of whom would go on to become a Hollywood legend. Paul Brinegar, Sheb Wooley and Clint Eastwood were regulars on "Rawhide," the long-running series which followed the adventures of cowboys on a cattle drive from Texas which would end in Sedalia, MO "Rawhide" was a top-10 rated show when Brinegar, Wooley and Eastwood came to Sikeston.

Brinegar played George Washington Wishbone, a cantankerous fellow who served as both cook and doctor for the trail hands. Before landing the Wishbone role in 1959, Brinegar had been a busy character actor, working since 1946. Western fans knew him from his recurring role of Jim "Dog" Kelly in "The Life and Legend of Wyatt Earp," but he had also appeared in many dramas such as "Perry Mason," "Alfred Hitchcock Presents" and others. When the "Rawhide" series ended in 1965, Brinegar picked up where he left off as a character actor, appearing in television roles into the '80s. He found the occasional big screen role as well, such as the bartender in the 1973 Eastwood Western "High Plains Drifter" and the stagecoach driver in 1994's Mel Gibson film "Maverick."

Wooley, who played scout Pete Nolan on "Rawhide", had two claims to fame before "Rawhide." Like Brinegar, he had appeared in many movie and TV Westerns, including the Gary Cooper classic "High Noon." But he also had been a successful country singer, and in 1958 he recorded "Purple People Eater" – a popular novelty song that went to #1 on the pop charts. Wooley had a country hit in 1962 with "That's My Pa" and recorded a number of country songs in later years under the name of his alter ego, Ben Colder.

Eastwood had appeared in a handful of low-budget films and commercials before being cast in the role of ramrod Rowdy Yates on "Rawhide," which established him as a genuine TV star. When he was cast in a series of "spaghetti Westerns" by Italian director Sergio Leone in the mid-sixties, Eastwood became a movie star. First came "A Fist Full of Dollars," followed by the sequel "For a Few Dollars More." With the third Leone film, "The Good, the Bad and the Ugly," the man who played "the man with no name" had become of of the biggest names in Hollywood.

In the '70s, Eastwood's career kicked into high gear with the "Dirty Harry" series, which made him a bona fide superstar. He added the position of "director" to his resume in 1971 with "Play Misty for Me" and has continued to act and direct on into 2012. Eastwood has won two Best Director Oscars to date – for "Unforgiven" in 1993 and "Million Dollar Baby" in 2005.

Rex Allen and band From the Loy Baugher collection.

REX ALLEN – 1962

Rex Allen was well-known to fans of Hollywood Westerns, having appeared in 19 films from 1950-54. With the growing popularity of television and the decline of singing cowboy movies, Allen's career in front of the camera was pretty much over by the time he appeared at the 1962 Jaycee Bootheel Rodeo. But he was still a popular country recording artist, with a song on the charts that would eventually make it to #4 nationally – "Don't Go Near the Indians." When he donned his white Stetson hat and saddled his famous horse KoKo, Allen could still draw the crowds.

Allen had been a singer and songwriter before his movie career and continued to record into the '70s, totaling a dozen albums and two top-10 hits. Younger rodeo fans who didn't know Allen from his movies were very familiar with his soothing baritone voice, which they knew from his work as narrator of over 100 popular weekly Walt Disney nature films on Sunday nights. He kept busy with voice-over work for the rest of his life, working in commercials and narrating feature films such as 1973's "Charlotte's Web,"

If being a singer, songwriter, actor and voice-over artist didn't display enough versatility, Allen may have been one of the few entertainers to perform at the Jaycee Bootheel Rodeo who had actually competed in rodeo in his youth. Rex Allen truly lived up to the nickname "The Arizona Cowboy.

JAY NORTH – 1963

The Sikeston Jaycees mixed things up a little bit by bringing in Jay North – the youthful star known to millions as "Dennis the Menace" – for the rodeo's opening night in 1963.

"Dennis the Menace" was the TV adaptation of the Hank Ketcham comic strip about a mischievous boy who couldn't help getting into trouble despite his best intentions. The show debuted in 1959 and finished in the top 20 of the Nielsen ratings for its first three seasons. Ratings slipped in the 1962-63 season, with North getting older and less believable. Apparently audiences thought Dennis Mitchell was old enough to know better than to pull the stunts that he did. By the time North played the Jaycee Bootheel Rodeo in the fall of 1963 the series had been canceled.

North continued working as an actor into the 1970s but struggled with being typecast as the boy with the overalls and slingshot. Except for an occasional cameo appearance he is retired from show business.

LORNE GREENE & DAN BLOCKER – 1963

Lorne Greene and Dan Blocker were half of the starring cast of the popular Sunday night Western "Bonanza," which was unique among TV Westerns at the time in that it was filmed in color and ran a full hour. Greene played Ben Cartwright, widower, owner of the sprawling Nevada ranch the Ponderosa and father to three sons (each by a different mother). Blocker played middle son Hoss, who was a giant of a man with a big heart but strong as an ox.

Greene was a leading newscaster in Canada before moving to the U.S. to work in theater and films. With the debut of "Bonanza" in 1959, Greene and the other cast members became household names. The show ran 14 seasons – 10 of them finishing in the top 10 highest-rated shows – and was on top of the ratings when he and Blocker came to Sikeston.

If having a top-rated TV show wasn't enough success for Greene, he hit #1 on the pop music charts with a spoken word ballad called "Ringo" in December 1964. The title referred to western character "Johnny Ringo", but sales of the record might have been helped by the coincidence that that the record was released at the height of Beatlemania.

Though the character of Hoss had presumably the lowest IQ of the Cartwright boys, in real life Blocker held a master's degree in theater and had moved to Los Angeles to pursue his PhD at UCLA when he was noticed in a phone booth wearing jeans and a cowboy hat. He appeared in character roles in many of the popular Westerns of the late 1950s before getting the role on "Bonanza." Blocker played Hoss until his sudden death in 1972, and the series didn't make it another season.

Homer and Jethro

HOMER & JETHRO – 1964

There has always been a place in country music for satire. The most successful country satirists ever – Homer and Jethro – brought their act to the Jaycee Bootheel Rodeo in 1964.

Homer Haynes and Jethro Burns had been a team since the 1930s, earning a loyal following on popular radio programs of the day. Their music career took a back seat to World War II for a few years, but after the war they picked up where they left off, returning to radio and starting to record, first on the small King Records label and then with RCA Victor, where they remained for the rest of their careers.

With Homer on guitar and Jethro on mandolin (occasionally a banjo), the duo made a career of sending up the popular songs of the day. Despite being classified as country artists they enjoyed a broad crossover audience, passing up the rhinestones and sequins of the popular country attire of the day in favor of conservative suits. Two of their most popular parodies were "How Much is That Hound Dog in the Winder" in 1953 and "The Battle of Kookamonga" in 1959. The latter song poked fun at the Johnny Horton hit "The Battle of New Orleans" and earned Homer and Jethro a Grammy Award. Homer and Jethro starred in a series of commercials for Kellogg's Corn Flakes that were popular in the mid-60s, featuring the catchphrase "Ooh, that's corny!"

After appearing at the Sikeston rodeo, Homer and Jethro continued to enjoy broad popular and recording success. The recorded 19 more albums for RCA before Homer's death in 1971. They were inducted into the Country Music Hall of Fame in 2001.

JIM NABORS – 1965

One of the country's most popular TV stars came to Sikeston in 1965 as Jim Nabors performed at the Jaycee Bootheel Rodeo.

Nabors was the star of "Gomer Pyle, U.S.M.C." when he came to Sikeston. "Gomer Pyle" debuted a year earlier and was the No. 3 rated show on TV for the 1964-65 season, just ahead of the show it spun off from – "The Andy Griffith Show." Griffith had spotted Nabors singing at a nightspot in Santa Monica, Cal. and invited him to play a one-shot role on his show as a simple gas station attendant named Gomer Pyle in 1962. The character was so popular that Nabors appeared 26 more times as Gomer before getting his own show in 1964. Gomer traded his mechanic's clothes for a U.S. Marine uniform, but the character was the same – a goodhearted but inept country boy who always seemed to mess things up despite his best intentions.

On a number of occasions the plot of "The Andy Griffith Show" or "Gomer Pyle, U.S.M.C." allowed Gomer's character to sing, giving Nabors the opportunity to showcase his beautiful baritone voice and versatility as a performer. When he quit the sitcom after five seasons (all in the top 10) Nabors hosted a variety show, "The Jim Nabors Hour," which ran for another two seasons.

Nabors has recorded 28 albums as a singer, including three gold and one platinum. When not making records he found time to appear in three feature length movies starring Burt Reynolds in the 80s – "The Best Little Whorehouse in Texas," "Stroker Ace" and "Cannonball Run II."

BUDDY EBSEN – 1966

When entertainment veteran Buddy Ebsen came to perform at the Jaycee Bootheel Rodeo in 1966, he had starred in a classic adventure TV film series and a classic sitcom, which probably made him feel better about the role in a classic big screen film that slipped away.

Ebsen starred as Jed Clampett, patriarch of the family known as "The Beverly Hillbillies." Debuting in 1962, the show told the story of a mountain man who struck oil one day while he "was shootin' at some food," according to the theme song. The Clampetts moved to "Californy" and an instant hit show was the result. "The Beverly Hillbillies" was the No. 1 rated show its first two seasons and was still in the top 10 when Ebsen came to Sikeston.

Buddy Ebsen was already familiar to audiences and no stranger to hit shows when "Hillbillies" began its nine-season run. In 1955 he starred alongside Fess Parker in the three-part Disney TV film "Davy Crockett: King of the Wild Frontier." The series was a huge family hit and made big stars of both Ebsen, who played sidekick George Russell, and Parker, who himself would appear at the Jaycee Bootheel Rodeo in 1969.

The "big one that got away" in terms of roles for Ebsen surrounded the 1939 classic "The Wizard of Oz." Ebsen was originally signed to play the scarecrow, but traded roles with Ray Bolger, who originally was the be the tin man. Unfortunately, a severe reaction to the silver makeup worn for the tin man role landed Ebsen in the hospital for a lengthy stay, and the producers decided to re-cast Jack Haley in the role rather that put the film months behind schedule.

Missing out on the "Wizard of Oz" role was a bad break for Ebsen, but as it turned out he did okay for himself. After "The Beverly Hillbillies" completed its run, Ebsen starred in another successful series as private investigator Barnaby Jones.

MOLLY BEE – 1967

Entertaining at the Thursday evening performance of the 1966 Jaycee Bootheel Rodeo was Molly Bee, a country singer who was co-star of a popular daytime country music TV show.

"Swingin' Country" was a country variety show hosted by Bee, Roy Clark and Rusty Draper. The show had launched a year before Bee played the rodeo, reestablishing her as a country star. But "Swingin' Country was not her first experience being on a popular TV program. The rodeo audience remembered the pretty blonde as a regular on the '50s children's program "The Pinky Lee Show," then as a frequent guest on two different series hosted by Tennessee Ernie Ford. She had previously been best known for recording the Christmas classic "I Saw Mommy Kissing Santa Claus" as a teenager in 1952.

ROBERT CONRAD – 1967

The handsome star of a hot new Western series took the stage to entertain at the final three performances of the 1967 rodeo.

Robert Conrad was the star of "The Wild Wild West," a series that followed the adventures of a pair of U.S Secret Service agents – James West, played by Conrad, and partner Artemus Gor-

Charlie Walls, Robert Conrad and an out-of-costume clown Rick Young. From the Loy Baugher collection.

don (Ross Martin). Debuting in 1965, "The Wild Wild West" was somewhat unique among Westerns in that the heroes traveled not on horse or stagecoach, but on a specially-equipped railroad car. This was necessary because, as Secret Service agents on assignment by President U. S. Grant, they had access to a lot of gadgetry to help them foil the villains. Also, Gordon's character frequently worked in disguise, so he needed a lot of wardrobe space. "The Wild Wild West" ran for four seasons.

The Sikeston audience knew Conrad not only as James West but also as Tom Lopaka, a private detective who was introduced as a recurring character on the youth-oriented series "77 Sunset Strip" then spun off into his own series, "Hawaiian Eye," which ran for four seasons.

After "The Wild Wild West" Conrad was part of another popular series – "Black Sheep Squadron."

KEN CURTIS – 1968 & 1971

Ken Curtis became the fifth different "Gunsmoke" cast member to appear at the Jaycee Bootheel Rodeo as he entertained the crowd in 1968. Curtis succeeded James Arness, who had performed 10 years earlier, and Milburn Stone, Amanda Blake and Dennis Weaver, who all performed in 1959.

Weaver, who played deputy Chester Goode, had left "Gunsmoke" in 1964. Since Matt Dillon needed a deputy, the job eventually went to Festus Haggen, a recurring character of Curtis who had originally appeared on "Gunsmoke" in December of 1962. In '64 Haggen was written into the scripts on a regular basis, eventually becoming Dodge City's deputy marshal.

The character of Festus Haggen was not your typical lawman. He wore a scruffy beard and rode a mule rather than a horse. Festus was illiterate, and he was notorious for mooching a beer from Doc or Miss Kitty. But he was good with a gun, was tough, had a good heart and was loyal to his friends, especially "Matthew," as he called Matt Dillon. He became a competent deputy and remained on "Gunsmoke for 304 episodes.

Festus may have been Ken Curtis' most famous role, but he was a successful singer and actor before "Gunsmoke." He succeeded Frank Sinatra briefly as Tommy Dorsey's lead vocalist in 1941. After serving in World War II he returned to show business, appearing in a number of low-budget singing cowboy Westerns starting in 1945. He later appeared in several classic Westerns such as "Rio Grande," "The

Ken Curtis greets young fans. From the Loy Baugher collection.

Searchers," "How the West was Won" and "The Alamo." Curtis somehow found time in his busy film career to record with the legendary Western singing group Sons of the Pioneers.

The versatile Curtis wasn't limited to Western roles. He co-starred with Henry Fonda, James Cagney and Jack Lemmon in the 1955 Navy comedy "Mister Roberts," then starred in "Ripcord," an early '60s series about a skydiving service.

In 1971 Curtis earned the distinction of being the first performer to be invited to return to the rodeo.

FESS PARKER – 1969

Fess Parker performance. From the Loy Baugher collection.

The man who would be forever identified with a long-barrel rifle and coonskin cap took the stage at the Jaycee Bootheel Rodeo in 1969.

When he appeared at the rodeo, Fess Parker was the star of "Daniel Boone," a hit series that he not only starred in but also co-produced. A curious series of events that began 15 years earlier led Parker to produce "Daniel Boone."

Parker had been acting in small-budget motion pictures, including a small part in a film that would become a sci-fi cult classic, "Them!" It only took one day's work for Parker on the film, but it turned out to be a fortuitous one. Walt Disney watched the film, eyeing James Arness for an upcoming film about the life of frontier legend Davy Crockett. But Disney saw something in Parker that he liked and cast him in the role that made him an overnight star. "Davy Crockett: King of the Wild Frontier" ran as a three-part TV movie in 1955 and sparked a nationwide craze for coonskin caps. Parker became famous in the role of Crockett, who, according to the theme song, "kilt him a bar when he was only three." As for Arness, he didn't do to badly, since missing the role of Davy Crockett made him available to star in "Gunsmoke."

After making "Old Yeller" in 1957, Parker's career hit the wall, a casualty of being typecast as a frontiersman. After years of failing to get meaty parts, Parker took matters into his own hands with "Daniel Boone," which ran for six popular seasons. Parker's version of Dan'l had him wearing the famous coonskin cap again.

After "Daniel Boone" ended its run, Parker retired from show business to become a developer of a popular resort in California and an award-winning winery.

MICHAEL LANDON – 1970

Seven years after his "Bonanza" co-stars Lorne Green and Dan Blocker played the Jaycee Bootheel Rodeo, another of the Cartwrights came to Sikeston to entertain the fans.

Michael Landon played the youngest of the Cartwright sons – Joseph, or "Little Joe" as he was normally called. Little Joe was probably the most impetuous of Ben Cartwright's TV sons, the most strong-willed and to the female fans of the show, the most popular. "Bonanza" was still a ratings juggernaut when Landon came to Sikeston, having completed the previous season at #3 – a ninth

Michael Landon, aka "Little Joe

straight top-10 season. Landon played Little Joe for 14 seasons and 430 episodes before the show ended its run.

Landon had enjoyed some success in films and TV before "Bonanza," and the workaholic actor wasted no time in moving on to his next project – "Little House on the Prairie" – which debuted in 1974. "Little House" was the story of a prairie family and was based on the series of books by Laura Ingalls Wilder. Landon not only starred in the series but also served as producer, writer and director. "Little House" also proved to have staying power, lasting eight seasons.

Landon launched yet another family-oriented series after "Little House on the Prairie," this time breaking from the Western genre. He played Jonathan Smith, an angel who came to earth on special assignment from God (or as Smith called him, "my boss"). "Highway to Heaven" ran for five successful seasons before co-star Victor French died of cancer and Landon decided not to continue the show.

Sadly, two years after French's death, Landon himself died of cancer.

BARBARA MANDRELL & JOHNNY PAYCHECK – 1972

The two country singers who appeared at the 1972 Jaycee Bootheel Rodeo found bigger success in the years following their visit to Sikeston.

Barbara Mandrell had toured as a 12-year-old with Johnny Cash, giving her the opportunity to rub elbows and learn from the legendary Patsy Cline and other country greats. She recorded her first single in 1966, and was still gaining popularity when she played the Sikeston rodeo. Mandrell had just been made a member of the Grand Ole Opry during the summer of '72.

In 1973 Mandrell had her first top-10 hit with "The Midnight Oil," then broke through in a big way in the late '70s and early '80s with classic hits such as "Sleepin' Single in a Double Bed," "(If Lovin' You is Wrong) I Don't Want to Be Right," and "I Was Country When Country Wasn't Cool." All in all she had six chart-topping singles and recorded 26 albums. Mandrell was inducted into the Country Music Hall of Fame in 2009.

Johnny Paycheck, who shared the rodeo bill with Mandrell, was finally enjoying the rewards of success after a long climb. He was an ex-convict who had flopped in his first attempts at recording in the '50s. He played bass in George Jones' band, the Jones Boys, then tried recording as a solo artist again in the '60s after changing names and record labels. He broke through with a top-10 country hit in 1966 called "the Lovin' Machine," then had a few more hits before scoring big in 1971 with "She's All I Got," which made it to #2. He followed that song with another hit, "Someone to Give My Love To," in the spring of 1972.

With Willie Nelson and Waylon Jennings, Paycheck was part of the outlaw country movement in the '70s and enjoyed a string of top-10 records. He finally hit #1 with "Take This Job and Shove It" in 1977. After his only chart-topping song, run-ins with the law and problems with drinking and drugs stalled the momentum he had built, and his career was never the same.

ROY ROGERS & DALE EVANS – 1973

Legendary performers who were known as "the King of the Cowboys" and "the Queen of the West" brought a sense of nostalgia to the Jaycee Bootheel Rodeo in 1973.

Since Roy Rogers' famous horse Trigger was unable to make the trip to Sikeston, Jaycee Charlie McGill gave Roy the use of his palomino Clementine for the traditional ride around the arena fence. From the Loy Baugher collection.

Apart from Gene Autry, Roy Rogers have have been the most famous of all the singing cowboys from the golden age of movie Westerns. He also had a successful TV series, "The Roy Rogers Show," from the '50s that was still in syndication for years. Real-life wife Dale Evans co-starred with Rogers in the TV series and in many of the films, and the twosome were famous for the classic duet that become Rogers' signature song, "Happy Trails," which was written by Evans. By the time the pair came to Sikeston their film and TV career were all but over, except for the occasional guest appearance or cameo, but they were still household names and continued to perform regularly at fairs and rodeos.

Rogers started in show business as an original member of the Sons of the Pioneers, who were known for their classic Western songs "Cool Water," "Tumbling Tumbleweeds" and others. He began making appearances as a singing cowboy in movies in 1935, making 11 films before his first starring role in 1938. With the role in "Under the Western Stars," which came as a result of a walkout by Gene Autry, a new singing cowboy star was born. Rogers cranked out 91 feature films from 1938-52 before focusing on his television show.

The Pat Boone Family

So popular was Rogers during the golden age of Westerns that he was the top Hollywood box office draw from 1943 through the early '50s.

Rogers had married Evans in 1947, a year after his first wife had died giving birth to his son Roy, Jr., or "Dusty." Dusty Rogers performed at the Sikeston rodeo along with Rogers and Evansv, as did the Sons of the Pioneers.

THE PAT BOONE FAMILY – 1974

Given his squeaky-clean image as a teen idol nearly two decades earlier, Pat Boone's devotion to his family should come as no surprise.

One of the music industry's biggest-selling artists of all time took his wife and four daughters with him on the road in 1974, not just to tag along, but as part of the show.

Boone had 16 top-10 hits from 1955-62, including standards such as "Love Letters in the Sand" and "April Love." His cover versions of songs by black rhythm and blues artists are credited with helping to make rock and roll acceptable to mainstream audiences, since most radio stations wouldn't play records by black artists. He hit #1 in 1955 with Fats Domino's "Ain't That a Shame" and #4 the next year with Little Richard's "Tutti Frutti." Established as a star, Boone then focused on romantic ballads and inspirational records.

The Boone Family Act consisted of Pat, his wife Shirley, and daughters Cherry, Lindy, Debby and Laury. The show was oriented toward spiritual music, but did include some secular tunes as well. Three years after their appearance in Sikeston, Debby Boone had one of the biggest hits in music history with "You Light Up My Life." That song spent an incredible 10 weeks at #1 – a record to that point.

In addition to his recordings, Pat Boone had a successful film career, appearing in 14 feature films and four documentaries from 1955-70.

BOBBY VINTON – 1975

Only a year separated from his fifth #1 single, crooner Bobby Vinton brought his show to the Jaycee Bootheel Rodeo in 1975.

Known as "The Polish Prince," Vinton had hit the top spot on the adult contemporary charts in 1974 with "My Melody of Love," a song that contained a few Polish lyrics and a catchy melody. The song also reached #3 on the pop charts.

Vinton had gained initial success as a singer of romantic ballads in 1962 with "Roses are Red (My Love)," which hit #1 on both the pop and A.C. Charts. Vinton had three more #1 records in the next three years, starting with what would become his signature song, "Blue Velvet," in 1963. He kept the hits rolling with "There! I've Said it Again" and "Mr. Lonely" in 1964. "There! I've Said it Again" had the distinction of being knocked out of the #1 spot by the Beatles' "I Want to Hold Your Hand," which marked the start of the British invasion and turned the pop charts upside-down for the next several years.

He launched a syndicated television variety show, "The Bobby Vinton Show," the same year he played the Sikeston rodeo. The show aired 52 episodes before ending in 1978.

As of 2012, Vinton continues to be in demand as a performer in theaters and casinos, although his days as a maker of hit records were done when he came to Sikeston.

TANYA TUCKER – 1976, 1989 & 1992

Tanya Tucker

Like Brenda Lee before her and like LeeAnn Rimes and Taylor Swift after her, Tanya Tucker was a young female country singer who found popularity before she was old enough to drive and enjoyed crossover success.

When she made her first appearance at the Jaycee Bootheel Rodeo at the ripe old age of 17, Tucker was already a stage veteran with a slew of hits. "Delta Dawn" was the first of two top-10 country hits in 1972, paving the way for three straight #1s the next year – "What's Your Mama's Name?," "Blood Red and Goin' Down" and "Would You Lay With Me (in a Field of Stone)." She had a total of six #1s and eight studio albums under her belt by the time she came to Sikeston, making her one of country's brightest stars.

Tanya didn't crank out the hits quite as fast after she left her teenage years, but she found the top of the charts three more times in the mid-'80s as she bounced back in a big way. Her 1986 album "Girls Like Me" resulted in four top-10 country singles, and she had three straight #1s later in the decade – "I Won't Take Less Than Your Love," "If It Don't Come Easy" and "Strong Enough to Bend." Thirteen more top-10 singles came in the '90s, a decade that saw Tucker honored as the Country Music Association's Female Vocalist of the Year in 1991. In 1989 and 1992 she made encore appearances at the Jaycee Bootheel Rodeo.

KENNY ROGERS – 1977

The appearance of Kenny Rogers and the 1977 Jaycee Bootheel Rodeo was significant not just because a superstar came to Sikeston but because the sequence of events that followed.

Rogers had initially found success as a member of the New Christy Minstrels, a folk-pop group. He and three other members of the New Christy Minstrels left the group in 1967 to form the First Edition. The first single of the new group was a psychedelic tune called "Just Dropped In (to See What Condition My Condition Was In," a song which hit #5 on the pop charts early in 1968. After "Just Dropped In," the First Edition moved toward a more country flavor with their next two singles – "Ruby, Don't Take Your Love to Town" and "Ruben James." With Rogers singing lead on all the songs, the group was re-billed as Kenny Rogers and the First Edition.

In the early '70s the First Edition had their own syndicated TV show, "Rollin'," an ironic title given that the First Edition's hit records had all but stopped by that time. The group broke up after Rogers left in 1974 to go solo. His big breakthrough as a solo artist didn't come until 1977, the year he played the rodeo. With "Lucille" – a song he introduced to the rodeo audience as "a good old-fashioned beer-drinking song" – Rogers hit #1 on the country charts and #5 on the pop charts. His rodeo performance also included his most recent chart-topper, "Daytime Friends and Nighttime Lovers."

Kenny Rogers

Rogers had five straight singles in 1978-80 – "Love or Something Like It," "The Gambler," "She Believes in Me," "You Decorated My Life" and "Coward of the County" – that all hit No. 1 on the country charts, not to mention a string of hit duets with Dottie West. With the First Edition well in his rearview mirror, Kenny Rogers career was indeed "rollin'."

While in Sikeston in 1977, Rogers was impressed with the charitable work done by the Sikeston Jaycees and wanted to help. A horse breeder, Rogers donated one of his valuable Arabian stallions to the Jaycees with instructions to use it in any way that they thought might help in their work. The horse was eventually auctioned for $75,000, which the Jaycees donated to the recently-opened Scott-Mississippi-New Madrid Counties United Cerebral Palsy Center as seed money for a new building. Rogers returned to Sikeston to perform with West in fundraisers held at the Sikeston High School Field House in both 1978 and '79 – a time when their duets were topping the charts. The new center opened in 1979 and was named the Kenny Rogers United Cerebral Palsy Center of Southeast Missouri. The singer has continued to support the center through the years, appearing at two more benefit concerts in 2001 and 2009.

As for his entertainment career, the hits kept coming for Rogers in the '80s, with at least one #1 country song each year between 1981-86. He also showed his versatility as an artist by starring in a number of television specials and TV movies, the most notable being "The Gambler." He was selected for induction into the Country Music Hall of Fame in 2013.

Dottie West

DOTTIE WEST – 1978

Due in part to her popular duets with the star who preceded her as entertainer at the Jaycee Bootheel Rodeo, Dottie West was enjoying her second wave of popularity when she appeared in Sikeston in 1978.

West was a close friend of Patsy Cline in the early '60s as a struggling singer and songwriter in Nashville before breaking through with "Here Comes My Baby," a top-10 song that earned her a Grammy in 1965 for Best Female Country Vocal Performance. She hit the top 10 on the country charts again in 1966 with "Would You Hold it Against Me" and again in '67 with "Paper Mansions." West didn't have a top-10 solo record again until 1973 with "Country Sunshine," a song she wrote that had been part of a commercial for Coca-Cola. But she did hit the #2 spot with "Rings of Gold," a duet with Don Gibson, in 1969. Duets would play an important role in the resurrection of her career in the '70s.

With the solo hits drying up, Dottie turned again to duets, this time teaming with with Kenny Rogers. Their 1978 album "Every Time Two Fools Collide" went gold, hit No. 1 on the country charts and spawned two monster hits. The title track went to #1 and "Anyone Who Isn't Me Tonight" made it to #2. After her rodeo performance in '78, Kenny and Dottie's follow-up album went platinum in

'79. "Classics" yielded the hit singles "All I Ever Need is You" (#1) and "Till I Can Make it On My Own" (#3). The two collaboration albums earned Rogers and West CMA Awards in both '78 and '79 for Vocal Duo of the Year.

With the jump start given her career by the duets with Rogers, Dottie returned to the top of the charts as a soloist in 1980 with a pair of #1s – "A Lesson in Leavin'" and "Are You Happy Baby." The next year she teamed up with Rogers for another #1 record, "What Are We Doin' in Love," which turned out to be her last top-10 single.

LARRY GATLIN & THE GATLIN BROTHERS – 1979

The Gatlin Brothers

Larry Gatlin and brothers Steve and Rudy honed their three-part harmonies singing in churches and local radio programs growing up in Abilene, Tex. When friend Kris Kristofferson helped Larry get a record deal as a solo artist, Steve and Rudy moved to Nashville to sing backup.

Gatlin's first chart-topping country single was "Broken Lady," a song that earned him a 1976 Grammy Award. The next year brought more #1 success with "I Just Wish You Were Someone I Love," and "Night Time Magic" made it to #2. With three big hits under their belt, Larry, Rudy and Steve officially became a group – The Gatlin Brothers.

The group was riding high in 1979 when they appeared at the Jaycee Bootheel Rodeo. The single "All the Gold in California" went to #1, was the Academy of Country Music's Single of the Year and helped Larry win Male Vocalist of the Year honors. The album "Straight Ahead" went platinum.

After their Sikeston performance The Gatlin Brothers had eight more top-10 records before retiring, including a #1 in 1983, "Houston (Means I'm One Day Closer to You)." The group returned in Sikeston in April of 1980 for a benefit concert to raise money for the Kenny Rogers Children's Center.

THE KENDALLS – 1979

The Kendalls

The Kendalls were two years removed from the release of their signature song – "Heaven's Just a Sin Away" – and were on a hot streak when they entertained at the Jaycee Bootheel Rodeo.

Father Royce Kendall had been part of a country duet with his brother before getting off the road to be with his family and becoming a barber. As daughter Jeannie grew up and began to show musical talent, the two found that they harmonized beautifully, and wound up with a record contract. But they had only modest success on the charts until "Heaven's Just a Sin Away" went to #1 and earned the Kendalls and

Grammy and a CMA award. Their next four singles all made it into the top 10, including "Sweet Desire" in '78, which made it to #1. The Kendalls were one of country music's hottest acts when they came to Sikeston.

The Kendalls released five more top-10 hits in the next five years, the last being "Thank God for the Radio," which made it to #1 in 1984. The duo never hit the top 10 again, although they continued to record and make public appearances until Royce's death in 1998.

TOM T. HALL – 1979

A prolific songwriter, Tom T. Hall had already recorded seven #1 records by the time he made it to the Jaycee Bootheel Rodeo to perform in 1979. But two of his biggest selling compositions would turn out to be ones recorded by other artists.

Known as a balladeer who told powerful stories, Hall made the top 10 for the first time in 1968 with "The Ballad of Forty Dollars." Then came a string of seven #1s over the next decade – "A Week in a Country Jail" ('69), "The Year Clayton Delaney Died" ('71), "(Old Dogs, Children and) Watermelon Wine" ('72), "I Love" ('73), "Country Is" and "I Care" ('74) and "Faster Horses (the Cowboy and the Poet)" ('75). "I Love" was a big crossover hit, making it to #12 on the pop charts.

But it was a song recorded by Jeannie C. Riley, "Harper Valley PTA," that sold over six million copies in 1968 and earned Hall a Grammy nomination for Song of the Year. Hall also wrote "Little Bitty," a song that went to #1 for Alan Jackson in 1996.

Tom T. Hall was inducted into the Country Music Hall of Fame in 2008.

Ronnie Milsap

RONNIE MILSAP – 1979, 1981, 1983 & 1990

When Ronnie Milsap came to Sikeston in 1979 to appear for the first of four times at the Jaycee Bootheel Rodeo he was a country star. When he returned two years later he was also a pop star.

Although Milsap was known as a blues and rock and roll performer when he moved to Nashville in 1972 at the urging of Charley Pride, country had been a part of his musical roots. He impressed RCA records enough to sign a contract in '73, and in short time had his first top-10 single, "I Hate You." Milsap's breakthrough came in 1974 with his first two #1 songs – "Pure Love" and "Please Don't Tell Me How the Story Ends." Another chart-topper came the next year with "Daydreams About Night Things."

Milsap could do little wrong for the remainder of the decade of the '70s. Of his next nine singles, eight went to #1 on the country charts (the ninth one "flopped" and only made it to #2). The most notable of that string of hits was "It Was Almost Like a Song," which gave a preview of the crossover success that Milsap would enjoy in the '80s by making it to #16 on the pop charts. He was CMA Male Vocalist of the Year three times in the '70s and Entertainer of the Year in '77. He also won six Grammy Awards during the decade.

Picking up where he left off, Milsap had an astounding 23 #1 country songs in the '80s, despite the fact that his music was migrating more toward easy-listening and pop. Songs that found success on the pop charts included "Smoky Mountain Rain," "(There's) No Getting Over Me," "I Wouldn't Have Missed It For the World" and "Any Day Now." Milsap was still hitting the charts with regularity when he made his fourth rodeo appearance in 1990.

DON WILLIAMS – 1980

Called "The Gentle Giant" due to his 6-foot-1 stature, his deep-but-mellow voice and soft-spoken stage presence, Don Williams was at the peak of his career when he played the Jaycee Bootheel Rodeo in 1980.

Williams began his professional singing career as a member of the Pozo-Seco Singers – a Texas pop trio – in the '60s before launching a solo career in 1973. He released three forgettable singles before breaking into the top 10 with "We Should Be Together," which made it to #5 on the country charts in '74. With the ice broken, Williams had another 18 top-10 singles by the time he took the Sikeston stage. Included in those hits were classics like "Some Broken Hearts Never Mend" ('77), "Tulsa Time" ('78) and "I Believe in You" ('80). "Tulsa Time" was the Country Music Association's Single of the Year in 1978, and Williams won Male Vocalist of the Year honors.

Don Williams

Williams scored six more #1s after his rodeo appearance. During his career 42 of 46 singles he released made it into the top 10, consistency seldom matched in the industry.

Williams songs tended to have simple orchestrations, which fit in well with his stage presence. He normally sang from a stool, played guitar and was dressed in his trademark blue jeans, boots, denim jacket and hat. In an era in country music where glitz and showmanship were popular, Williams was the common man's star, endearing him to fans. He was inducted into the Country Music Hall of Fame in 2010.

Jim Ed Brown and Helen Cornelius

JIM ED BROWN & HELEN CORNELIUS – 1980

Jim Ed Brown came to the Sikeston Rodeo as half of one of country's most popular duets in the '70s. But harmonizing with females was nothing new to the stage veteran.

Brown's first success in recording came with sister Maxine as a duet, then as a trio when younger sister Bonnie joined and the group was billed as Jim Edward, Maxine and Bonnie Brown. The trio had several top-10 records in the mid-1950s, including "I Heard the Bluebirds Sing" and "I'll Take the Chance." In '59 they began to call themselves simply "The Browns," and the first single released that year made music history. "The Three Bells," a poignant ballad about the birth, marriage and death of a simple man (who ironically was named Jimmy Brown), not only topped the country charts, but was also #1 on the pop and adult contemporary charts, an unprecedented accomplishment.

The Browns followed up "The Three Bells" with a few more hits before Maxine and Bonnie left the group to focus on their families and Jim Ed set out on a solo career in 1965. He hit the country top 10 four times during the next decade, the biggest hit being 1967's "Pop a Top," which made it to #3. Having failed to produce an consistent string of hits on his own, Jim Ed tried harmonizing again, this time with Helen Cornelius. Their debut single, "I Don't Want to Have to Marry You" went to #1 in 1976, and the duo had six more top-10 singles before their appearance at the Sikeston rodeo.

Brenda Lee

BRENDA LEE – 1980

To say Brenda Lee started out in show business when she was young would be an understatement. She was singing in talent shows when she was only five, and by the time she was 11 she was on national TV, singing on Red Foley's "Ozark Jubilee" in 1956. Later that year she got her first recording contract and released her first single.

Diminutive in stature, audiences couldn't understand how such a little girl could have such a big, booming voice. When her single "Dynamite" was released in 1957, she was given the nickname "Little Miss Dynamite" which stuck with her throughout a long career.

Brenda finally began to have some success on the charts in 1960, first with "Sweet Nothin's" (#4 on the pop charts) and then what would become her signature song, "I'm Sorry." That song went to #1 in 1960 and stayed on Billboard's Hot 100 list for six months. Later in 1960, a Christmas song she had recorded two years earlier, "Rockin' Around the Christmas Tree," was re-released, taking advantage of her newfound popularity. It was a huge hit and remains a holiday standard to this day. Another 1960 release, "I Want to Be Wanted," also hit #1. In all, Brenda Lee had 10 top-10 pop hits from 1960-63. She was the biggest-selling female singer of the '60s.

Although the hit records stopped coming in the '70s, Lee was still a popular concert attraction when she appeared at the rodeo. She was inducted into the Country Music Hall of Fame in 1997 and the Rock and Roll Hall of Fame in 2002.

THE STATLER BROTHERS – 1980 & 1986

The Statler Brothers

One of country's most prolific and enduring groups entertained the Sikeston audience at the 1986 Jaycee Bootheel Rodeo.

Brothers Harold and Don Reid, along with Phil Balsley and Lew DeWitt, performed as a gospel quartet in Virginia in the late '50s and early '60s. They called themselves the Kingsmen, but when a pop group with the same name had a huge hit record in "Louie, Louie" in 1963, the group decided to change their name to avoid confusion. Spotting a box of Statler brand facial tissue in a hotel room, they decided to call themselves the Statler Brothers. Harold Reid joked years later, "We could just as easily have been called the Kleenex Brothers."

The new name wasn't the only change coming for the group. They had been experimenting with using four-part gospel harmonies in country songs, a formula that got them their first big hit in 1965 with "Flowers On the Wall." The song was #2 on the country charts and also a huge pop favorite at #4, no small feat for a country artist at a time when British pop groups ruled the charts. At that time the Statler Brothers were the opening act for Johnny Cash, and when he launched his popular "The Johnny Cash Show" in 1969 they were regulars on the show, giving them weekly national television exposure. Their next big country hit didn't come until 1970's "Bed of Rose's" made it to #9.

The Statler Brothers were a fixture on the country charts during the '70s, with hits such as "Do You Remember These?," "Class of '57," "I'll Go to My Grave Loving You" and their second #1, "Do You Know You Are My Sunshine." More hits followed in the '80s before their Sikeston appearance, including a three #1 country singles – "Elizabeth" ('83), "My Only Love" ('84) and "Too Much on My Heart" ('85).

In addition to their country success, the Statler Brothers kept in touch with their gospel roots, recording several gospel albums. They were inducted into the Gospel Hall of Fame in 2007, a year before being inducted into the Country Music Hall of Fame. They won the CMA Vocal Group of the Year a staggering nine times between 1972 and 1984.

It is noteworthy that the Statler Brothers didn't experience the frequent lineup changes common with groups that record over several decades. The only change the group ever made was made out of necessity. Jimmy Fortune replaced Lew DeWitt as the group's tenor in the early '80s after DeWitt became too ill to perform.

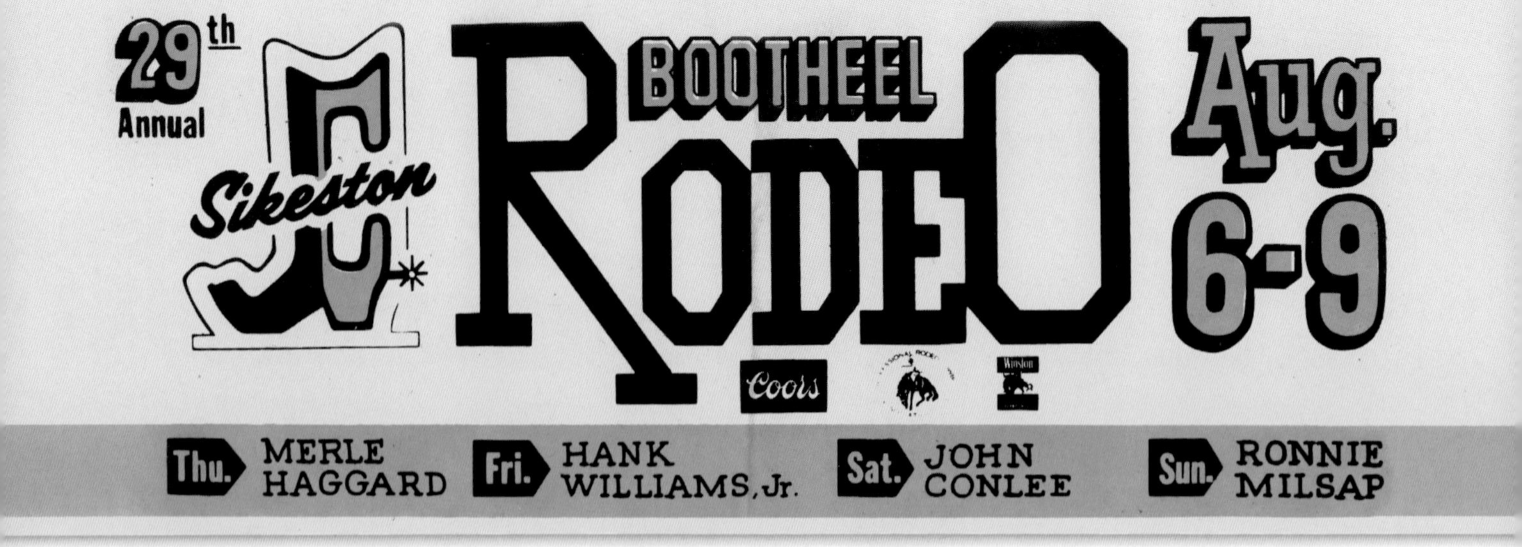

MERLE HAGGARD – 1981

Merle Haggard already had 26 #1 country hits in the bank when he came to Sikeston to play the Jaycee Bootheel Rodeo in 1981. And he wasn't nearly done.

After his father's sudden death when Merle was nine years old, Haggard rebelled against authority and spent his time in reform schools and eventually prison. He turned to his love of music to turn his life around, and at the urging of Johnny Cash, began to write songs dealing with the themes of prison and his troubled youth. The advice turned out to be not only therapeutic for Haggard, but also profitable. "I'm a Lonesome Fugitive" hit #1 on the country charts in 1966, and two more prison songs topped the charts in '67 – "Branded Man" and "Sing Me Back Home." "Mama Tried" in '68, another #1, was an apology of sorts to his mother for his rebellious youth.

While Haggard certainly understood rebellion, he had little room for the anti-Vietnam war protests that marked the late '60s. "Okie From Muskogee" ('69) and "The Fightin' Side of Me" ('70) were both slams at the the hippie movement, the drug culture and what Haggard perceived as an anti-American element. Both songs resonated with conservative country fans, and both hit #1.

The hits were still pouring in for Haggard when he came to Sikeston, with two in 1980 and another in '81. He won the Academy of Country Music's Male Vocalist of the Year that year, the fourth time he'd been so honored. The Sikeston audience caught Haggard at a high point in his career. The singer became ill shortly before he was to take the stage, but went on with the show, which turned out to be shortened by rain. Unfortunately for the fans, the show was stopped before he had the opportunity to sing many of his classic hits.

All told, Merle Haggard produced 38 #1 singles. He was inducted into the Country Music Hall of Fame in 1994.

HANK WILLIAMS, JR. – 1981

Growing up as the namesake of a country music icon, Hank Williams, Jr. had a hard time living and being a musician in his daddy's shadow. It wasn't until he threw off that shadow and decided to be his own man that he began to live up to his talent and built his own legend.

Hank, Jr. was only three when his famous father died. When he showed a talent for music at an early age, his mother wanted him to become what amounted to a Hank Williams tribute act. Although he was enjoying success, with a #1 single in 1970 and another in '72, the pressures of being compared to his dad were mounting and Hank turned to pills and alcohol to help him cope. He nearly died twice in his mid-20s – once a failed suicide attempt and the other a mountain climbing accident – before coming to grips with the fact he couldn't be his father. That being the case, he decided to be himself.

Two 1979 albums – "Whiskey Bent and Hell Bound" and "Family Tradition" – featured many tracks that addressed Hank's troubled past and substance abuse problems. The "Whiskey Bent and Hell Bound" album went platinum. Williams had two more gold albums before coming to Sikeston in 1981. He had just released another album, "Habits Old and New," before his Jaycee Bootheel Rodeo appearance. That album went platinum and featured two classics – "All My Rowdy Friends (Have Settled Down)" and "A Country Boy Can Survive."

Hank Williams, Jr. had an astounding 17 consecutive albums that went gold or platinum over a 13-year period – success his daddy could only dream of.

Hank Williams, Jr.

JOHN CONLEE – 1981

In the late 1970s, disc jockey John Conlee went from spinning records to recording them. When he played the Jaycee Bootheel Rodeo in 1981 Conlee's third album was on the charts, and he had produced a pair of #1 singles and four #2s.

"Rose Colored Glasses" was Conlee's first hit and remains his signature song, although it wasn't one of his chart-toppers. "Back Side of Thirty" and "Lady Lay Down" did make it to the top spot from his first album. "With Love," Conlee's fourth album, was released in '81 and featured the #2 hit "Miss Emily's Picture."

John Conlee has recorded 11 albums that have spawned a total of eight #1 country singles.

CONWAY TWITTY – 1982, 1984 & 1987

To say that Conway Twitty had an impressive life resume before making it big as a country music star would be putting it mildly.

As Harold Jenkins, he was an exceptional baseball player and was drafted by the Philadelphia Phillies before being drafted into the army. After his military service he was a contemporary of Elvis Presley, Johnny Cash and Jerry Lee Lewis at Sun Records in the early days of rock and roll. His first hit as a solo recording artist, "It's Only Make Believe," was #1 on practically every pop chart on the planet and made "Conway Twitty" an international star who was the inspiration for Conrad Birdie, the lead character in the hit Broadway musical "Bye, Bye Birdie."

But country music was in Twitty's blood, and he made the transition from rock and roll to country in 1965. His first country #1 release, "Next In Line," came out in 1968, followed by 28 more #1 country singles before appearing at the Jaycee Bootheel Rodeo in 1982. Included in that long list of hits are songs considered classics today, including "Hello, Darlin'," "You've Never Been This Far Before," "Linda On My Mind," "Happy Birthday Darlin'," "I'd Love to Lay You Down," "Tight Fittin' Jeans" and "Slow Hand." Twitty also had five straight #1s with duet partner Loretta Lynn during the '70s.

Conway Twitty continued to crank out country hits through the '80s to accumulate a career total of 44 #1 singles in the US and 55 worldwide. He was inducted into the Country Music Hall of Fame in 1999, six years after his sudden death.

T. G. SHEPPARD – 1982

Bill Browder was somewhat of a music industry chameleon before he finally found his niche and became country star T. G. Sheppard.

He was a pop performer in the early '60s under the name Brian Stacy, opening for Jan and Dean, the Beach Boys and other stars. He tried his hand at being a record promoter using his own name later in the decade, but never shook his desire to perform. After unsuccessfully trying for 18 months to find someone to record a song by a songwriter he represented, he decided to record "Devil in the Bottle" himself on the Melodyland label, which was owned by Berry Gordy's legendary Motown Records. That record went to #1 in 1975, Bill Browder was history, and country star T. G. Sheppard arrived. The follow-up single, "Tryin' to Beat the Morning Home" also hit No. 1.

After a drought of over three years without a #1 single, Sheppard found his stride in 1989. Starting with "Last Cheater's Waltz," 11 of his next 13 singles went to #1. He was on a roll of eight straight chart toppers when he appeared at the Jaycee Bootheel Rodeo in 1982, the biggest being "I Loved 'Em Every One," which also made the Top 40 on the pop charts.

Although Sheppard recorded most of his big hits on Warner Brothers and Columbia Records after Motown abandoned its experiment with country music, R & B was still a part of his musical style. His blend of R & B, pop and country proved popular until the traditionalist country movement took hold in the mid-80s. He charted a total of 20 #1 country singles before retiring from recording.

MOE BANDY – 1982

The former bull rider from Texas came to the Jaycee Bootheel Rodeo in 1982 not as a cowboy, but as a country star who stayed true to his honky tonk roots.

Moe Bandy cut his first record with borrowed money and printed 500 copies. A copy of "I Just Started Hatin' Cheatin' Songs Today" got the attention of an Atlanta record label, which released it, and the song made it to #17. Moe sang and played honky tonk at a time when country pop was the rage, but his songs about drinking and cheating found a niche audience and popularity not just as a recording artist but also as a live performer. "It's a Cheating' Situation," a duet with Janie Fricke, went to #2 in 1979 (#1 in Canada), and "I Cheated Me Right Out of You" was #1 later that year.

But it was hit duets with Joe Stampley that really put Bandy on the map. "Just Good Ol' Boys" went to #1 in '79, and the duo had another hit in '81 with "Hey Joe (Hey Moe)."

MICKEY GILLEY & JOHNNY LEE – 1982

With the enormous success of the 1980 film "Urban Cowboy," 1982 seemed like a good year to bring in two of the stars of the hit soundtrack album to entertain at the Jaycee Bootheel Rodeo.

Mickey Gilley and Johnny Lee accounted for five of the 18 tracks on the album and in the film, which was inspired by Gilley's nightclub in surburban Houston, Tex. "Stand By Me," a remake of the classic Ben E. King R & B standard, made it to #1 on both the country and adult contemporary record charts in 1980 for Gilley. Lee's "Lookin' for Love" was a country #1 hit that also achieved crossover success.

Gilley had been a journeyman piano player in the South's honky tonks during the '60s, but didn't find fame until he opened the nightclub that bears his name. He had seven #1 country singles during the '70s before "Urban Cowboy" and its success.

Lee had been a sideman for Gilley at the club and on the road before "Lookin' for Love" brought him success as a solo performer. He had two more #1s before joining Gilley on the Sikeston stage – "One in a Million" and "Bet Your Heart on Me."

Gilley and Lee both continued to have success on the country charts until the mid-80s. Gilley's career totals included 16 #1 country singles. Lee hit the top spot four times total.

DAVID FRIZZELL & SHELLY WEST – 1983

One of country music's hottest duets in the early 1980s, David Frizzell and Shelly West came to record together as a result of marriage, but not the traditional way. She was married to David's brother.

David was the younger brother of popular singer Lefty Frizzell and played in his band. Shelly had a country music pedigree also, being the daughter of Dottie West. Shelly fell in love and married a third Frizzell brother, Allen, who was the lead guitarist in Dottie's band. By 1977 David had struck out on his own, and Shelly and Allen both joined his band.

David and his sister-in-law Shelly tried their hand as a duet, at first without success. But a demo record of "You're the Reason God Made Oklahoma" got the attention of Clint Eastwood, who liked the song and made it part of the soundtrack to his film "Any Which Way You Can." "You're the Reason God Made Oklahoma" went to #1 and launched David and Shelly's career as a duet. The 1981 album "Carrying On the Family Names" featured another top-10 country hit, "A Texas State of Mind." The team took the honors from both the CMA and ACM in '81 and '82 and best vocal duo.

David and Shelly recorded five albums together through 1985 that yielded two more top-10 singles. But the name recognition achieved through their success as a partnership also paid off in their solo careers. Shelly hit #1 with "Jose Cuervo" in 1983, while Frizzell's "I'm Gonna Hire a Wino to Decorate Our Home" was a chart topper a year earlier and nominated for a Grammy.

LEE GREENWOOD – 1983, 1984 & 1985

Lee Greenwood was perhaps the hottest male singer in country music when he performed a record three straight years at the Jaycee Bootheel Rodeo, the first time in 1983. He was '83's Male Vocalist of the Year at both the Country Music Association and the Academy of Country Music Awards shows, and repeated at the CMAs in '84. His hit "I.O.U." won the Grammy in '85 for Top Male Vocal Performance.

Greenwood's big music break came in 1979 when Mel Tillis' bass player, Larry McFaden, saw him playing at a Nevada casino and talked him into going to Nashville. He was signed to a record deal with MCA Records and his first album, "Inside Out," produced three top–ten country singles. That was the beginning of a string of 17 straight singles that made the top 10, including seven chart toppers.

Oddly enough, the patriotic standard that became Greenwood's signature song, "God Bless the USA," wasn't one of those #1s, only making it to #7 during its original release in 1984. But the song made a comeback during the first Persian Gulf War (a.k.a. Desert Storm). Its inclusion in "The Best of Lee Greenwood" album in 2001 coincided with the terrorist attacks of 9/11/2001, and the song zoomed to the top 10 again, even hitting #16 on the pop charts.

LORETTA LYNN – 1983

Loretta Lynn's place as the first lady of country music was well established when she performed at the Jaycee Bootheel Rodeo in 1983. But getting there was a long road.

She married when she was 14 and already had four children when she started pursuing a singing career in 1961, singing near her home in Washington, where husband "Doo" Lynn had moved the family looking for work. Loretta was spotted performing in a talent competition in Tacoma, and soon recorded her first song, "I'm a Honky Tonk Girl." The Lynns traveled around the country self-promoting the single to disc jockeys, a trip depicted in her biographical film, "Coal Miner's Daughter." When they reached Nashville the song was on the charts, and soon she had a recording contract with Decca.

The rest, as they say, is history. Loretta's vocal style, combined with songs that sympathized with the struggles of women, struck a chord with audiences. She released 38 top-10 country singles by the time she came to Sikeston, including 11 that went to #1. Among her classics that topped the charts are "Don't Come Home a Drinkin' (with Lovin' On Your Mind)," "Fist City," "Woman of the World (Leave My World Alone)" and her signature song, "Coal Miner's Daughter." She also had great success as a duet partner – first with Ernest Tubb and later with Conway Twitty.

Loretta Lynn's body of work has included 54 studio albums and 23 #1 country singles. She has been honored by the music industry with 54 different awards and was inducted into the Country Music Hall of Fame in 1988.

JOHN ANDERSON – 1984 & 1996

On the basis of his recent #1 hit "Swingin'," John Anderson swung into Sikeston in 1984 as a rising country star.

"Swingin'," which was released in '83, helped Anderson win two Country Music Association awards, including the Horizon Award for the most promising newcomer. The title track of the album "Wild and Blue" had also hit #1 in late '82. He had enjoyed a third #1 song, "Black Sheep," and a #3, "She Sure Got Away With My Heart," by the time he took the Jaycee Bootheel Rodeo stage.

Anderson didn't flirt with the top of the country charts again for the rest of the '80s, and seemed to be a has-been until his "Seminole Wind" album in 1991. That album featured four top-10 songs, including "Straight Tequila Night." His next album would feature his last #1 single, "Money in the Bank," and two more songs that made the top five. Anderson returned to Sikeston in 1996 for an encore rodeo performance.

GEORGE STRAIT – 1984

Jaycee Bootheel Rodeo fans in 1984 got an early glimpse of an artist who would go on to become arguably the greatest country singer ever.

George Strait was riding high in the summer of '84 when he came to Sikeston, with four straight #1 country singles. His "Right or Wrong" album had gone platinum, the third album of his to do so in three releases. Most artists would consider that a pretty good career, but for Strait, it was only the start.

George Strait was a college student in Texas when he saw an ad wanting a singer for a country band called Stoney Ridge. He joined the band, soon became the lead singer, and changed the band's name to Ace in the Hole. The band gained a strong following in south Texas, playing in clubs and bars. One of the bar owners had formerly worked with MCA Records and convinced the company to check out Strait. MCA signed Strait to a deal in early 1981, and the Ace in the Hole Band came with the deal.

Whatever money MCA spent to come and audition George Strait was likely the best investment the company ever made. He has remained with the label through his entire career, and every one of the 37 albums he has released through 2011 has been certified by the RIAA as either Gold, Platinum or Multi-Platinum. His 59 #1 singles through 2011 are the most of any recording artist of any genre in history, ahead of Elvis Presley.

Soon after Strait's Sikeston rodeo appearance he released the album "Does Fort Worth Ever Cross Your Mind?" The single of the same name went to #1, and the album went platinum, setting the tone for the next three decades. His portfolio of classic hits includes "Unwound," "Amarillo by Morning," "Oceanfront Property," "The Chair," "Check Yes or No," "All My Exes Live in Texas," "Living and Living Well" and "Give It Away." A model of consistency, Strait has had at least one top-10 record every year for 31 years.

George Strait's impact on country music can be measured not just in record sales but also in the awards he has won. He is the most nominated and most awarded performer in both the Country Music Association and the Academy of Country Music. In 2006 he was inducted into the Country Music Hall of Fame, only the second performer to be so honored while still actively recording.

MICHAEL MARTIN MURPHEY – 1985

At one time country music was called country and western, a recognition of the influence that cowboy music played on the genre. Artists like Bob Wills, Gene Autry, the Sons of the Pioneers and Marty Robins played a large role in the popularity of the music. Michael Martin Murphey, who was a throwback to the singing cowboy, brought his act to the Jaycee Bootheel Rodeo in 1985.

Murphey's first charting single, 1975's "Wildfire," reached #1 on the adult contemporary charts and #3 on the pop charts. After "Carolina in the Pines" also became a hit, Murphey was a bona fide star, but still hadn't made a ripple in the country charts. That didn't change until 1982, when "What's Forever For" was a #1 country single, and "Still Taking Chances" made it to #3. At the time of his Sikeston appearance he had a "Best Of" album on the charts which included a re-release of "Carolina in the Pines." That song made it to #9 on the country charts in '85.

Murphey had one more #1 single in the years following his Sikeston appearance – 1987's "A Long Line of Love."

EDDY RAVEN – 1985

Eddy Raven brought his brand of country mixed with a dash of cajun music to the Jaycee Bootheel Rodeo in 1985. His arrival on the country scene as a star in the early '80s proves that perseverance pays off.

Raven had been a successful songwriter before starting his own recording career. He released 20 singles before finally cracking the top 20 in 1981-82 with four difference songs from his

"Desperate Dreams" album. Raven's 1984 album "I Could Use Another You" yielded three top-10 country hits, including his first #1, "I Got Mexico." When he took the Sikeston stage in '85 his current album was "Love and Other Hard Times," which produced three more top-10 singles.

From 1984-90 Eddy Raven had 17 straight top-10 hits, including three consecutive #1s during 1987-88 – "Shine, Shine, Shine," "I'm Gonna Get You" and "Joe Knows How to Live." His last top-10 song was in 1990.

RAY CHARLES – 1985

In a departure from the usual Jaycee Bootheel Rodeo lineup that featured country music almost exclusively, the Sikeston Jaycees brought one of the most celebrated performers of his generation of any musical genre to entertain rodeo fans.

Rolling Stone Magazine listed Ray Charles as #2 on their list of the 100 Greatest Singers of All Time in 2008. The same magazine ranked Charles as #10 when they listed the 100 Greatest Artists of All Time. He won 16 Grammy Awards, including the Lifetime Achievement Award. The list of awards and honors Charles has received goes on and on, making him perhaps the most honored artist that has appeared on any stage in Sikeston. That would include the budding superstar Elvis Presley, who appeared at the Armory twice in 1955.

Charles was totally blind by the age of 10 and was an orphan by the time he was 15. At the Florida School for the Deaf and Blind he developed a talent for music. Moving from Florida to Seattle in 1947 after his mother's death, he began playing in jazz bands. He had a #2 R&B hit as part of a trio in 1949, then two more top-10 R&B singles under his own name in '51. His 1955 song "I Got a Woman" was the first of what would be many #1 songs for Ray Charles. Some of Charles' records in the late '50s began to make the pop charts, proving it wasn't just black audiences that dug his music. The 1959 release "What'd I Say" was a #1 on the R&B charts and #6 on the pop charts. "Georgia On My Mind" (1960) and "Hit the Road Jack" (1961) were both pop #1s.

After switching from Atlantic Records to ABC and getting more creative control over his recordings, he confounded the music industry by releasing a pair of country albums in 1962, "Modern Sounds in Country and Western Music," volumes one and two. Volume one reached #1 on the pop album charts; volume two made it to #2. "I Can't Stop Loving You" from volume one made a clean sweep on the charts, hitting #1 on the pop, R&B and adult contemporary charts.

The 1980s saw a return to country music for Ray Charles, with five different country albums. None met with the success that his '60s country albums did, but his collaboration with George Jones and Chet Atkins in '84 produced a top-10 country single, "We Didn't See a Thing." In '85, a duet with Willie Nelson titled "Seven Spanish Angels" went to #1.

The winner of a dozen Grammy Awards, Ray Charles was one of the original inductees into the Rock and Roll Hall of Fame in 1986.

RICKY SKAGGS – 1986

The reigning Country Music Association Entertainer of the Year winner and his band brought bluegrass and gospel music to the Jaycee Bootheel Rodeo stage in 1986.

Ricky Skaggs learned the play the mandolin when he was five, played on stage with bluegrass legend Bill Monroe when he was six and performed on the Grand Ole Opry when he was seven. He was a frequent guest on the syndicated TV show of Lester Flatt and Earl Scruggs, billed as "Little Ricky Skaggs." Along with Keith Whitley, he joined Ralph Stanley's bluegrass band in 1971 and got a taste of being a traveling musician and studio recording. His big breakthrough as a solo artist came in 1981 with the country album "Waiting for the Sun to Shine," which went gold and featured his first pair of #1 country hits – "Crying My Heart Out Over You" and "I Don't Care."

Skaggs had eight more #1 country singles before his appearance in Sikeston: " Heartbroke," "I Wouldn't Change You If I Could," "Highway 40 Blues," "Don't Cheat in Our Hometown," "Honey (Open That Door)," "Uncle Pen," "Country Boy" and "Cajun Moon." He was the CMA's Male Vocalist of the Year and Horizon Award winner in 1982, the first two of what would be a total of seven CMAs he would win.

His last country #1, "Let It Be You," was in '89, but that didn't mean the end of Skaggs' success as an artist. Having already won three Grammy Awards as a country performer, he captured seven more Grammys in bluegrass categories through 2009.

RAY STEVENS – 1986 & 1988

Ray Stevens, who performed at the Jaycee Rodeo in 1986 and 1988, may be best known for his novelty songs about exhibitionists, misbehaving Shriners and mischievous squirrels. But his resume as a serious musician and singer is about as impressive as they come.

Stevens was still a high school student in 1957 when he made his first record, a song called "Silver Bracelets" that he had co-written and which became a regional hit in the Atlanta area. While studying classical piano and music theory at Georgia State he recorded a novelty song called "Jeremiah Peabody's Poly Unsaturated Quick Dissolving Fast Acting Pleasant Tasting Green and Purple Pills." The song made the top 40 in 1961, but more importantly got him a job with Mercury Records that allowed him to get experience as a session musican, singing, playing piano and arranging. Another of his own novelty songs, "Ahab the Arab," made it to #5 in 1962. Stevens spent more of his time in the '60s producing than he did working on his own songs, but he hit the top 10 again in '69 with "Gitarzan," a song about a guitar-playing ape.

But it was a serious song that made Stevens a star in 1970. "Everything is Beautiful" was Stevens' first #1 pop record and won him the Grammy Award for Male Vocalist of the Year. His arrangement of "Misty" won another Grammy in 1975. Then a novelty song from 1974, "The Streak," brought Stevens back into the comedy spotlight. "The Streak" was a #1, and he enjoyed more comedy hits in the '70s and '80s with "Shriner's Convention," "The Mississippi Squirrel Revival" and "It's Me Again Margaret."

Exile with Kenny Rogers in 1986. Courtesy Steve Goetzman.

EXILE – 1986

A hard-working rock and roll band that enjoyed its biggest success after turning to country music in the '80s performed at the Jaycee Bootheel Rodeo in 1986.

Exile's first country album in 1984, "Exile," produced the #1 country singles "Woke Up in Love" and "I Don't Want to Be a Memory." Once established on the country scene, their next album, "Kentucky Hearts," yielded another three more #1 hits – "Give Me One More Chance," "Crazy For Your Love" and "She's a Miracle." The title track of their "Hang On to Your Heart" album in '85 hit #1, and two more songs from the album – "I Could Get Used to You' and "It'll Be Me" – also had made it to #1 by the time the group came to Sikeston. The group had another pair of #1 singles in '87 before starting to fade.

The route Exile took to country music success was not a traditional one. As a rock and roll group originally known as the Exiles, the band toured as the opening act for popular groups of the day such as the Young Rascals and B. J. Thomas. Experimenting with musical styles and record labels throughout the next two decades, they struck gold in 1978 with "Kiss You All Over," which was #1 on the pop charts for four weeks. But they didn't find consistent success until they embraced country music in the '80s.

RANDY TRAVIS – 1987

A major contributor to the traditionalist movement in country music in the '80s, Randy Travis was enjoying his first real taste of success when he came to Sikeston to appear at the Jaycee Bootheel Rodeo in 1987.

Travis' album "Storms of Life," released in 1986, was in the process of achieving triple-platinum sales. His "Always and Forever" album, released in the spring of '87, achieved even greater heights, selling over 5 million cop-

Randy Travis

ies. His first #1 single, "Diggin' Up Bones," came from "Storms of Life." "Always and Forever produced four #1 songs – "Forever and Ever, Amen," "I Won't Need You Anymore (Always and Forever)," "Too Gone Too Long" and "I Told You So."

Travis' emergence as a country superstar came after a long struggle that had him narrowly avoiding prison and then being rejected time after time by Nashville studios who thought he sounded "too country." But Warner Brothers Records heard a live album of the singer that had been recorded on an independent label, and the company was impressed enough to sign Travis to a contract in 1982. Their gamble on Travis paid off handsomely. He had 10 more #1 country singles over the next two decades, to go with eight platinum and four gold albums.

Travis has won 41 music industry awards, including Grammys, CMA, ACM and Music City News awards. He turned his attention toward spiritual music later in his career and has been honored with eight Dove Awards from the Gospel Music Association.

SAWYER BROWN – 1987 & 1992

Country-pop group Sawyer Brown had released four albums in two years before appearing for the first time at the Jaycee Bootheel Rodeo in 1987. Three of the four albums made the top 10 country album charts, and the '85 single "Step By Step" had gone to #1. The band had arrived as stars when they came to Sikeston.

Sawyer Brown's members had been the backup band for Don King before he stopped touring in 1981. Liking their chemistry, the five musicians decided to try to make a go of it as a group. Their big break came on Ed McMahon's TV talent show "Star Search," which they entered just because they figured they'd get a good promotional tape out of the deal. But they won the competition, along with the $100,000 price and record contract that went with it.

Sawyer Brown

The band enjoyed their biggest success in the '90s, when albums "The Dirt Road" and "Outskirts of Town" both went gold, as did a greatest hits album. Sawyer Brown was nominated for best vocal group almost every year in the decade by all three major country awards shows (CMA, ACM and Music City News) and won seven times. Sawyer Brown's career body of work has included 22 albums and 53 singles, 51 of which charted.

KENNY LOGGINS – 1987

Although he found his first fame as a member of a popular pop duo, Kenny Loggins had found a niche as a composer and performer of film songs when he appeared at the Jaycee Bootheel Rodeo in 1987.

Loggins had big hits with "I'm Alright" from "Caddyshack" in 1980, the title song "Footloose" in 1984 and "Danger Zone from "Top Gun" in '86. Before the big screen helped to popularize those songs, Loggins' first three Columbia Records albums went platinum. The second album, 1978"s "Nightwatch," contained a top-10 duet with Stevie Nicks – "Whenever I Call You Friend," while the third LP, "Keep the Fire," yielded another hit single – "This Is It."

But it was Loggins' partnership with Jim Messina that jumpstarted his career in the '70s. Messina was a producer with Columbia after recording with Buffalo Springfield and Poco. Loggins was one of Columbia's new artists, and Messina produced his first album. As the album evolved, Messina's role brought him out of the control room and into the studio as an arranger and singer, in addition to writing some of the songs. The album was titled "Kenny Loggins with Jim Messina Sittin' In." The collaboration proved popular with the fans, and the duo cranked out eight more albums as Loggins and Messina through 1977. The 1972 Loggins and Messina single "Your Mama Don't Dance" was a top-10 hit.

RICKY VAN SHELTON – 1988

When he stepped onto the Jaycee Bootheel Rodeo stage in August of 1988, Ricky Van Shelton was an up-and-coming country star whose first album had gone platinum and was days away from releasing a single which would be his fourth straight #1 hit.

Van Shelton's 1987 debut album "Wild-Eyed Dream" hit #1 on the country album charts and sold over two million copies in North America. "Wild-Eyed Dream" featured the #1 singles "Somebody Lied," "Life Turned Her That Way" and "Don't We All Have the Right." His follow-up LP "Loving Proof" was released in September following his Sikeston appearance and also was RIAA certified platinum. The first single off "Loving Proof," "I'll Leave This World Loving You," was about to be released in August of '88. That song, along with "From a Jack to a King" and "Living Proof," all went to #1, making five consecutive chart toppers for Van Shelton and helping him earned the Country Music Association's Male Vocalist of the Year award in 1989.

Van Shelton continued on a roll into the '90s, with two more platinum albums to go with a pair of golds. "RVS III" was a #1 country album, and "Backroads" made it to #3. He charted three more country #1 singles – "I've Cried My Last Tear for You" ('90), "I Am a Simple Man" ('91) and "Keep it Between the Lines" ('91) – before sales began to fall off in the middle of the decade.

RESTLESS HEART – 1988 & 1991

Country-pop quintet Restless Heart's third studio album had been released when they appeared at the 1988 Jaycee Bootheel Rodeo. The group didn't have a long career, but they made the most of their period of popularity in the '80s.

The group's self-titled first album in 1985 produced three top-10 country singles, the most popular being 1986's "(Back to the) Heartbreak Kid." Restless Heart went on to have six #1 singles over the next two years – "The Rock That Won't Roll" ('86), "I'll Still Be Loving You and "Why Does It Have to Be Wrong or Right" from '87, and "Wheels," "The Bluest Eyes in Texas" and "A Tender Lie " from '88. Restless Heart had established themselves as one of country's hottest groups when they came to Sikeston.

The group went on to record seven more top-10 singles through 1998, to go with four gold albums.

WILLIE NELSON – 1989 & 1990

Only a handful of musicians are so well-known that if you mention only their first name, people know who you mean. Mention "Willie" to country fans, and only one man comes to mind. Music legend Willie Nelson took to the Jaycee Bootheel Rodeo stage in back-to-back years and thrilled the Jaycee Bootheel Rodeo crowd.

Willie was somewhat of a jack-of-all-trades while getting his feet wet in the music business during the late '50s and early '60s. He worked as a disc jockey by day and a honky tonk singer by night in his home state of Texas before signing with a music publisher and joining country star Ray Price's band in 1960. Nelson didn't achieve much success as a performer during this time, even though he did get a record deal as a solo artist. But he wrote songs for others that have become standards, including Patsy Cline's "Crazy" and Faron Young's "Hello Walls'. But only one of his own singles reached the country top 10, and Willie had given up on recording by the end of the '60s.

Rejuvenated by the outlaw country movement and a recording contract with Columbia that gave him creative control over his music, Willie's career was resurrected in the '70s. While Willie had seen other artists have success with his songs in the '60s, in an ironic twist several of his biggest hits from the '70s were covers of classics, such as Fred Rose's "Blue Eyes Crying in the Rain" ('75), Lefty Frizzell's "If You've Got the Money, I've Got the Time" ('76) and Hoagy Carmichael's "Georgia on My Mind" ('78).

More Willie Nelson smash hits came in the '80s. "My Heroes Have Always Been Cowboys," "Angel Flying Too Close to the Ground," "Always On My Mind" and "City of New Orleans," "Forgiving You Was Easy," "Living in the Promiseland" and "Nothing I Can Do About it Now" all reached #1. And Nelson's duets with the biggest pop stars of the day helped bring him crossover success and making him one of the biggest stars of any genre. He teamed with Latin star Julio Iglesias on "To All the Girls I've Loved Before" and with jazz and R&B legend Ray Charles on "Seven Spanish Angels," both of which went to #1 on the country charts and the pop top 10.

Willie's broad international appeal is born out by the sales of his 1978 album "Stardust," which sold over 11 million copies in Australia and New Zealand.

THE CHARLIE DANIELS BAND – 1988, 1989, 1991, 1998 & 2001

The Charlie Daniels Band, pioneers in the southern rock movement, hold the record for most Jaycee Bootheel Rodeo appearances. Their 1988 appearance was the first of five times they graced the Sikeston stage.

Though Charlie Daniels is primarily known as a country fiddler, the performer played guitar while bouncing around in bands that played rock, bluegrass, jazz and R&B until his early '30s, when he landed a job as a Nashville session musician. Daniels played on Bob Dylan's "Nashville Skyline" album, and with legends such as Marty Robbins and Ringo Starr. His first album as a solo performer, "Charlie Daniels," is one of the earliest records to be identified as southern rock. That record also coincided with the formation of the Charlie Daniels Band.

The group's first three albums went nowhere on the charts, but a single from the third album, "Uneasy Rider," made it to #9 on the pop charts in 1973. The song told about a long-haired boy's encounter with rednecks in the south on a car trip to Los Angeles and established Daniels as a storyteller. Between 1974 and 1982 the band had six albums to go either gold or platinum, including '79's "Million Mile Reflections." That album went triple platinum and featured the song that became his biggest hit ever – "The Devil Went Down to Georgia." That song was #1 on the country charts and #3 on the pop charts.

The album "Simple Man," which would eventually go platinum, was the Charlie Daniels Band's current album during the first visit to Sikeston in 1989. It was the band's last big studio album, but they had two compilation albums that each sold in excess of a million copies. The Charlie Daniels Band was also well-known for their popular "Tennessee Jam" concerts, which were an annual tradition during the '70s and '80s.

EARL THOMAS CONLEY – 1989

Earl Thomas Conley played the Jaycee Bootheel Rodeo in 1989, a year that capped a phenomenal decade of success. His 18 #1 country singles were the most chart toppers by any artist in any musical genre during the '80s.

Conley started gaining success as a songwriter in the '70s, writing hits for Conway Twitty and Mel Street. He had recorded a few singles on an independent label that went nowhere before gaining some traction in 1980 with a top-10 country single, "Silent Treatment." The next year the title song of the "Fire and Smoke" album was Conley's first #1 and the first in a long string of chart toppers during the decade. Beginning with "Somewhere Between Right and Wrong" in '82, 17 of the next 19 Earl Thomas Conley singles were country #1s. Including in that string of hits were classics like "Holding Her and Loving You," "Nobody Falls Like a Fool" and "Right From the Start."

Making Earl Thomas Conley's run of success in the '80s particularly noteworthy was the fact that he was bucking the traditionalist movement in country music. His songs often were fusions of pop, R&B and adult contemporary, and he seemed more intent of doing the music he wanted to do than what he thought would sell. It turns out he got the best of both worlds. But personal problems combined with burnout led him to take a hiatus from recording in the '90s at the height of his popularity.

SHENANDOAH – 1990

In the summer of 1990, the country band Shenandoah had a new album on the charts and a hit single that stayed at #1 for four weeks. Jaycee Bootheel Rodeo fans had a chance to see of one country music's hottest groups.

The five-piece band's self-titled debut album in 1987 didn't chart, but 1989's "The Road Not Taken" LP went gold and produced three #1 country singles – "The Church on Cumberland Road," "Sunday in the South" and "Two Dozen Roses." Shenandoah's 1990 album "The Extra Mile" also went gold and produced the single "Next to You, Next to Me" that was still a big hit when the group appeared in Sikeston.

Shenandoah continued to record throughout the '90s, despite lineup changes and legal battles related to their name. They had one more #1 country hit – 1994's "If Bubba Can Dance (I Can Too)."

GARTH BROOKS – 1990

Jaycee Bootheel Rodeo fans fortunate enough to see a 28-year-old Garth Brooks in 1990 knew they were seeing one of country's hottest young stars. Who knew that they were also seeing a legend in the making?

Brooks' 1989 debut album "Garth Brooks" contained a pair of poignant ballads – "If Tomorrow Never Comes" and "The Dance." Both songs became #1 country hits. The album did well initially, making it to #2 and the country charts and #13 on the pop charts, and eventually achieved RIAA diamond status, reflecting over 10 million copies sold. Brooks was a hot newcomer when he took the Sikeston stage in August of 1990, roughly three weeks before the release of the landmark album "No Fences."

"No Fences" featured four #1 country singles – "Friends in Low Places," "Unanswered Prayers," "Two of a Kind, Workin' On a Full House" and "The Thunder Rolls." The album reached #1 on the charts, #3 on the pop charts and has sold over 24 million copies in North America alone. The album established Garth Brooks as a superstar. Over the next ten years Brooks recorded nine more studio albums, including a pair of Christmas LPs and another album under the pseudonym Chris Gaines. All were multi-platinum, and seven were #1 on the country album charts. The run of success would include a dozen more #1 singles, including the classics "Shameless," "American Honky-Tonk Bar Association" and "Longneck Bottle."

After several years of retirement beginning in 2000 (other than a few charity performances) Brooks began performing in Las Vegas on weekends while devoting time to his family during the week. As of March 2012, he has sold over 128 million albums, second only to Elvis Presley among solo performers and third among all artists (the Beatles are #1). He was inducted into the Country Music Hall of Fame in 2012.

TRAVIS TRITT – 1991

When Travis Tritt signed his first recording contract with Warner Brothers, the deal was to record six songs, three of which would be released as singles. Only if one of the three became a hit would he record an album. As it turned out, one single was all he needed to invoke the album clause.

Released in September of 1989 – almost two years before his appearance at the Jaycee Bootheel Rodeo – Tritt's single "Country Club" was a top-10 country hit and was the title song for his 1990 debut album, which was certified platinum by the time of his rodeo appearance. The success of "Country Club" helped Tritt win Billboard's Top New Male Artist of 1990. Tritt's follow-up album "It's All About to Change" was released 10 weeks before his Sikeston appearance and would yield more country hits, including "Here's a Quarter (Call Someone Who Cares)" and a #1, "Anymore." A third single from the album, "The Whiskey Ain't Workin'." was a duet that won the Grammy for Best Country Collaboration for Tritt and composer Marty Stuart.

Five of the next six albums released by Travis Tritt went platinum and included #1 country singles "Can I Trust You With My Heart," "Foolish Pride" and "Best of Intentions." He has also demonstrated a talent for acting and has appeared in a number of television shows such as "The Jeff Foxworthy Show" and "Dr. Quinn, Medicine Woman."

DOUG STONE – 1991

Jaycee Bootheel Rodeo fans got to hear a preview of Doug Stone's upcoming album when he performed in 1991. "I Thought It Was You," the performer's second album, was released three days after his appearance in Sikeston.

Stone's first LP, "Doug Stone," ultimately sold over a million copies. The debut single "I'd Be Better Off (in a Pine Box)" was a Grammy nominee for Best Country Song, and his first #1 hit, "In a Different Light." The "I Thought It Was You" album also went platinum and included "A Jukebox With a Country Song," Stone's second #1 country single.

The next two albums from the performer were certified gold and featured #1 singles "Too Busy Being in Love" and "Why Didn't I Think of That."

MARK CHESNUTT – 1992 & 1993

Mark Chesnutt

Mark Chesnutt appeared at the Jaycee Bootheel Rodeo in back-to-back years during what turned out to be the height of his success.

Chesnutt's 1990 debut album, "Too Cold at Home," spawned five #1 country singles, including the title track, which went to #3. Then came "Brother Jukebox," which became the first of eight #1s he would have in the '90s. Another #1, "I'll Think of Something," was a current hit during Chesnutt's first rodeo appearance in 1992. The album "Long Necks and Short Stories" became his second platinum album in as many releases.

During his return engagement in Sikeston in 1993, Chesnutt's third album "Almost Goodbye" was climbing the charts. Three singles from the album made it to the #1 position – "It Sure is Monday," "Almost Goodbye" and "I Just Wanted You to Know." It was Chesnutt's

Festus Haggen holding up some of the locals. From the Loy Baugher collection.

1992 Junior Miss Rodeo Frannie Trum gets a tour of Mark Chesnutt's tour bus.

third straight platinum album and marked the pinnacle of his chart success. Although his album sales dropped off, he had three more #1 singles in the '90s.

MARK COLLIE – 1992

Mark Collie's performance at the Jaycee Bootheel Rodeo in 1992 came just weeks before the release of what would be his highest-charting single, "Even the Man in the Moon is Crying," which made it to #5. The album the single came off of, "Mark Collie," wasn't released until '93, and proved to be his only top-40 country album.

While Collie never found super stardom as a singer, he has shown his versatility in show business through his acting career. He has appeared in two feature films – "The Punisher" and "Fire Down Below" – as well as a number of guest-star appearances in television series such as "Jag," "Walker, Texas Ranger" and "The Strip."

PAM TILLIS – 1993

When Tracy Lawrence was a late cancellation for the '93 rodeo, the Jaycees were left scrambling for a replacement. When they were able to book Pam Tillis, they got one of the hottest female singers in the country music industry.

Daughter of legendary country singer and songwriter Mel Tillis, Pam Tillis was a successful composer in her own right during the '80s, but the pop album she recorded went nowhere before she found her niche as a singer by switching to country.

Her debut country album, "Put Yourself in My Place," made it to #10 in 1991, and produced a pair of hit country singles – "Don't Tell Me What to Do" (#5) and "Maybe It Was Memphis" (#3). A second album, "Homeward Looking Angel," went gold the next year and was Tillis' current release when she appeared at the 1993 Jaycee Bootheel Rodeo. A pair of top five country singles came from that album – "Shake the Sugar Tree" and "Let That Pony Run."

Tillis' 1994 album, "Sweetheart's Dance" was her second platinum album and contained her only #1 country single, "Mi Vida Loca (My Crazy Life)." A greatest hits album in 1997 also was platinum. As her record sales slowed down late in the '90s she had several acting roles on TV shows such as "Diagnosis: Murder" and "LA Law."

LORRIE MORGAN – 1993 & 1999

Despite the advantages of having a father who was a country star, Lorrie Morgan was a late bloomer as a performer. It was 10 years between the release of her first single and her first top-10 record in 1989.

But George Morgan's daughter made up for lost time. She had 11 top-10 country singles by the time she appeared for the first time at the Jaycee Bootheel Rodeo in 1993, including a pair of #1 smashes – "Five Minutes" in 1990 and "What Part of No" in 1992. Another #1 single, "I Didn't Know My Own Strength," followed in 1995. Morgan's first three albums achieved platinum certification, and three more went gold.

Morgan's return visit to perform at the 1999 rodeo was as part of the bill with Sammy Kershaw, her duet partner and future husband. She had been married a total of six times as of 2010, including Keith Whitley until his 1989 death.

SAMMY KERSHAW – 1993, 1995 & 1999

Sammy Kershaw was riding high for his first of three Jaycee Bootheel Rodeo appearances in August of 1993. "She Don't Know She's Beautiful," the first single from his second album, "Haunted Heart," had reached #1 in April. The album would go platinum, his second LP to sell at least a million copies.

When Kershaw returned to Sikeston in '95, he was still enjoying the success of his third album, 1994's "Feelin' Good Train." That album featured a pair of #2 hits – "National Working Woman's Holiday" and "Third Rate Romance." When he appeared at the rodeo for the third time in 1999, he did so on the bill with Lorrie Morgan, with whom he had recorded a top 20 single that year – "Maybe Not Tonight." Kershaw and Morgan would later be married for six years and recorded an album of duets together, 2001's "I Finally Found Someone."

All but one of Kershaw's six studio albums during '90s were certified either gold or platinum by the RIAA.

JOE DIFFIE – 1994 & 1996

Joe Diffie's fourth album, "Third Rock From the Sun," had only been on the charts for two weeks when he appeared for the first time at the Jaycee Bootheel Rodeo in 1996. The album turned out to be his highest-charting LP ever (#6) and became his second-straight platinum-certified record. Two singles from the album – the title track and "Pickup Man" – went to the top of the country charts.

Diffie burst onto the country music scene in a big way in 1990 as his first single release, "Home," was a #1 hit. The next year saw him top the charts again with "If the Devil Danced (In Empty Pockets)." Four straight Joe Diffie albums would be certified either gold or platinum during the '90s, including "Life's So Funny," which was his current release when he returned to Sikeston in 1996. "Life's So Funny" featured the #1 single "Bigger Than the Beatles." That was his final #1 hit, but he did have two more top-10 singles later in the decade.

Joe Diffie also had some success with duets, the first being "I Don't Need Your Rockin' Chair," for which he and George Jones won the Academy of Country Music's Vocal Event of the Year in 1993. In 1998 he and Marty Stuart won a Grammy for Best Country Collaboration with the record "Same Old Train."

TRACY LAWRENCE – 1994 & 2010

When musicians swap stories backstage about the adversities they had to overcome before they found success, Tracy Lawrence can top them all.

Lawrence's career was barely started when it almost ended. While recording his debut album "Sticks and Stones" in 1991 he was walking a female acquaintance to her hotel room when armed muggers attacked the pair. Lawrence resisted and was shot four times. He recovered from his wounds and completed the album, which was released in December of '91 and sold over a million copies. The title track became Lawrence's first #1 country single.

The next Tracy Lawrence album, "Alibis," resulted in a grand slam of sorts. All four singles from the 1993 album – "Alibis," "Can't Break It to My Heart," "My Second Home" and "If the

Tracy Lawrence

Good Die Young" – made it to #1, helping the album go double platinum. Lawrence also had a top-10 single from the Mel Gibson film "Maverick" that year, "Renegades, Rebels and Rogues." He was scheduled to perform at the Jaycee Bootheel Rodeo that year, but illness forced him to cancel. But the Jaycees were able to book him for the '94 rodeo, bringing him in at the peak of his career. Lawrence's third straight album to go platinum, "I See It Now," was released shortly after his first Sikeston appearance.

Sixteen years later, Lawrence returned to Sikeston to play the rodeo in 2010, marking the longest interval for a rodeo entertainer between their first appearance and their last. All seven studio albums he released in the years between rodeo appearances made it into the top 20 country charts, and three more singles were country chart toppers – "Texas Tornado" ('95), "Time Marches On" ('96) and "Find Out Who Your Friends Are" (2006).

MARTINA McBRIDE – 1994

Martina McBride's journey to music stardom was a result of talent, good looks, hard work and a little help from superstar Garth Brooks.

McBride's husband was Brooks' concert production manager, and Martina often went along on the road selling the souvenirs. Brooks recognized her work ethic, as well as her ability as a singer, and offered her a position as his opening act. But she would need a recording contract. RCA Nashville Records listened to a demo tape made by Martina's husband and signed her to a record deal in 1991.

Her first album didn't make much of a splash on the charts, although one single cracked he top 40. But McBride's second LP, 1993's "The Way That I Am," rode the success of three particular songs to platinum sales. "My Baby Loves Me" and "Life #9" went to #2 and #6, respectively. The third song, "Independence Day," didn't make the top 10 but became an anthem of battered women and was honored with Country Music Association and Grammy awards. Martina McBride was a rising country star when she appeared at the Jaycee Bootheel Rodeo in 1994.

Beginning with 1995's "Wild Angels," the next five Martina McBride albums achieved platinum certification. As her sound began to move away from traditional country and more toward pop, her records began to achieve more crossover success in the late '90s. Country chart-toppers "Wrong Again" ('98), "I Love You" ('99) and "Blessed" (2001) all cracked the Billboard top 40. "This One's For the Girls" in 2003 topped out at #3 on the country charts but was #1 on the Adult Contemporary list.

Through 2011, Martina McBride has sold over 14 million albums in the U.S. She has won 17 major music industry awards.

MARTY STUART – 1994

Marty Stuart had five top-10 country singles and three gold albums under his belt when he appeared at 1994's Jaycee Bootheel Rodeo. His album "Love and Luck" was on the charts, but he had already reached his peak of popularity.

Stuart cut his teeth as a performer and recording artist in bluegrass, as a mandolin and guitar player in Lester Flatt's Nashville Grass. He played in Johnny Cash's touring band in the early '80s, but left to pursue a solo career, securing a contract with Columbia. The 1985 album "Marty Stuart" brought him his first taste of chart success, giving him a top 20 single, "Arlene," and a top 40 album. The next LP, 1989's "Hillbilly Rock," went gold and the title track made it to #8 on the country charts. Stuart's 1991 LP "Tempted" and 1992's "This One's Gonna Hurt You" were RIAA certified gold.

The single "This One's Gonna Hurt You (For a Long, Long Time)," a duet with Travis Tritt, reached #7 on the country charts, marking his last top-10 record.

CONFEDERATE RAILROAD – 1995

The country rock band Confederate Railroad came to Sikeston in 1995 to perform at the Jaycee Bootheel Rodeo with two RIAA certified platinum albums under their belt. Their third release, "When and Where," had been released two months previous. In retrospect the title is somewhat ironic, since the group may be wondering when and where they'll have another hit. But for two years they were one of country's hottest bands.

After being the backup band for David Allan Coe and Johnny Paycheck, Confederate Railroad struck out on their own and got a record contract with Atlantic in 1992. Their debut album, "Confederate Railroad" produced a half-dozen top-10 country hits, including what proved to be their highest-charting single ever, "Queen of Memphis," which made it to #2. The follow-up album, 1992's "Notorious," also went platinum, and the single "Daddy Never Was the Cadillac Kind" made the top 10. But starting with the "When and Where" album, the hits dried up. The group released four more LPs through 2007, but none cracked the top 20 album charts.

TRACY BYRD – 1995 & 1999

When Tracy Byrd took the Jaycee Bootheel Rodeo stage for the first time in August of 1995, his third album, "Love Lessons," had just been released. Byrd's first two albums had gone platinum and had yielded five top-10 country singles, so he had plenty of popular material to draw on for his performance, as well as songs from the new album.

Byrd's career developed, in part, due to a demo he made at a Texas shopping mall recording studio. His rendition of Hank Williams' "Your Cheatin' Heart" was good enough that the studio owner entered Tracy into a local talent contest. He caught the attention of MCA Records and signed with them in 1992.

MCA released Byrd's first album, "Tracy Byrd" in 1993. The third release from the LP, "Holdin' Heaven," went to #1 and helped the album achieve RIAA gold certification. His second album, "No Ordinary Man," went platinum and featured four top five country hits – "Lifestyles of the Not So Rich and Famous," "Watermelon Crawl," "The First Step" and the romantic ballad "The Keeper of the Stars."

As it turned out, Byrd's third album couldn't build on the success of "No Ordinary Man," although the title track "Love Lessons" went to #9. It did, however, achieve gold certification. Byrd had two more albums and five more top-10 singles before his 1999 return engagement at the rodeo.

KEN MELLONS – 1995

Ken Mellons was somewhat unusual among performers who have appeared at the Jaycee Bootheel Rodeo in that he was a "one-hit wonder."

On the strength of his performance in Opryland USA's Country Music USA show, Mellons signed a record deal with Epic in 1993. One song from his debut album was a hit – "Jukebox Junkie." That song made it to #8 on the country charts. Mellons never had another song make it into the top 40, and none of his succeeding four albums even showed up on the charts.

CLAY WALKER – 1996, 2000 & 2007

With five #1 country singles and three hit albums under his belt, Clay Walker was a bona fide country star when he first sang at the Jaycee Bootheel Rodeo in 1996.

Discovered singing at a Texas bar by a record producer in 1992, Walker signed with Giant Records. "What's It to You" and "Live Until I Die," his first two singles from the debut album , both went to #1, as did a fourth single, "Dreaming With My Eyes Wide Open." The album, "Clay Walker," was certified platinum and helped him win Academy of Country Music honors for Top New Male Vocalist in 1994.

Walker's follow-up album "If I Could Make a Living" produced two more #1 singles – the title track and "This Woman and This Man." The album made it to #2 and, like the first, went platinum. A third album, "Hypnotize the Moon," made it three straight platinum-certified LPs in 1995.

Three more successful studio albums and seven top-10 country singles were released by Walker before his second Sikeston performance in 2000. The title cut from the 1997 album "Rumor Has It" was a #1 hit. Although that was his last #1 single, Walker's album sales remained strong, with four more charting albums after 2000. Walker's 2010 release, "She Won't Be Lonely Long" made it to #5 on the country album charts in time for his rodeo appearance that year.

CHRIS LeDOUX – 1996 & 2003

While the early days of the Jaycee Bootheel Rodeo featured Western movie stars who frequently sang in their films, Chris LeDoux brought a whole new meaning to the term "singing cowboy."

LeDoux was a professional rodeo cowboy for 10 years during the '70s. As he traveled the rodeo circuit – which included the Sikeston rodeo – he wrote songs about the lives of cowboys and about the sport. He and his father established an independent record label just for the purpose of recording Chris' songs, and he would sell the records out of the back of his truck at rodeos. When he won the world bareback riding championship in 1976, the sales of his self-recorded albums took off. When he retired from rodeo competition in 1980 he continued to make records and began to do concerts. By the end of the '80s LeDoux had made 22 albums. He might be the only recording artist who can honestly say that he literally "sold" over 250,000 albums. He also holds the distinction of being the only person confirmed to have appeared at the Jaycee Bootheel Rodeo as both a competitor and as a performer (Moe Bandy was a bull rider before making it as a singer, but there is no record verifying that he competed in Sikeston).

Chris resisted offers to sign with major record labels until his mention in a Garth Brooks song changed his career. Brooks' debut single "Much Too Young to Feel This Damn Old" contained a line about "worn-out tapes of Chris LeDoux" and another proclaiming "God bless Chris LeDoux!" The exposure made his name one recognized not just by rodeo fans but by music fans in general. He signed with Liberty Records in 1991 and recorded 10 albums on that label and Capitol in the next 13 years. While his highest-charting single was a duet with Brooks, "Whatcha Gonna Do With a Cowboy," (#7) his albums all made it into the country top 40.

LeDoux underwent a liver transplant in the fall of 2000 after being diagnosed with liver disease earlier that year. He recovered enough to record and tour again, including a return appearance in Sikeston in 2003. But 14 months later he was diagnosed with liver cancer, which claimed his life in 2005.

GEORGE JONES – 1997

Many fans call him "the Possum." Some have called him "No-Show Jones." But when it comes to George Jones, most are in agreement that one word in particular described him. That word is "legend."

The man legendary for not only his music but for his hard-drinking lifestyle entertained at the Jaycee Bootheel Rodeo in 1997. By then, George Jones had mostly shed his "no-show" reputation, which he earned as a result of many concerts missed due to his alcohol and substance abuse problems. He had become a reliable concert attraction again, despite the fact that he occasionally fell off the wagon.

After establishing a foothold on the country scene in the '50s with hits like "Why Baby Why" and "White Lightning," Jones became a star in the '60s. He topped the charts with classics such as "She Thinks I Still Care" and "Walk Through This World with Me" while cranking out 27 albums. Jones cut back on the quantity of his recording in favor of quality in the '70s and '80s, and five #1 singles were the result. "He Stopped Loving Her Today" has been ranked in multiple surveys as the greatest country song of all time, and Jones himself said the 1980 song revived his career after a six-year drought between #1s in the late '70s.

While George Jones had great success as a solo performer, he has been a part of several duet partnerships, most notably with Tammy Wynette. The pair was married six years and produced nine duet albums, including #1 singles "We're Gonna Hold On," "Golden Ring" and "Near You." Jones also partnered with Melba Montgomery and with pop star Gene Pitney on multiple albums.

DIAMOND RIO – 1997

Country music's hottest vocal group of the '90s entertained fans at the Jaycee Bootheel Rodeo two days before their greatest hits album was released. The album sold over 5 million copies, which was not surprising due to the stockpile of hits Diamond Rio had produced in a few short years.

The five-piece band had signed a record contract in 1988 but didn't release its first album until '91 due to health problems and accidents involving three of the members. The debut single, "Meet In the Middle," became the first debut single by a country group ever to make it to #1, and four more singles from the album made the country top 10. Titled "Diamond Rio," the album was RIAA certified platinum.

Sales for the group's second album fell short of their debut, but "Close to the Edge" still sold over a half million copies and accounted for several top 20 singles. Their third LP, 1994's "Love a Little Stronger," went platinum, and the title single was a #2 hit. Diamond Rio's fourth album, titled simply "IV," produced four more top-10 hits and became the band's fourth LP to be certified either gold or platinum.

The 1997 album "Diamond Rio's Greatest Hits" included two new songs to go along with the compilation of previous favorites. One of those new cuts, "How Your Love Makes Me Feel," became the group's second #1 single and the biggest hit of any country group that year. The song was released three months before Diamond Rio's Sikeston performance.

Diamond Rio won six country music industry awards for leading vocal group during the '90s. They continued their chart success after the turn of the century with three more #1 country singles during the 2000s – "One More Day," "A Beautiful Mess" and "I Believe."

TERRI CLARK – 1997 & 2006

Up-and-coming country songstress Terri Clark entertained Jaycee Bootheel Rodeo fans for the first time in 1997. When she returned nine years later her career was on the downswing, but her portfolio of hit records still made her a popular concert draw.

Clark's dress and vocal stylings broke the mold for female country singers. She passed on the traditional feminine dress of contemporaries like Reba McIntyre, Shania Twain and Martina McBride for stage attire that typically included blue jeans, boots, a tight-fitting top and, of course, a cowboy hat. A native of Canada, Terri Clark didn't sound like it. She exhibited a powerful low and mid register in her vocals, and she sang with a "twang." On her debut single, she sang "I've got better thangs to do."

"Better Things to Do" was off her 1995 self-titled debut album, which eventually went platinum both in the US and her native Canada. Clark's second album in 1996, "Just the Same," included "Poor Pitiful Me" and "Emotional Girl." Both singles went to #1 in Canada and were in the top 10 in the US. Like her debut album, "Just the Same" went platinum in both the US and Canada.

Terri Clark produced four more top-10 albums before her return to Sikeston in 2006. The 1998 LP "How I Feel" contained another #1 single, "You're Easy on the Eyes" and a #2, "Every Time I Cry." The 2004 single "Girls Lie Too," a new track featured on a greatest hits package, was her most recent #1 and most recent top 20 single as of 2012.

WADE HAYES – 1997

Most of Wade Hayes success in country music was already behind him when he appeared at the 1997 Jaycee Bootheel Rodeo.

Hayes signed with Columbia Records in 1994 and recorded his first album that same year. The title track, "Old Enough to Know Better," was also his first single and made it to #1 on the country charts in 1995. Three more singles from the album made it into the top 10 – "I'm Still Dancin' With You," "Don't Stop" and "What I Meant to Say." The title track of his second LP in 1996, "On a Good Night," was a #2 hit, but was the only song from the disc to get into the top 40. Both of Hayes' first two albums were RIAA certified gold.

After Hayes' Sikeston appearance he released two more albums. "When the Wrong One Loves You Right" actually charted higher than either of the first two (#9) but sales dropped. The single "The Day That She Left Tulsa (in a Chevy)" made it to #5, marking Hayes final top 10 single. Neither that album, nor his final one, 2000's "Highways and Heartaches," was a commercial success.

CLINT BLACK – 1998

With seven platinum albums and a dozen #1 country singles to his credit, Clint Black had plenty of material to draw own when he performed at the Jaycee Bootheel Rodeo in 1998.

Black burst on the country music scene from out of nowhere in 1989-90, with the first four singles from his debut album "Killin' Time" going to #1. He had struggled for six years supporting himself with odd jobs during the day and singing in clubs at night. When he finally did get his break, he made the most of it. "Killin' Time" was a triple-platinum album while going to #1 on the country album charts and into the top 40 pop album charts. The singles "A Better Man," "Killin' Time," "Nobody's Home" and "Walkin' Away" all were #1 hits. Black won six Country Music Association awards that year.

"Put Yourself in My Shoes," Clint Black's second album, featured two more #1 singles – "Loving Blind" and "Where Are You Now." More #1 country singles followed as the decade continued, with hits such as "When My Ship Comes In" ('93), "A Good Run of Bad Luck" ('94), "Summer's Comin'" ('95) and "Like the Rain" ('96). When he appeared in Sikeston in 1998, Black's current album was "Nothin' But the Taillights," which had two more #1 singles – the title track and "The Shoes You're Wearing." "Nothin' But the Taillights" was Clint Black's seventh straight album to be RIAA certified platinum, including his Greatest Hits album in 1996.

"Nothin' But the Taillights" was Black's last platinum album, but he did have one more #1 single to come, 1999's "When I Said I Do," a duet with wife Lisa Hartman Black.

In addition to his music, Clint Black has also been featured as an actor in numerous roles. He has been in feature films such as "Maverick" and "Anger Management," along with a starring role in the made-for-TV movies "Still Holding On: The Legend of Cadillac Jack" and "Going Home."

RICOCHET – 1998

The country band Ricochet burst on the music scene with a gold debut album and a #1 single in 1995-96, but the group was already out of new hits when they played the Jaycee Bootheel Rodeo in 1998.

The six-piece band's debut album, "Ricochet," featured the #1 country single "Daddy's Money," as well as two other top-10 singles. The group's 1997 follow-up release, "In the Blink of an Eye," didn't have a top-10 single, and neither did the third, "What You Leave Behind," which was a commercial failure.

Like many performers who find success, Ricochet's popularity was short-lived, gone "in the blink of an eye."

DAVID LEE MURPHY – 1998

The country music career of David Lee Murphy, who appeared at the 1998 Jaycee Bootheel Rodeo, literally started "Out With a Bang," which was the title of his debut album. Unfortunately for the Herrin, Ill. native, Murphy couldn't repeat the success of his first release.

"Out With a Bang," which was released in 1994, featured the #1 country single "Dust on the Bottle," as well as a #6 hit, "Party Crowd." The album made it into the country top 10 and was certified platinum by the RIAA for selling over a million copies. Murphy's second LP, "Getting Out the Good Stuff" in 1996, had two more hit singles – "Every Time I Get Around You" (#2) and "The Road You Leave Behind" (#5). But the album didn't match the chart or sales success of "Out With a Bang."

A third David Lee Murphy album, "We Can't All Be Angels," was released in 1997 and was a commercial failure. He was let go by his label, MCA Records, but he was still a popular touring performer when he played the rodeo.

After focusing on songwriting for a few years, Murphy enjoyed a short-lived comeback in 2004 with a new album on a new label. "Tryin' to Get There" had a #5 single, "Loco," but the album wasn't successful enough to record another one. But David Lee Murphy has continued to be a successful composer, writing hits for stars like Kenny Chesney, Gary Allan, Blake Shelton and others.

TOBY KEITH – 1999

Still a country superstar in 2013 when this book was published, Toby Keith was already one of the industry's hottest acts in 1999 when he performed at the Jaycee Bootheel Rodeo.

An oil field worker and semi-pro football player before moving to Nashville, Keith burst onto the music scene in 1993 with a platinum debut album, "Toby Keith," and a #1 single, "Should've Been a Cowboy." The single not only topped the charts in '93, but was the most played song of the decade according to Broadcast Music Inc. Three more hit albums and a dozen top-10 singles followed before Keith's Sikeston appearance. The LPs "Boomtown" and "Blue Moon" were RIAA certified platinum, while 1997's "Dream Walkin'" went gold.

Released about 10 weeks after his rodeo performance, Keith's 1999 album title asked the question "How Do You Like Me Now?!" For country fans, the answer was – plenty. The platinum-certified LP, which also made it into the pop top 40 album charts, had a pair of #1 singles – the title track and "You Shouldn't Kiss Me Like This." The latter was the first of a string of 10-out-of-11 single releases that made it to #1. The run of chart-toppers included "I Wanna Talk About Me," "Who's Your Daddy?" and a big duet with Willie Nelson, "Beer For My Horses." During the decade following the turn of the century Keith had five platinum or multi-platinum albums. The albums "Unleashed" ('92) and "Shock'n Y'all" ('93) each sold over 4 million copies in the US and were #1 on both the country and pop charts.

As of the publication of this book, Toby Keith continues to be a force on the country and pop charts. The 2011 album "Clancy's Tavern," with hit singles "Made in America" and "Red Solo Cup," was certified gold. "Made in America" became the 22nd Toby Keith single to hit #1 on the country charts.

KENNY CHESNEY – 1999

When Kenny Chesney stepped onto the stage at the 1999 Jaycee Bootheel Rodeo, he had an album on the charts that was on the way to selling two million copies. But unlike some country performers who found chart success with their debut albums, Chesney's road to stardom was a long one.

Chesney's first two albums barely made a ripple on the charts, although the second one, 1995's "All I Need to Know," had a pair of top-10 singles. It was the third LP that was the charm. "Me and You," released in '96, featured a pair of #2 country hits – the title track and "When I Close My Eyes." The album was certified platinum, and fans jumping on the Chesney bandwagon helped "All I Need to Know" achieve gold status. Chesney's next two albums went platinum – 1997's "I Will Stand" and '99's "Everywhere We Go." Those releases netted Kenny his first three #1 singles – "She's Got It All," "How Forever Feels" and "You Had Me From Hello," his current single at the time of his Sikeston appearance.

Chesney has been one of country's most consistent hit-makers since then. From 2000 to 2010 he had seven straight #1 country albums, with four going multi-platinum. He won eight Entertainer of the Year awards during the decade, four each from the Country Music Association and the Academy of Country Music. He scored 18 #1 country singles during the decade, with mega-hits such as "The Good Stuff," "Living in Fast Forward," "Beer in Mexico" and "Summertime," the latter selling over a million copies. Chesney has not only been a prolific record-seller, but is also one of country's hottest touring acts.

JOHN MICHAEL MONTGOMERY – 2000

With three multi-platinum albums in his first three releases, John Michael Montgomery exploded onto the country music scene in the early '90s. By the time he appeared at the Jaycee Bootheel Rodeo in 2000 his record sales had slowed, but he was still a popular concert attraction.

Montgomery's first album, 1992's "Life's a Dance," sold over three million copies in the U.S. The title song peaked at #4 on the country charts, but the romantic ballad "I Love the Way You Love Me" became the Kentuckian's first #1 single. The 1994 LP "Kickin' It Up" sold over 6 million units in the U.S and Canada and would prove to be his most successful album ever. "Kickin' It Up" had three #1 singles – "I Swear," "Be My Baby Tonight" and "If You've Got Love."

In 1995, the singles "I Can Love You Like That" and "Sold (The Grundy County Auction Incident)," from Montgomery's self-titled third album, both went to #1, making it four straight chart-toppers and proving to be the high point of his career. He had 11 more top-10 singles during the '90s, but didn't hit #1 again until 2000's "The Little Girl," released about three weeks after his Sikeston appearance. The album the single was from, "Brand New Me," was appropriately titled, representing somewhat of a comeback for the singer after his previous album had disappointing sales.

Montgomery continued to record into the 2000s, but battled hearing troubles as well as legal and substance abuse problems. Of his three albums during the decade, "Letters From Home" was his most successful, hitting #3 on the country charts.

JO DEE MESSINA – 2000

Rising country singer Jo Dee Messina had just released her third album and was on the was to winning the CMA's Horizon Award for best new artist when she stepped on the Jaycee Bootheel Rodeo stage in 2000.

The single "That's the Way" had already climbed to the top of the country charts when Messina played the Sikeston rodeo. The album "Burn" would produce another #1 country single in 2011, a duet with Tim McGraw titled "Bring On the Rain," and be RIAA certified platinum.

Messina's self-titled debut LP in 1996 went gold, with the #2 hit "Heads Carolina, Tails California" leading the way. The follow up LP, "I'm Alright," sold over 2 million copies and featured three straight #1 singles in 1998– "Bye, Bye," "I'm Alright" and "Stand Beside Me."

With the exception of a holiday album and a greatest hits compilation, Jo Dee Messina went almost five years before her next LP, which contained the 2005 #1 hit "My Give a Damn's Busted." She released a series of three extended play recordings in 2010 that barely made a ripple on the country charts.

MONTGOMERY GENTRY – 2000, 2005 & 2009

Country duo Montgomery Gentry was still gaining traction in the music business in 2000 when they played the Jaycee Bootheel Rodeo for the first of three times. When they returned in 2005, their career was in high gear.

Eddie Montgomery had been in a band with younger brother John Michael Montgomery and Troy Gentry before the former left to pursue what would become a successful solo career. Eddie and Troy decided to try going it as a duo and signed a record deal with Columbia in 1999. Their debut album, 1999's "Tattoos and Scars," had only one top-10 single, but the album eventually achieved platinum certification as the act gained popularity. Montgomery Gentry took home best new artist awards from the both the CMA and ACM awards in 2000.

The team produced three more hit country albums before their return to Sikeston, including the platinum LPs "My Town" (2002) and "You Do Your Thing" (2004). The singles "If You Ever Stop Loving Me" and "Something To Be Proud Of" off the 2004 release became Montgomery Gentry's first two #1 country singles.

The group had two more top five country albums before they made their third Sikeston appearance in 2009, with more #1 singles such as "Lucky Man," "Back When I Knew it All" and "Roll With Me."

COLLIN RAYE – 2001

Collin Raye's days as a country hitmaker were drawing to a close when he appeared at the Jaycee Bootheel Rodeo in 2001. But with four platinum albums and 21 top-10 singles to his credit, the singer had plenty of material to draw from as he entertained the Sikeston audience.

Raye came from a musical family. His mother opened the show for many of the legendary Sun Records artists in the '50s, and he and his brothers were part of a family act in the '80s. The Wrays released several singles that flopped before Collin changed the spelling of his last name, signed a new contract with Epic Records and released his first solo album in 1992. "All I Can Be" was the first of four-straight platinum-certified LPs in the '90s for Raye. The singles "Love, Me" ('91), "In This Life" ('92), "My Kind of Girl" ('94) and "I Can Still Feel You" ('98) all made it to #1.

Raye's 2000 album "Tracks" was the singer's last studio album to crack the country top 10. He has released five more albums through 2011, but none have been commercial successes.

LONESTAR – 2001 & 2002

The five-piece country band Lonestar was on quite a roll in August of 2001 when they appeared at the Jaycee Bootheel Rodeo the first time, enjoying the success of their fifth straight #1 country single and another hit album on the charts.

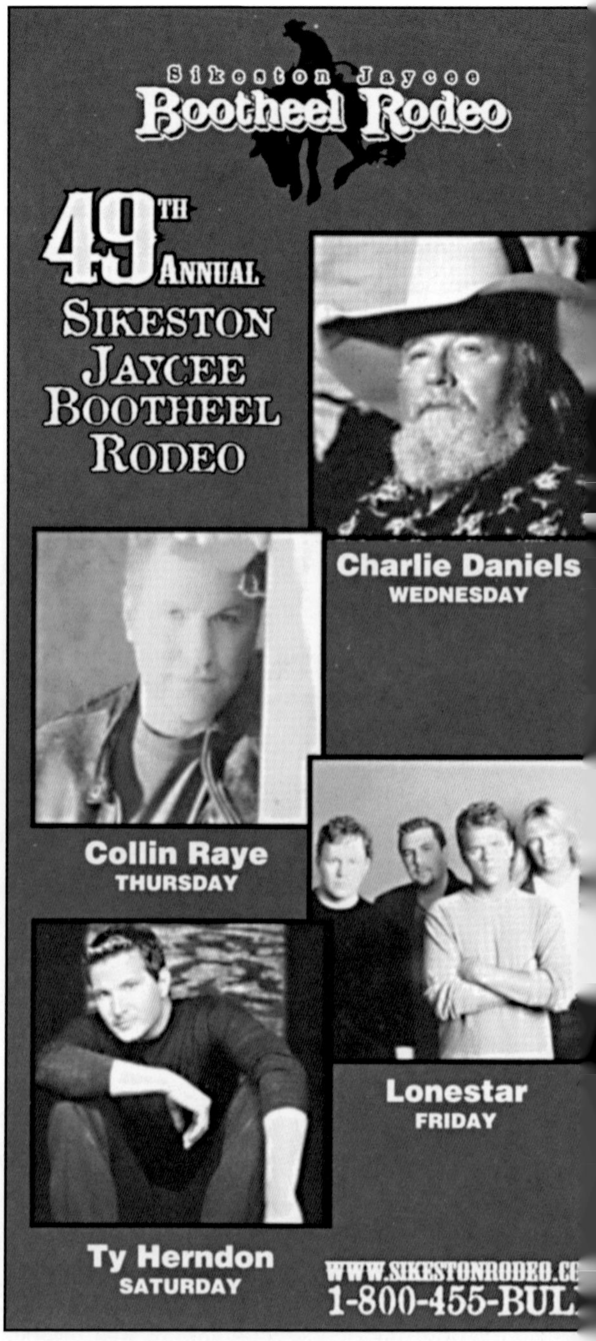

Lonestar had released a pair of successful country albums – "Lonestar" ('95) and "Crazy Nights" ('97) – along with the #1 singles "No News" and "Come Cryin' to Me" before firing vocalist and bass player John Rich, who was later part of the successful duo Big and Rich. But Richie McDonald, Michael Britt, Keech Rainwater and Dean Sams reached bigger heights without Rich. All four singles from the 1999 "Lonely Grill" album – "Amazed," "Smile," "What About Now" and "Tell Her" – went to the top of the country charts. When "Amazed was re-released in 2000 to target Top 40 stations, it reached #1 on Billboard's Hot 100, the first country record to do so since the Kenny Rogers/Dolly Parton duet "Islands in the Stream" 18 years earlier. "Lonely Grill" became Lonestar's biggest-selling album, achieving RIAA triple-platinum status.

"I'm Already There," the leadoff single from the album of the same name, made it five consecutive country chart-toppers for Lonestar before their first rodeo appearance. They returned to Sikeston for the 2002 rodeo and released three more studio albums in the decade, but none met with sales success of "Lonely Grill" and "I'm Already There."

TY HERNDON – 2001

Ty Herndon enjoyed a brief period of success as a country performer in the mid-to-late '90s and had three #1 country singles when he entertained at the Jaycee Bootheel Rodeo in 2001.

After ten years of struggling in Nashville after high school without breaking in to the music business, Herndon moved to Texas and became a popular singer in the state's numerous honky-tonks, earning him a contract with Epic Records 1993. His debut album in 1995, "What Mattered Most," became a top-10 LP, and the title track went to #1. His next two LPs – "Living in a Moment" ('96) and "Big Hopes" ('98) – also were popular and each yielded a #1 single.

But after his 1999 album "Steam" didn't sell well and failed to produce any hit singles, Epic released Ty Herndon. Unfortunately, his days as a country hitmaker were gone by the time of his Sikeston appearance.

ALABAMA – 2002

The most successful band in the history of country music made the Jaycee Bootheel Rodeo a stop on their much-publicized farewell tour in August of 2002.

Alabama, with record sales of over 73 million, is the biggest-selling country group ever. Among all types of music, the boys from Fort Payne, Alabama have sold more records than legendary rock bands such as the Who, Led Zeppelin, Pink Floyd, the Doors and Queen. They are credited with expanding the popularity of country music by tapping into the youth market. Five of their hits from the '80s cracked Billboard's adult contemporary top 10, and "Love in the First Degree" climbed into the Hot 100 pop chart.

Randy Owen, Teddy Gentry and Jeff Cook were a popular band in the south before signing with RCA in 1980. Alabama's first album, appropriately titled "My Home's in Alabama," featured two #1 singles – "Tennessee River" and "Why Lady Why." The LP's title track didn't make it to #1 but proved to be one of the band's most requested songs on tour. The album eventually sold over 2 million copies to earn double-platinum certification from the RIAA.

The string of successful recordings that followed was without precedent. The next eight Alabama albums in the '80s all topped the country charts, and all went platinum or higher. Of 28 singles released by the group in the decade, 27 were country #1s, including a record-breaking string of 21 in a row. Included in the string of chart-toppers were classics such as "Old Flame," "When We Make Love," "Feels So Right," "Dixieland Delight," "If You're Gonna Play in Texas (You Gotta Have a Fiddle in the Band)" and "40 Hour Week (For a Livin')."

Alabama turned out five more #1 country singles in the '90s, to go with five more platinum or multiplatinum albums. The Sikeston audience in August of 2002 was treated to an extended set of the band's hits.

GARY ALLAN – 2002 & 2008

Rising country star Gary Allan was starting to enjoy the fruits of stardom when he first appeared at the Jaycee Bootheel Rodeo in August of 2002.

Allan's first two albums released after signing with Decca didn't exactly make him a household name, but did result in two top-10 singles – "Her Man" ('96) and "It Would Be You" ('98). But after switching to the MCA Nashville label his career found another gear. Allan's 1999 album "Smoke Rings in the Dark" climbed to #9 on the country charts, and the single "Right Where I Need to Be" was his highest-charting single yet. The album eventually went platinum. Then the 2001 LP "Alright Guy" gave Allan his first #1 single, "Man to Man," and helped Allan win the CMA's Horizon Award for best new artist. The platinum album was on the charts when Allan played the Sikeston rodeo, with "Man to Man" being released in the fall.

Gary Allan has continued to enjoy record sales and concert success. He had four more hit albums through 2010, including the platinum-certified "See If I Care" and the #1 "Tough All Over." "See If I Care" featured two more #1 singles from Allan – "Tough Little Boys" and "Nothing On But the Radio." He returned to Sikeston in 2008 for an encore Jaycee Bootheel Rodeo appearance. In the spring of 2013 the Jaycees announced that Allan had been booked for a third rodeo appearance.

TRACE ADKINS – 2002 & 2006

Louisiana native Trace Adkins brought his deep voice to the Jaycee Bootheel Rodeo stage twice – first in 2002 and again in 2008.

Adkins made his first splash in the country music world in 1996 with his debut album "Dreamin' Out Loud," which featured three smash singles. "Every Light in the House" rose to #3 on the country charts, followed by Adkins' first #1, "(This Ain't) No Thinkin' Thing)" and "I Left Something Turned On At Home," a #2 hit. "Dreamin' Out Loud" went platinum, as did his follow-up LP in 1997, "Big Time."

Trace Adkins showed that he wasn't a flash in the pan, consistently turning out hit albums after the turn of the century. Of the seven studio albums Adkins released between 2000 and 2012, three topped the country charts and all were in the top 10. The LPs "Comin' On Strong" ('03) and "Songs About Me" ('05) both were RIAA certified platinum. The single "You're Gonna Miss This" was a #1 single in April of 2008, four months before Adkins played the rodeo a second time. "Ladies Love Country Boys" had topped the charts for Adkins in 2006.

BRAD PAISLEY – 2003

One of country's most promising young singers, Brad Paisley stepped onto the stage of the Jaycee Bootheel Rodeo in 2003 having just released his third album, "Mud On the Tires."

Hailing from West Virginia, Paisley had been a regular on the famous Jamboree USA radio program while still in high school. He earned a degree in music business from Belmont University in Nashville with the assistance of a scholarship from ASCAP and then interned at both ASCAP and Atlantic Records. Paisley wrote a couple of songs for other artists, then got his own record deal with Arista Records in 1999.

Paisley's debut album in 1999, "Who Needs Pictures," went platinum, as did 2001's LP, "Part II." A pair of #1 country singles came from the first album – "He Didn't Have to Be" and "We Danced." "Part II featured "I'm Gonna Miss Her (The Fishin' Song)," which not only went to #1 but also became the CMA Video of the Year. Paisley won both the CMA Horizon Award and the Academy of Country Music's best new male vocalist in 2000, and in 2001 he became the youngest person to be inducted into the Grand Ole Opry.

Sikeston rodeo fans were treated to several selections from Paisley's current album, "Mud On the Tires," which went double-platinum and became the first of six consecutive #1 country albums for the star through 2011. The 2005 duet with Dolly Parton, "When I Get Where I'm Going," started a string of 10 straight #1 singles, including the hits "She's Everything" ('06), "Ticks" ('07), "I'm Still a Guy" ('08) and "Then" ('09). Paisley charted four more #1 country singles in 2010-11, including the Carrie Underwood duet "Remind Me" that went platinum.

TRICK PONY – 2003

For the three-piece country band Trick Pony, their musical career was "three and out." That is to say, three albums and they were out of the business. Sikeston rodeo audiences were entertained by the group in between their second and final LPs.

Original members Keith Burns, Ira Dean and Heidi Newfield signed a Warner Brothers recording contract in 2000 and released their first album, "Trick Pony," the same year. The biggest hit off the debut LP was "On a Night Like This," which rose to #4 on the country singles chart and turned out to be the band's only top-10 hit. The album was eventually RIAA certified gold. Trick Pony's second album, "On a Mission," had only the title track crack the top 20. After Warner Brothers dropped the group, they released a third LP in 2005 with Asylum-Curb records titled "R.I.D.E.." That LP had decent sales but no hits, and the band disintegrated after lead singer Newfield left the group at the end of 2006.

CHRIS CAGLE – 2003 & 2004

The performer who entertained Jaycee Bootheel Rodeo audiences in both 2003 and 2004, Chris Cagle, began his professional music as a songwriter. Cagle worked odd jobs in Nashville including nannying, bartending and waiting tables while honing his songwriting skills. After a meeting with legendary country composer Harlan Howard he got a publishing contract, then a recording contract with Virgin Records in 2000.

Cagle's first album, "Play It Loud," featured his only #1 single, "I Breathe In, I Breathe Out." His self-titled second LP on the Capitol Nashville label had a pair of top five singles, including "Chicks Dig It," which was his current hit when he appeared in Sikeston for the first time in 2003. Cagle recorded two more albums for Capitol Nashville that did well in terms of airplay but were not commercial successes. The highest-charting single of the two LPs was 2007's "What Kinda Gone," which made it to #3.

EMERSON DRIVE WITH JOE NICHOLS – 2004

A country band on the decline and a singer whose career was on the rise shared the bill on the opening night of the 2004 Jaycee Bootheel Rodeo.

A Canadian band formerly known as 12 Gauge, Emerson Drive had already gone through several lineup changes by 2004. Although they were very popular north of the border, none of their first three albums made it into the American top 10. However, two singles from their self-titled debut album did crack the American top five – "I Should Be Sleeping" and "Fall Into Me." Emerson Drive's only US #1 hit came in 2006 with "Moments."

Joe Nichols, on the other hand, was coming off a platinum album "Man With a Memory" and a #1 country single "Brokenheartsville" when he took the Sikeston stage. His just-released second LP, "Revelation," was headed to the #3 position on the country album charts and featured the singles "If Nobody Believed in You" and "What's a Guy Gotta Do," with both making the top 10. Nichols went on to score two more #1 singles in the decade – "Tequila Makes Her Clothes Fall Off" ('05) and "Gimmie that Girl" ('09).

BLAKE SHELTON – 2004 & 2009

Only a few weeks after the release of what would become his third #1 country single, Blake Shelton entertained Jaycee Bootheel Rodeo fans in August of 2004.

"Some Beach," a single from the album "Blake Shelton's Barn and Grill," sold over a million copies, helping the LP become his third straight gold-certified album. Two more singles from the album made the country top 10.

Blake Shelton's first single, "Austin," spent five weeks at #1 on the Billboard country charts and helped his self-titled first album go gold. Following 2002's "The Baby," "Some Beach" became the third Shelton single to top the charts. The Oklahoma native hit his peak in popularity in 2008-11 when seven of eight singles went to the #1 spot. That run was capped by the 2011 million sellers "Honey Bee" and "God Gave Me You," helping him win the Country Music Association's Male Vocalist of the Year and the American Music Awards Favorite Country Male Artist

Shelton has also been known in recent years for his role as a reality TV judge on "The Voice" and for his high-profile marriage to country superstar Miranda Lambert.

PHIL VASSER – 2004

Phil Vasser had already shown that he could write a good country song, but when he got the chance to record his own songs, he showed that he could sing them just as well as the next guy.

Vasser, who performed at the 2004 Jaycee Bootheel Rodeo, had penned a number of country hits. "I'm Alright" and "Bye, Bye" for Jo Dee Messina and "Right On the Money" for Alan Jackson all were #1 country hits. "Bye, Bye" was ASCAP's 1999 Song of the Year, and he also won Songwriter of the Year. That year also saw Vasser sign a recording contract with Arista Nashville.

His first single off his debut album "Phil Vasser" was "Carlene," which made it to #5 on the Billboard country chart. The next single, "Just Another Day in Paradise," became his first #1 as a singer. Two more singles from the RIAA gold certified album made it into the top 10. The title song from his 2002 follow-up LP, "American Child," made it to #5. The leadoff single for Vassar's third album, "Shaken Not Stirred" was climbing the charts when he appeared in Sikeston in August of 2004. "In a Real Love" would reach #1 in November of that year, giving him his second #1.

Vassar released two more studio albums that decade, but the only noteworthy hits were "The Last Day of My Life" ('06) and "Love is a Beautiful Thing" ('07). Both of those songs climbed to #2.

SARA EVANS – 2005

For Missourian Sara Evans, country music stardom didn't come quickly. But hard work and perseverance ultimately paid off for the singer who performed at the 2005 Jaycee Bootheel Rodeo.

After what she went through as a child, overcoming adversity in her music career was a piece of cake. Evans was struck by a car when she was eight and spent months in hospitals and wheelchairs recovering. She had been singing in the family's band since she was five, and even from her wheelchair she continued to perform to help pay her own medical bills. Moving to Nashville in 1995 seeking to make it big, Sara recorded demo after demo before Harlan Howard heard one and used his connections to get her a contract with RCA. But it seemed nothing came easy for Evans. She released four singles starting in 1997 that didn't crack the top 40 before the public found one they liked enough to make a hit. The title track off her second album, "No Place That Far," went to #1 in '98 and set the stage for Evans' career to really take off in 2000.

Evans third LP, "Born to Fly," featured a #1 title track and two more singles that made the country top five – "I Could Not Ask For More" and "I Keep Looking." Another #1 hit, "Suds in the Bucket," came from the 2003 album "Restless." "Born to Fly" went double-platinum, and "Restless" was RIAA certified platinum.

A fifth album, "Real Fine Place," was released shortly after Evans' Sikeston appearance, but the single "Real Fine Place to Start" had already been released and was climbing the charts quickly. "Real Fine Place to Start" made it to #1 a month after she played the rodeo, giving her four chart-topping singles. The album went on to become Sara Evans' third-straight platinum LP.

After a five-year hiatus from new studio recording that was marked by reality TV appearances, political campaigning and a bitter divorce from her second husband, Evans returned to the studio and released her sixth album, "Stronger," in 2011. The album went to #1, and so did the single "A Little Bit Stronger."

DIERKS BENTLEY – 2005 & 2007

The year 2005 – the year he appeared at the Jaycee Bootheel Rodeo for the first time – was a big one for rising country singer Dierks Bentley.

In July, a month before his Sikeston appearance, Bentley released the single "Come a Little Bit Closer," which would be his second country #1. The album "Modern Day Drifter," released in the spring of that year, achieved platinum-certified sales and went to #1. In October, he became the third-youngest performer ever inducted into the Grand Ole Opry, and in November he received the Country Music Association's Horizon Award for best new artist.

Bentley's self-titled first album on Capitol Records in 2003 rose to #4 on the country album charts and the single "What Was I Thinkin'" went to #1. The next three LPs released by Bentley all went to #1, including "Long Trip Alone," which made it to the top spot only a month after its release in 2006 and was his current release when he returned to Sikeston for 2007's rodeo.

As of 2013, 10 of Dierks Bentley's 19 career singles have been #1 country hits.

DARRYL WORLEY – 2005

Darryl Worley's set list when the performed at the 2005 Jaycee Bootheel Rodeo no doubt included his three #1 country singles and material from two chart-topping albums.

Worley's 2000 debut album, "Hard Rain Don't Last," had three top 20 singles but was hardly a smash. But his second release, 2002's "I Miss My Friend," went to #1, led by the title track, which became the singer's first #1 single. "Have You Forgotten?," Worley's third album in 2003, also went to #1 and achieved RIAA gold certification. The title track to that album also went to #1.

The 2004 album "Darryl Worley" failed to match the success of his previous two releases, but the single "Awful, Beautiful Life" went to #1. None of the singer's subsequent singles or LPs have made it into the top 10.

CRAIG MORGAN – 2006 & 2011

Craig Morgan is one of the few singers who can list a 10-year military career on their resume before making as a star.

Morgan, who appeared at the 2006 and 2011 Jaycee Bootheel Rodeos, served in two different airborne divisions of the U.S. Army. He wrote songs and sang while in the Army and while stationed in Korea opened a show for Sawyer Brown.

His self-titled debut album with Atlantic Records' Nashville division in 2000 failed to chart, and only one single from the disc made it into the top 40. Atlantic closed their Nashville label, and Morgan didn't release another album until 2003. That LP on the Broken Bow label got into the top 20 and the single "Almost Home" made it to #6, giving Morgan his first legitimate country hit. His third album, 2005's "My Kind of Livin'," provided Morgan with his first #1 single – "That's What I Love About Sunday" – and "Redneck Yacht Club," which made it to #2. The album was RIAA certified gold.

Three subsequent albums by Craig Morgan have had modest success and yielded three top-10 singles.

KEITH ANDERSON – 2006

The multi-talented Keith Anderson, who performed at the 2006 Jaycee Bootheel Rodeo, might have been a professional baseball player if a bad break hadn't derailed his sports career.

Anderson, who played in a church band, played college baseball at Oklahoma State and was being scouted by the Kansas City Royals before a shoulder injury ended his baseball aspirations. But there was still music, and after a brief career as an engineer, he began writing songs and formed a band. He was one of several writers who collaborated on "Beer Run (B Double E Double R You In?)," which was a hit for George Jones and Garth Brooks in 2001. Anderson signed a recording contract with Arista Nashville in 2004.

Anderson's debut album, "Three Chord Country and American Rock & Roll," featured the hits "Pickin' Wildflowers" (#8) and "Every Time I Hear Your Name" (#7). The album eventually was certified gold and was on the charts when Anderson made his Sikeston appearance in 2006. His follow-up LP "C'mon!" went to #3 and contained what was the biggest hit of Anderson's career, 2008's "I Still Miss You."

While Anderson hasn't released another album as of 2012, he continued to be a successful songwriter. His biggest credit as a writing was "Lost in This Moment," which was a #1 hit for Big and Rich.

SUGARLAND – 2007

After starting out as a trio, Sugarland had become a duo when they appeared at the Jaycee Bootheel Rodeo in 2007.

The original three members of Sugarland – Kristen Hall, Jennifer Nettles and Kristian Bush – signed a recording contract with Mercury Nashville in 2004. "Baby Girl," the first single from the debut album "Twice the Speed of Life," rose to #2 on the country charts, making it the highest-charting debut single by a group in 13 years. The singles "Something More" and "Just Might (Make Me Believe)" also made the top 10, propelling "Twice the Speed of Life" to triple-platinum certification. Lead singer Nettles joined with Bon Jovi on their 2005 song "Who Says You Can't Go Home," which became a #1 country single.

Hall left the group at the end of 2005, and Sugarland's 2006 album "Enjoy the Ride" featured only Nettles and Bush. That album also went triple-platinum, and all four singles made the top 10, including the #1 hits "Want To" and "Settlin'." "Settlin'" reached #1 three months before the duo's Sikeston appearance.

Sugarland released two more platinum albums between 2007 and 2012, and both went platinum. "Love on the Inside" was helped by three straight #1 singles – "All I Want to Do," "Already Gone" and "It Happens." The duo won 18 major music industry awards through 2011.

ERIC CHURCH – 2007

Eric Church was a fresh new face on the country music scene and was promoting his debut album when he performed at the 2007 Jaycee Bootheel Rodeo.

Church's debut album in 2006 – "Sinners Like Me" – climbed to #7 on the country charts, although none of the four singles released from the record threatened the top 10. But the North Carolinian worked hard on the road, touring with Brad Paisley and Rascal Flatts. When he released his next LP, 2009's "Carolina," audiences were ready. The first two singles from the album – "Love Your Love the Most" and "Hell on the Heart" – made it to #10, helping the album achieve gold certification.

Church completed his steady climb up the ladder of success with the 2011 album "Chief," which made it to #1 and gave the singer his first #1 single, "Drink in My Hand." "Chief" was still selling well when it achieved gold certification early in 2012 and was nominated for a Grammy for Best Country Album.

LITTLE BIG TOWN – 2008

With two guys, two girls, rotating lead singers and tight four-part harmonies, the quartet called Little Big Town might be called country's answer to the 60's pop group The Mamas and the Papas. The group entertained fans at the 2008 Jaycee Bootheel Rodeo with three albums to their credit, but their best yet to come.

Karen Fairchild, Kimberly Schlapman, Jimi Westbrook and Phillip Sweet released their self-titled debut album in 2002, but "Little Big Town" didn't catch on with the fans. But their 2005 release "The Road to Here" put the group on the map in a big way with the top-10 singles "Bring It On Home" and "Boondocks." The Road to Here eventually was certified platinum by the RIAA. The 2007 LP "A Place to Land," Little Big Town's current release at the time of their Sikeston appearance, had no breakout hits but still made it to #10 on the country charts.

Little Big Town's fourth album, 2010's "The Reason Why," became the group's first #1 country album and contained "Little White Church," a single which rose to #6 and went gold.

38 SPECIAL – 2008

Country music stepped aside to make way for '80s classic rock as 38 Special took the stage on Thursday evening of the 2008 Jaycee Bootheel Rodeo.

Starting with the 1981 album "Wild-Eyed Southern Boys," 38 special released three straight platinum-certified LPs during the early part of the decade. "Hold On Loosely" became the band's first major hit, climbing to #3 on Billboard's new Hot Mainstream Rock Tracks chart. The singles "Caught Up in You" and "If I'd Been the One," from 38 Special's next two platinum albums, went to #1 on the same chart.

The group produced nine more top-10 singles from 1982-91. In addition to their three platinum studio albums, a "Best of" LP in '87 also sold over a million copies. Although their last significant studio album was 1991's "Bone Against Steel," 38 Special has continued to be a popular concert draw. In addition to their rodeo appearance, the group was also busy touring at that time with Lynyrd Skynyrd, Hank Williams, Jr., Styx and REO Speedwagon.

JASON ALDEAN – 2008

Jaycee Bootheel Rodeo fans welcomed one of country music's hottest young stars to the stage in 2008 as Jason Aldean performed at the Saturday evening show.

Aldean had released his self-titled debut album in 2005, and all three singles made it to the top 10. "Why" became the singer's first #1 single. "Amarillo Sky" only made it to #4, but was nominated for the Academy of Country Music's Song of the Year and Video of the Year awards in 2006, the same year that Aldean won the ACM's Top New Male Vocalist honors. He took the Country Music Association's Horizon Award honors in 2007.

Aldean's second LP, "Relentless," wasn't quite as successful as his debut release, but was still good enough to produce two top-10 singles. "Johnny Cash" and "Laughed Until We Cried," which both rose to #6, made it five straight top-10 hits. "Relentless" was Aldean's current LP in 2008.

The albums "Wide Open" ('09) and "My Kinda Party" ('10) established Jason Aldean as a superstar. Eight straight singles from the two LPs made it to either #1 or #2 covering a period from late 2008 into 2011. "Wide Open" went platinum, while "My Kinda Party" achieved double-platinum certification. One of those chart-toppers was "Don't You Wanna Stay," a duet with Kelly Clarkson that was the CMA's Musical Event of the Year in 2011, then took the same honors at the ACM Awards in 2012.

DARIUS RUCKER – 2009

Only two days before his debut country album was officially certified platinum, the artist best-known as the lead singer of the pop group Hootie and the Blowfish entertained Jaycee Bootheel Rodeo fans on opening night of the 2009 rodeo.

Darius Rucker's first country LP, "Learn to Live" had been released in 2008, marking a sabbatical for the singer from Hootie and the Blowfish. That group's 1994 LP "Cracked Rear View" is one of the most popular albums in music history with sales of over 16 million units. After five studio albums (three went platinum) over a period of 11 years, Rucker signed a contract with Capitol to record country music. "Don't Think I Don't Think About It," the leadoff single from the album, went to #1 on the country charts, marking the first #1 single by an African-American solo country artist in over a quarter of a century. The next two singles from the album – "It Won't Be Like This For Long" and "Alright" – also went to the top of the country hit list. He won the CMA New Artist of the Year award in November 2009, becoming the first black performer since Charley Pride to win a CMA award.

Rucker's second country album, "Charleston, SC 1966," also became a #1 country album in 2010. The disc featured two more chart-topping singles – "Come Back Song" and "This." While his country career has certainly thrived, he hasn't ruled out more recordings with Hootie and the Blowfish.

LUKE BRYAN – 2009

With the first single from his upcoming second album climbing the charts, Luke Bryan's popularity was rising when he appeared at the 2009 Jaycee Bootheel Rodeo.

"Do I" was released in May of 2009 and made a steady climb up the country singles hit list, peaking at #2 in November. "Do I" was from the LP "Doin' My Thing" released in October. The album's next two singles – "Rain Is a Good Thing" and "Someone Else Calling You Baby" – both went to #1 in 2010, and the album was certified platinum.

After having written hits for Travis Tritt and Billy Currington, Bryan released his first album as a singer in 2007. "I'll Stay Me" included a pair of top-10 hits, including "All My Friends Say," which made it to #5. After the success of the follow-up LP "Doin' My Thing," Bryan's third album in 2010 also went platinum. "Tailgates and Tanlines" was highlighted by the #1 single "I Don't Want This Night to End."

LYNYRD SKYNYRD – 2010

With only one member of their classic lineup still with the group, southern rock legends Lynyrd Skynyrd were touring again in 2010, performing classic hits and songs from their new album "God and Guns" at the Jaycee Bootheel Rodeo.

Lead singer Ronnie Van Zant and guitarist Steve Gaines were killed in a 1977 plane crash at the height of the group's popularity. Prior to the tragedy, Lynyrd Skynyrd had four platinum albums to their credit, featuring rock classics such as "Free Bird," "Sweet Home Alabama" and "What's Your Name?" Even though several band members survived the crash, Lynyrd Skynyrd as a musical act was mostly dead for 10 years until a 1987 reunion featuring Gary Rossington, Billy Powell, Leon Wilkeson, Artimus Pyle and Ed King. What was meant to be a one-time tour turned into act that continues to perform today, though Rossington is the only member from the classic '70s lineup left.

Lynyrd Skynyrd

Although none of the six studio albums released by Lynyrd Skynyrd have been hits, the enduring popularity of the band has been demonstrated by their successful live tours and by the fact that eight of the band's 24 compilation albums released through 2010 have been RIAA certified platinum. The 1989 greatest hits package "Skynyrd's Innyrds" sold over five million copies. The band was inducted into the Rock and Roll Hall of Fame in 2006.

JAMEY JOHNSON – 2010

Although he has three studio albums to his credit as a performer, 2010 Jaycee Bootheel Rodeo entertainer Jamey Johnson has enjoyed more success with songs he's written for other artists.

Johnson started writing songs during an eight-year hitch in the U.S. Marine Corps Reserves, then moved to Nashville to pursue a country music career. He co-wrote Trace Adkins' hits "Honky Tonk Badonkadonk" and "Ladies Love Country Boys" as well as the 2006 George Strait chart-topper "Give it Away." Johnson's highest-charting single as a singer was 2009's "In Color," which made it to #9.

Despite the fact that none of Jamey Johnson's singles have flirted with the top of the country charts, his album "The Guitar Song" – released a month after his Sikeston appearance, went to #1.

GRETCHEN WILSON – 2010 & 2011

Gretchen Wilson

The Grammy Award-winning singer famous for her signature hit "Redneck Woman" entertained Jaycee Bootheel Rodeo audiences twice, performing in 2010 and 2011.

Wilson, a southern Illinois native and die-hard St. Louis Cardinals baseball fan, hit a grand slam in her fast at bat as a recording artist. The 2004 debut album "Here For the Party" sold over five million copies and included five top five country singles, including the #1 "Redneck Woman." The success of the album helped Wilson sweep the CMA and ACM new artist awards for 2004 and best female vocalist honors for 2005, in addition to a 2004 Grammy for Best Female Vocal Performance. She sang "The Star-Spangled Banner" before Game 4 of the 2004 World Series at Busch Stadium and recorded a Cardinal-themed version of "Redneck Woman" called "Redbird Fever."

Wilson's 2005 studio album "All Jacked Up" fell well short of the success of "Here For the Part" but still had enough sales for platinum certification by the RIAA. The title song of the LP was her most recent top-10 single as of 2012, peaking at #8.

BIG and RICH – 2011

Kenneth Alphin (a.k.a. "Big Kenny") and John Rich – better known as Big and Rich – were in the midst of a reunion tour when they performed at the Jaycee Bootheel Rodeo. One of music's hottest duos from 2004-07, Big and Rich took a three-year hiatus to pursue solo projects before teaming up again to perform their unique blend of country and rock.

The Big and Rich reunion didn't include any new albums, but they did record a single called "Fake I.D." that was part of the soundtrack of the 2011 remake of "Footloose." The Sikeston performance marked a return to Sikeston for Rich, who had played the rodeo in 2001 and 2002 as a part of the band Lonestar.

Big and Rich's 2004 debut album "Horse of a Different Color" featured the hit "Save a Horse (Ride a Cowboy)." The record went triple-platinum, and the duo's next LP, "Comin' To Your City," went platinum. It was their third album, 2007's "Between Raising Hell and Amazing Grace," that got Big and Rich their first #1 single (and only one as of 2012), "Lost in This Moment."

PAT GREEN – 2011

Texan Pat Green, who had sold over a quarter million albums before he ever signed a recording contract, entertained fans at the 2011 Jaycee Bootheel Rodeo.

Green became a popular concert attraction in Texas after appearing at Willie Nelson's annual 4th of July picnic in 1998. Although he didn't have a record deal, he had a major sponsor in Miller Lite and recorded three self-produced albums that sold over 250,000 copies. When he finally signed a recording contract with Universal/Republic and released the album "Three Days" in the fall of 2001, the record made it into the country top 10 album charts. His follow-up release, "Wave On Wave," was RIAA certified gold, and the title track was a #3 country single, marking his highest-charting single.

Pat Green released four more albums through 2012, with three of the four making it into the country top 10.

RODNEY ATKINS – 2011

As country singers go, Rodney Atkins, who entertained at the 2011 Jaycee Bootheel Rodeo, might be considered a late bloomer.

It was six years from the release of his first single that Atkins finally had a top-10 country single, 2003's "Honesty (Write Me a List)." His first single in 1997 was from an album that wound up never being released. After an airplane discussion with Curb Records owner Mike Curb, Atkins got a change in producers and a change in musical style. When his first album "Honesty" was finally released in the fall of 2003, it didn't exactly set the charts on fire, although the title track made it to #4.

It was three more years before Atkins released another album – nine years after his first single. But the results were worth the wait. "If You're Going Through Hell" was a #1 country album and yielded four straight #1 singles – "If You're Going Through Hell (Before the Devil Even Knows)," "Watching You," "These Are My People" and "Cleaning This Gun (Come On In Boy)." The album was RIAA certified platinum.

Atkins released two more albums and had two more #1 singles through 2011 – "It's America" (2008) and "Take a Back Road" (2011).

THE BAND PERRY – 2012

Siblings Kimberly, Reid and Neil Perry, better known as The Band Perry, had already tasted the success of a platinum album when they performed at the 2012 Jaycee Bootheel Rodeo.

Reid and Neil were not yet 20 years old when they and big sister Kimberly signed with the Republic Nashville label in 2009. "If I Die Young," the second single from The Band Perry's self-titled debut album, went to #1 on the country charts in 2010. Another single from that album, "All Your Life," topped the charts in 2011. "Better Dig Two," an early release from their 2013 LP "Pioneer," made it to #1 in February 2013.

JERROD NIEMANN – 2012

Like many country stars, 2012 Jaycee Bootheel Rodeo performer Jerrod Niemann enjoyed success as a songwriter before it came as a singer.

Niemann co-wrote Garth Brooks' 2005 hit "Good Ride Cowboy," one of many compositions performed by other artists. His first two self-released albums as a singer went nowhere, but his performing career got a boost when he signed with Sea Gayle, a division of Arista Nashville. The 2010 album "Judge Jerrod & the Hung Jury" went to #1 and featured the chart-topper "Lover, Lover" and another hit, "What Do You Want."

Niemann released his second Sea Gayle album, "Free the Music, in October 2012.

EASTON CORBIN – 2012

Easton Corbin took the Jaycee Bootheel Rodeo stage in 2012 with a #4 debut album and two #1 singles under his belt.

A Floridian, Corbin signed with Mercury Nashville in 2009. His first single was the title track to an extended play CD, "A Little More Country Than That," released in August 2009. The EP was not a hit, but when the label released the song as the lead single on Corbin's debut album, it went to #1, as did the follow up single "Roll With It."

"Lovin' You Is Fun," the preview single from Corbin's second album, entered the country charts a month before Corbin's Sikeston appearance and eventually peaked at #7. The album, titled "All Over the Road," was released in September 2012 and peaked at #2.

JUSTIN MOORE – 2012

Justin Moore, who performed at the 2012 Jaycee Bootheel Rodeo, benefited from social networking on his way to becoming a successful performer.

Moore had moved to Nashville in 2002 and played in his uncle's southern rock band before signing a record contract with Valory Music in 2008. His first two singles weren't hits, but his debut album "Justin Moore" went to #3 in 2009 and the follow up, "Outlaws Like Me," topped the charts in 2011. The debut album was part of a social networking promotion called "So You Want to Be a Record Label Executive," which allowed fans to select 10 songs that were included on the album. The single "Small Town USA" hit #1 from the debut album, and "If Heaven Wasn't So Far Away" from the second LP also topped the country charts.

Moore's current hit during his rodeo appearance was "Til My Last Day," which peaked at #7 on the country charts but topped the Billboard country airplay lists.

Justin Moore

Terry Lape, Larry Miller, Woody Sigmon, Bud Werner, Alan Keenan, Terry Lee, Bill Burch, Steven Burch, Charlie McGill, Dan Lape, David Hough, Unknown.

Youths scramble to try to catch their swine during a grease pig contents in the '60s. From the Loy Baugher collection.

Don Durant and the Jaycee wives. From the Loy Baugher collection.

The Grand Entry at the Sikeston Jaycee Bootheel Rodeo. From the Loy Baugher collection.

Steve Taylor slips a rodeo vest on Bill Anderson, a.k.a. "Cousin Carl", while Charlie Stamp does the talking.

Roy Rogers and Dale Evans with Shriner Rich Lewis (left) and Jaycee Bill Lewis.

Sikeston police officer Lloyd Treece with Molly Bee.

"Johnny Ringo" star Don Durant signs for his young fans at the fence in 1960. From the Loy Baugher collection.

Winning cowboys show off their trophy buckles. From the Loy Baugher collection.

A youngster shows off his pony to James Arness. Officer Gerald Howard of the Sikeston Police Department is behind the boy. From the Loy Baugher collection.

Jaycees work to set fence posts during a rodeo work day, 1992.

Bottom row (kneeling) L-R: Dan Lape, Rob Mitchell, Steve Taylor, Dennis Ziegenhorn, Bud Werner, Rich Wrather, David Bird, Bob Fuchs. Second row (standing): ?, George Hale, ?, Charles Mitchell, Bill Sikes, ?, Robert Mitchell, John Harper, Bill Buneit, Stan Eudy, Rick Adams, Steve Sikes, Jim Cox.

Jim Nabors poses with Little Miss Western Tammy Clark and Little Mr. Western Michael Snider. From the Loy Baugher collection.

1994 General Chairman Tom Green and 1985 Jaycee President Mike Marshall look over the rodeo grounds.

Mike Kohlfeld of Kohlfeld Distributing (middle), representing national sponsor Coors Brewing Co., with 1992 General Chairman Gary Lasater (left) and Rex Dunn of the Coyote Hills Rodeo Co.

Marcie Lawson (center) holds the hat containing the names of those bidding to win a saddle in the 2010 rodeo's "Tough Enough to Wear Pink" giveway to benefit the American Cancer Society. Pictured from left are Jaycee President Ryan Merideth, Joyce Winchester, Marcie Lawson, Heather Wibbenmeyer and Jaycee Jason Pounds.

L-R: Dave Klueppel, Jayson Snyder, unidentified.

Rick Young makes like a laying hen, 2012.

Announcer Boyd Polhamus departs from his customer seat in the press box to interview a fan from the saddle in 2012.

Paul Brinegar of "Rawhide" with the mounted color guard, 1961. From the Loy Baugher collection.

Clowning around

Waitresses at a local restaurant get in the spirit of rodeo week. From the Loy Baugher collection.

Gunsmoke stars Dennis Weaver (left) and Milburn Stone at their motel room, 1959

Using the profits from the 1st rodeo, the Jaycees gave the City of Sikeston trashcans for the downtown area. L-R: Bill Bess, Bob Mitchell (1952-1953 Jaycees President) and Mayor of Sikeston, Charles Butler.

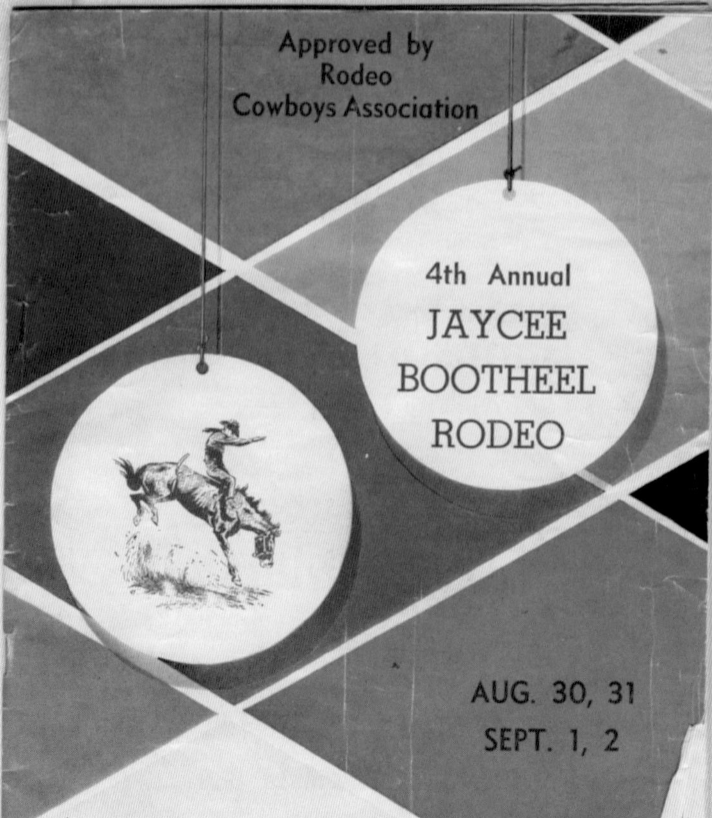

The arena crew, whose job is to untie the calves after the Tie-Down Roping event. L-R: Craig Cox, Zach Fayette, Blake Wethington, Kenny Graham, Trey Glaus, Justin Littleton.

A youthful rider and his pony participate in the grand entry.

Young cowboys show off their gunfighting skills.

The Grand Entry at an early Jaycee Bootheel Rodeo.

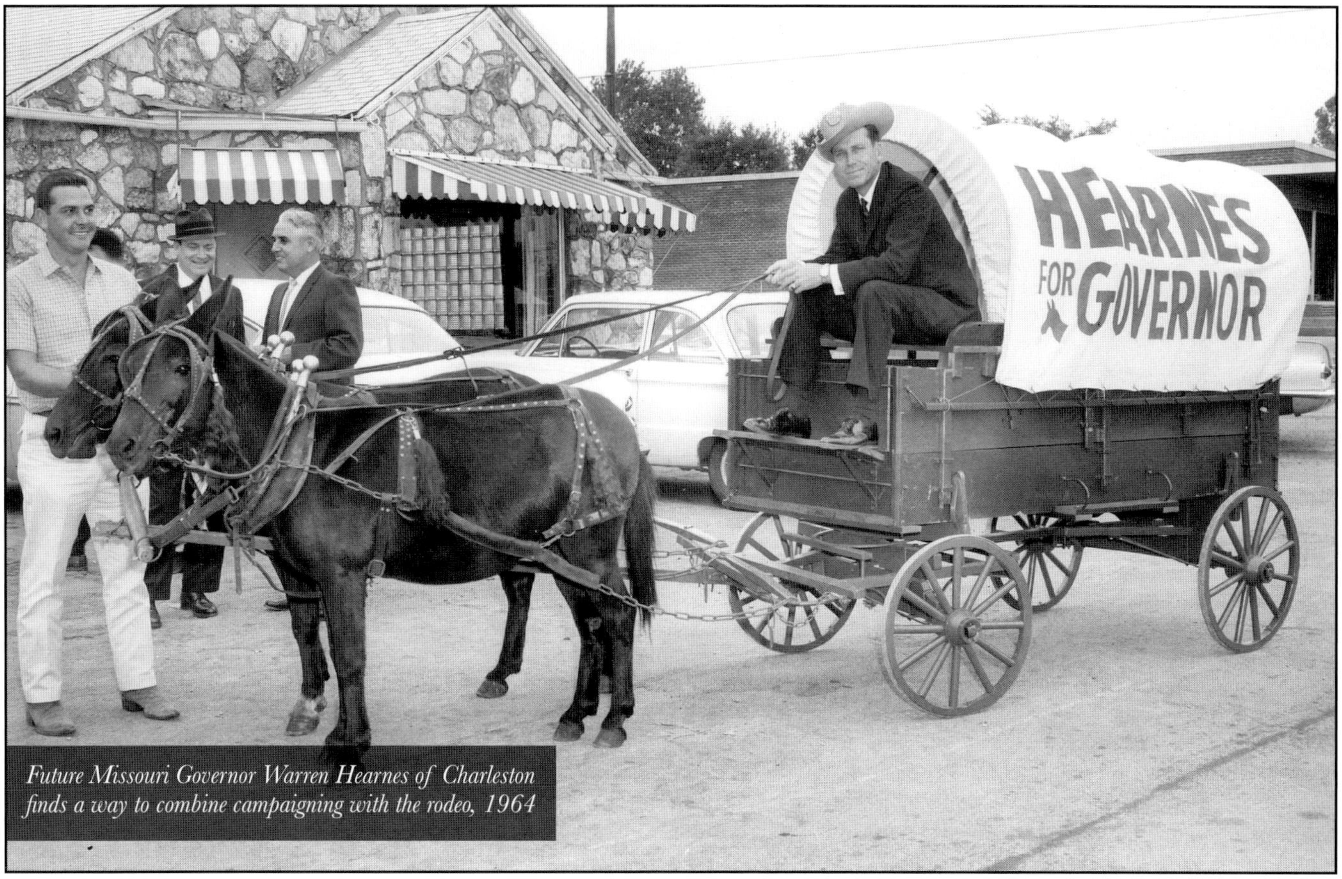

Future Missouri Governor Warren Hearnes of Charleston finds a way to combine campaigning with the rodeo, 1964

Larry Lasater and Jeff Sutton preparing the rodeo arena for the grand entry, 1992.

Sometimes rodeo clowns not only have to protect cowboys from bulls, but other clowns as well. In this sequence, the bull takes down clown Greek Ellick before other clowns distract him so their bullfighting partner can make a safe getaway.

Bullfighters Mike Johnson and Jimmy Anderson distract this bull so the cowboy can ride another day.

A view of the grand entry from ground level, inside the arena.

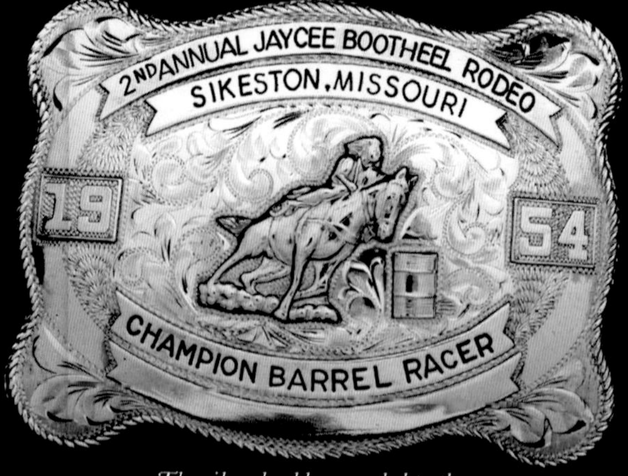

The silver buckle awarded to the barrel racing champion, 1954.

Bill Deane, Mark Deane, David Bizzell, Tony Powell, David Vaughn, Ken Lape, Bud Werner, David Hough - 1982 Grounds Crew.

Police chief Arthur Bruce with another "kidnapped family" at the El Capri Motel. From the Loy Baugher collection.

Jaycees and friends enjoy a break from their work in 1992: L-R: Matt Vowels, Julie Harper, Craig Stoker and Felecia Blanton.

Jaycees and friends discuss 1992 rodeo preparations over a beverage. L-R: Lisa Polivick, Linda Bridger, Danny Bridger, Jimmy Gipson and Lynn Gipson.

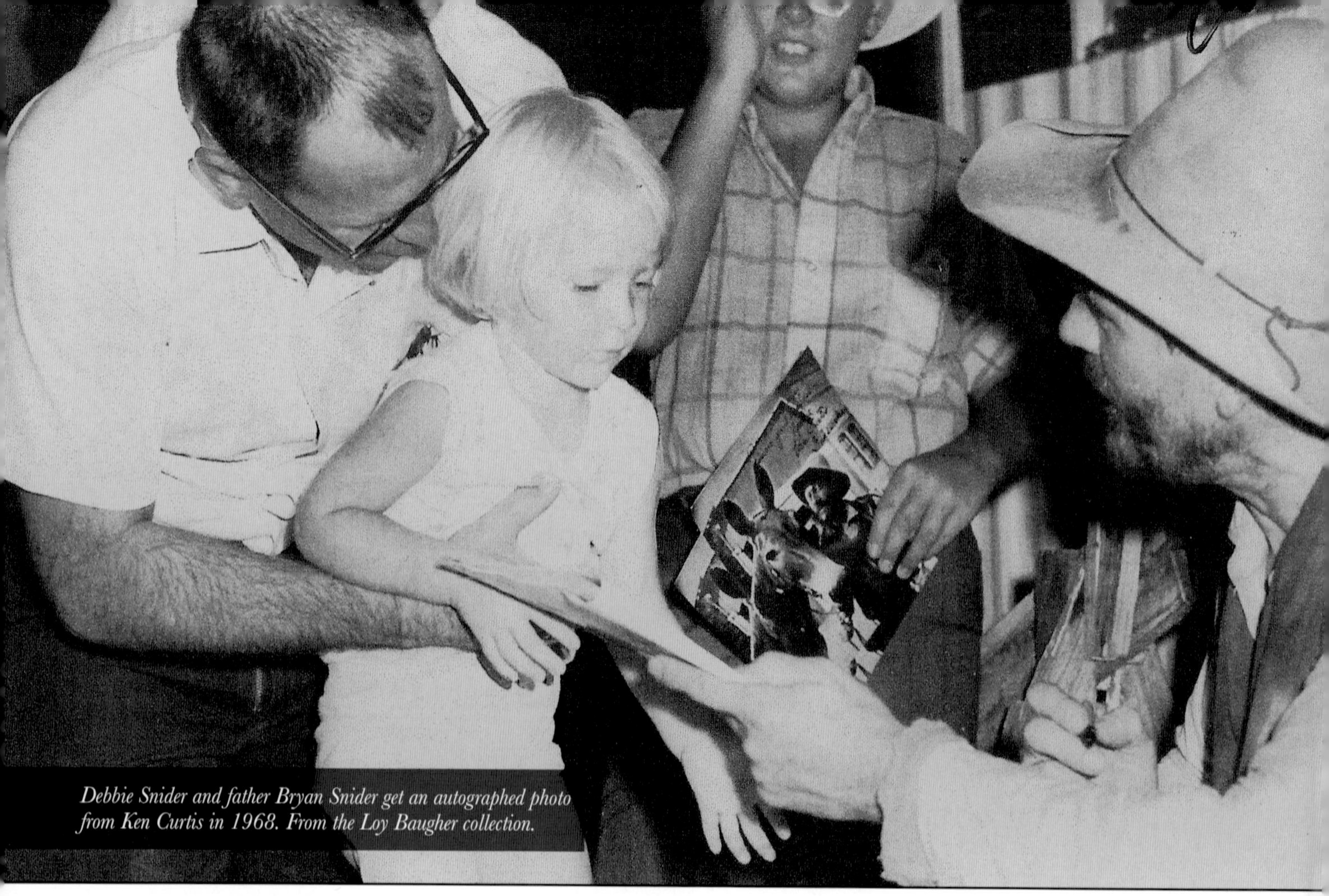

Debbie Snider and father Bryan Snider get an autographed photo from Ken Curtis in 1968. From the Loy Baugher collection.

Jeff Sutton preps the rodeo arena surface with a tractor and scratcher, 1992.

Festus Haggen (Ken Curtis) finds himself in a "Mexican Standoff" with "Bad Yogi," owned by James and Geneva Kincade of Malden, 1971. From the Loy Baugher collection.

Jaycees gather around a campfire for an organizational meeting, late 1950s. From the Loy Baugher collection.

Rick Young

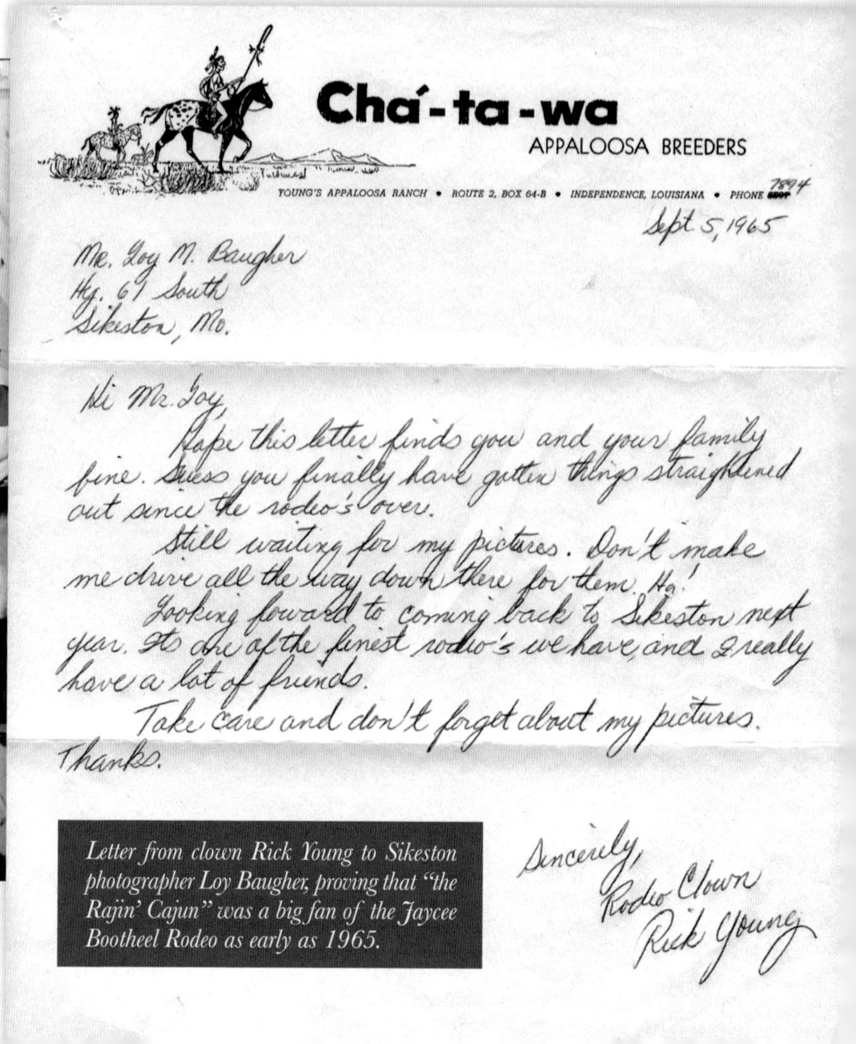

Chá-ta-wa
APPALOOSA BREEDERS
YOUNG'S APPALOOSA RANCH • ROUTE 2, BOX 64-B • INDEPENDENCE, LOUISIANA • PHONE 7894

Sept. 5, 1965

Mr. Loy M. Baugher
Hy. 61 South
Sikeston, Mo.

Hi Mr. Loy,

Hope this letter finds you and your family fine. Guess you finally have gotten things straightened out since the rodeo's over.

Still waiting for my pictures. Don't make me drive all the way down there for them. Ha!

Looking foward to coming back to Sikeston next year. Its one of the finest rodeo's we have, and I really have a lot of friends.

Take care and don't forget about my pictures. Thanks.

Sincerely,
Rodeo Clown
Rick Young

Letter from clown Rick Young to Sikeston photographer Loy Baugher, proving that "the Rajin' Cajun" was a big fan of the Jaycee Bootheel Rodeo as early as 1965.

A rodeo clown takes five to pose for a picture with a future cowboy and cowgirl.

Bronc rider Jason Havens rides duiring slack, 2012.

General Co-Chairman David Vaughn (right) discusses work in 1992. L-R: Jon Forrest, Dan Beussink, General Chairman Gary Lasater and Vaughn.

Because of the quantity of entrants, some rodeo competition is held before the gates open to the public. Tie-down roper Chris Neal lassos his calf, 2012.

2010 Miss Jaycee Bootheel Rodeo Lindsey Riley, followed by Junior Miss Rodeo Rachel Lowe, ride in the grand entry.

Todd Lenderman and Zach Fayette

Local women and children in front of Rodeo Headquarters. From the Loy Baugher collection.

Fans surround the stage as they await the night's entertainment.

Bull rider Chris Roundy comes out of the chute during slack competition, 2012.

Governor Jay Nixon addresses the rodeo crowd, 2012

Bulldogger Ben Shofner gets his steer by both horns in 2012.

Clint Cooper's leaves the saddle as his horse digs in during slack competition, 2012.

Young fans get up close and personal with Michael "Little Joe Cartwright" Landon, 1970. From the Loy Baugher collection.

A palomino shows off for the spectators during the rodeo parade, late 1950s. From the Loy Baugher collection.

Carolyn Pike, Larry Miller, Carolyn Miller, Debbie Keenan and Sandy Lape practice the Jaycee version of tailgating, 1992.

Mike Bohannon is congratulated by fellow Exhausted Roosters after receiving the 2010 Art Saunders Founder's Award.

L-R: 2012 Novelties Chairman Heath McGill, Jerome Henson, Blake Walker, Paul Myers, Terry Jones and David Teachout.

2012 General Chairman Chris Deen presents Jim Gleason, president of New Wave Communications, with the 2012 Rodeo Spirit Award.

Chester Kordahl of the American Legion (with bucket) and other members of the concessions crew at work preparing hamburgers for hungry rodeo fans.

Roy Rogers and Dale Evans pose with members of the SEMO Shrine Mounted Patrol. From the Loy Baugher collection.

INDEX

Numbers

4-H Club 65

A

Acord, Cliff 89
Acord, J.R. 89
Acord, June Ellen 89
Acord, Mildred 89
Acord, Ralph 89
Adams, Doc 31, 102
Adams, Lloyd 87
Adams, Mike 66
Adams, Pete 18
Adams, Richard 68
Adams, Samantha Star 97
Adams, Sharon 87
Adkins, Trace 152
Adkisson, Joshua Allan 97
Alabama 55, 151
Alcorn, Dale 16
Aldean, Jason 158
Aldrich, Ed 23, 68
Allan, Gary 151
All-Around Award 20, 81
Allen, Rex 32, 34, 92, 104, 105
Alphin, Kenneth "Big Kenny" 161
Alsup, Ross 21
American Bullfighting 52
American Cancer Society 170
American Legion 37, 188
American Quarter Horse Association 76
American Red Cross 65
America's Got Talent 49
Anderson, Bill 166
Anderson, Jimmy 8, 73, 86, 177
Anderson, John 125
Anderson, Keith 156
Anderson, Kirstie 97
Andrews, Burr 12, 13, 14, 16, 17, 19, 20
Andrews, Sam 17
Arabian Horse Journal 44
Arness, James 12, 25, 26, 27, 28, 29, 31, 101, 108, 109, 168
Atkins, Rodney 162
Aufdenberg, Alice 97
Aufdenberg, Jeanne 97
Autry, Gene 24, 111, 126

B

Bad Yogi 181
Bail, Jessie 87
Baker, Joe 30
Baker, Tom 95
Bandy, Moe 123
Bareback Horse of the Year Award 74, 84
Bareback Riding 74, 18, 77, 79, 82, 142
Barnett, Amanda 96, 97
Barrel Racing 18, 75, 82, 83, 100, 178
Baugher, Loy 5, 11, 16, 21, 22, 27, 28, 30, 33, 34, 35, 37, 38, 40, 52, 63, 69, 72, 82, 89, 91, 92, 93, 94, 95, 96, 99, 102, 104, 108, 109, 111, 136, 164, 165, 167, 168, 169, 171, 179, 180, 181, 182, 184, 186, 188
Baugher Studio, The 72
Beach Boys 45, 122
Beal, Clem 28, 68
Beaver, Joe 75
Beck, Daniel 2, 7, 56, 64, 66, 68
Beck, Lee 7, 51, 61, 62, 68, 70
Bedell, Brian 61
Bee, Molly 107, 166
Belvin, Leah 97
Benny, Claude 68
Bentley, Dierks 155
Berry, Marty 97
Bess, Bill 17, 21, 68, 172
Bethell, Dan 21
Beussink, Dan 61, 68, 183
"Beverly Hillbillies, The" 37, 41, 107
Big and Rich 150, 156, 161
Bird, G. David 68
Bird, Jalonda Kay 96
Bizzell, David 178
Black, Clint 145
Black, Phil 68, 71
Black, Zac 66
Blair, Jessica 97
Blake, Amanda 30, 31, 72, 99, 102, 108
Blanton, Felecia 179
Blanton, Joe 68
Bleacher Collapse 38
Blocker, Dan 33, 105, 109
Blodgett, Missouri 12, 69
Bloemer, Heather 97
Blumenberg, Charles 68
Boardman, Harold 13, 14
Bohannon, Don 68
Bohannon, Michael 60, 71, 187
"Bonanza" 33, 38, 40, 105, 109, 110
Bonner, Jim (J.W.) 15, 23, 68
Boone, Debbie 41
Boone, Pat 41
Borders, Chad 96
Borraabby 43, 44, 45
Bouckaert, Shaye 97
Boyd, Neal E. 48, 49
Boy Scouts 65
Bozo the Clown 23, 24
Bradley, Brian 68
Bradley, Bud 63
Branum, Bailey 97
Brazil, Trevor 12
Breakaway Roping 82
Bridger, Danny 61, 179
Bridger, Ken 68
Bridger, Kenny 48, 88
Bridger, Linda 179
Bridges, Glen 33, 94, 96
Bridges, Virginia 96
Brinegar, Paul 35, 103, 171
British Invasion 40
Brock, Judy 96
Bronc Riding 18, 74, 79, 80, 89, 183
Brooks, Garth 12, 53, 134, 140, 143, 156, 163
Browder, Bill 122
Brown, Ben 97
Brown, Bonnie 118
Brown, Jim Ed 118
Brown, Maxine 118
Bruce, Arthur 21, 72, 179
Bryan, Luke 159
Bryan, Micah 97
Bucking Bull of the Year Award 84
Bulldogging (Steer Wrestling) 18, 19, 77, 78, 89, 185
Bullfighting 52, 176, 177
Bull of the Year Award 74, 84
Bull Riding 18, 24, 74, 76, 79, 82, 83, 85, 86, 100, 123, 143, 185
Burch, Bill 24, 33, 34, 35, 39, 52, 68, 70, 164
Burch, Steven 68, 164
Burnette, Smiley 24, 25, 101
Burns, Jethro 106
Burns, Keith 153
Bush, Kristian 157
Butler, Charles 172
Byrd, Tracy 141

C

Cagle, Chris 153
Cain, Karen 95, 96
Calf Roping 18, 78, 79, 82, 89, 100
Cannon, Paul 15
Cartwright, Ben 33
Cartwright, Hoss 33
Cartwright, Joe 38
Cash, Johnny 110
Cashmer, Morgan 97
Cattle Baron Seats 52
Causey, Joey 95, 96
Center Street 43, 48
Cerebral Palsy 43, 44, 45, 48, 65, 114
Cervi, Sherry 75
Chandler, Leslie 13
Charles, Ray 127
Charleston, Missouri 159, 175
Charlie Daniels Band, The 133
Chasteen, Paige 97
Chesney, Kenny 147
Chesnutt, Mark 135, 136
Childs, Mark 13, 14, 68
Church, Eric 157
Clampett, Jed 37
Clarkson, Kelly 159
Clark, Tammy 94, 96, 169
Clark, Terri 144
Clay, Rob 68
Clay Walker 148
Cline, Patsy 110
Coe, David Allan 141
Collie, Mark 137
Committee of the Year Award 54
Community Counseling Center 65
Confederate Railroad 141
Conlee, John 121
Conley, Earl Thomas 133
Conrad, Robert 36, 107
Conway, Marshall 68
Conway, Mike 68
Cook, Ann Marie 97
Cook, Jeff 151
Cook, Lindsey Renee 97
Cooper, Allen 15
Cooper, Clay O'Brien 75
Cooper, Clint 185
Coors "Man in the Can" Award 75, 85, 86
Copeland, Greg 66, 97
Corbin, Easton 163
Corey, Clint 74
Cornelius, Helen 118
Cotton Carnival 37
Cousin Carl 166
Cowger, Kyleigh 97
Cowger, Mallory 97
Cox, Buddy 68
Cox, Craig 66, 173
Cox, Jay 66
Cox, Jim 57, 68, 70
Cox, Jimmy 68
Cox, Nathan 56, 64, 66
Coyote Hills Rodeo Company 169
Crader, Cal 55, 56, 64, 66, 68
Crider, Chantelle 96
Criss, Tami 97
Crosby, Chester 17
Crow, Chad 68
Crumpecker, Billie 20, 94, 96
Curb, Mike 162
Currington, Billy 55
Curtis, Ken 40, 108, 180, 181
Cutting Horse Event 18

D

Dace, Muzzy 16
Dalton, John 33
Dame, Melinda 97
"Daniel Boone" 37, 88, 109
Daniels, Charlie 133, 150
Davis, Taylor 97
Deane, Bill 178
Deane, Mark 178
Dean, Ira 153
Deen, Chris 56, 64, 66, 68, 187
Dempster, Robert 17
"Dennis the Menace" 33, 41, 105
DeRoush, Charlie 63
DeWitt, Bradley 96
Dewitt, Lew 119
Dexter 16, 88
Diamond Rio 144
Diffie, Joe 138
Dillon, Matt 25, 26, 27, 28, 101, 102, 108
Dittmer, Jillian Lee 97
Dobbs, Quail 75
Dockins, Brad 66
Dolan, David 68, 71
Dottie West 45, 47, 48, 49, 50, 114, 124
Douglas, Patrick 68
Dover, Brian 66
Drake, Matt 56, 64, 66, 68
Drury, Emma 97
Duncan, Andrea 97
Dunking of the Jaycees 15, 23
Dunn, Rex 169
Durant, Don 34, 102, 165, 167
Dye, Christopher 96
Dye, Tanner 13

E

Easton, Landy 97
East Prairie, Missouri 16
Eastwood, Clint 35, 103
Eastwood, Kris 64, 66
Ebsen, Buddy 37, 41, 107
Edward, Jim 118
Edwards, Tina 96
Eftink, Nathan 66
El Capri Motel 21, 179
Ellen, June 89
Elliott, Bill 83
Elliott, Wild Bill 83
Elms, Chick 62
Engram, Jan 96
Estes, Milford 13, 14
Eudy, Stan 68
Evans, Dale 41, 111, 166, 188
Evans, Sara 154, 155
Exhausted Roosters 56, 57, 69, 187
Exile 129

F

Fairchild, Karen 158
Famous Bulls:
  #68 84
  King Kong 84, 87
  No. 105 84
Famous Horses:
  Trigger 111
Faris, Ashton 97
Farrington, J.W. 78
Fayette, Zach 66, 173, 184
Ferrell, Chase 62, 97
Ferrell, Frank 30, 98
Ferrell, Jordi 97
Ferrell, Steve 61
Ferrell, William "Bill" 98
Fetters, Jacob 97
Fetters, Kyle 97
First Edition 42, 113, 114
Fister, Tamara 96
Fitzsimmons, Jay 96
Forrest, Jon 183
Francis, Donald 31
Francis, Ralph 31
Fraser, Dennis 68
Freeland, Terry 68
Freeman, Charline 96
French, Victor 110
Frizzell, David 124
Frizzell, Lefty 100, 124, 132
Frost, Lane 12, 75
Fuchs, Bob 68

G

Gadberry, Luke 97
Garner, Matthew 96
Garrett, Shannon 68
Gatlin Brothers, The 48, 115
Gatlin, Larry 45, 48, 115
Gatlin, Steve 115
Gay 90s Village 32

Gay, Donnie 12, 74
Gayle, Sea 163
Gentry, Teddy 151
Gentry, Troy 149
Gilley, Mickey 123
Gilliland, Myra Baugher 72
Gilmore, Tim 68
Gilmore, Weber 17
Gipson, Jimmy 54, 68, 71, 179
Gipson, Lynn 179
Girl Scouts 65
Girl's Rodeo Association (GRA) 82
Glaus, Trey 173
Gleason, Jim 187
Glenn, Doug 66
Golladay, Bill 16
Goode, Chester 31, 102, 108
Gordon, Artemus 107
Graham, Kenny 66, 173
Grand Entry 19, 51, 54, 98, 165, 173, 174, 175, 177, 184
Grand Ole Opry 100, 110, 128, 152, 155
Gray Ladies 94
Gray, Micayla 97
Greased Pig-Catching Contest 36, 164
Great Lakes Circuit Best Footing 54
Great Lakes Circuit Best Ground 54
Great Lakes Circuit Rodeo of The Year 54
Greene, Lorne 33, 105
Greenfield, Wyatt 97
Green, Lorne 33, 109
Green, Pat 161, 162
Green, Tom 54, 68, 71, 169
Greenwood, Lee 124
Griffin, Doug 68, 70
Grimes, Mark 66
Grojean, Jason 66
Grojean, Theon 12, 13, 14
Groves, Pat 13, 14
"Gunsmoke" 25, 27, 28, 30, 31, 40, 72, 99, 101, 102, 108, 109, 172

H

Hadley, Tom 74
Haggard, Merle 52, 120
Haggen, Festus 40, 136, 181
Hagy, Shori Lynn 96
Hale, Bill 68, 70
Hall, Betty 60
Hall, Dell 51, 60, 83, 84
Hall, Jeff 66
Hall, Jonathan 66
Hall, Kristen 157
Hall, Shelly 51, 60, 84
Hall, Tom T. 116
Hamby, Jess Jr. 16
Hamm, Cynthia 96
Hampton, Bruce 68, 70
Hampton, Jessica 97
Hamra, Mamie 60
Hanschen, Leslie 97
Hanselmar, Corey 97
Happy Trails 111
Harmon, Larry 23
Harper, Chris 68
Harper, John 29, 30, 33, 34, 39, 68, 70, 168
Harper, Julie 179
Harris Drug Store 20
Harris, Ed 16
Harris, Jodi 97
Harris, L.A. 20
Haunted Hayride 64
"Have Gun Will Travel" 40
Havens, Jason 183
Hawkins, Nathan 68
Hawthorne, George 61
Hayes, Wade 145
Hay, Jeff 66
Haynes, Homer 106
Hazer 78
Hearnes, Warren 175
Heckemeyer, Joe 61
Heckert, Joey 66
Hedemen, Tuff 75
Henley, Bob 70
Henley, Rob 15
Henson, Jerome 66, 187
Herndon, Ty 150
Heuring, John 66
Holliday, Pistol 18
Holsinger, Harry 25, 26, 32
Homer and Jethro 106
Hootie and the Blowfish 159
Horn, A.J. 66
Horse Breeds:
Arabian 43, 44, 45, 47, 48, 114
Barrel Horse 83
Bronc 10, 18, 22, 74, 76, 77, 79, 80, 82, 89, 183
Bucking Horse 83
Palomino 22, 88, 111, 186
Quarter Horse 76

Hough, David 61, 68, 71, 73, 164, 178
Hough, Morgan 62
Hough, Vivian 96
House of Refuge 65
Howard, Gerald 21, 168
Howard, Harlan 155
Huff, Bill 13, 14
Huff, Vivian 95
Humphries, Jill Ann 96
Hutchison, Eric 96

I

Irvin, Andrew 66
Ivey, Melinda Ann 96

J

Jackson, Debbie 97
James, Charmayne 75
James, Justin 97
James, Maverick 97
Jardine, Al 45
Jaycee Bootheel Rodeo Parade 17, 18, 50, 90, 92, 93, 94, 98, 186
Jaycee Bootheel Rodeo Sponsors and Partners:
Coors Brewing Company 52, 75, 85, 86, 169
Dodge 52, 82
Justin Boots 54
Winston 52
Jaycee Wives 27, 43, 88, 94
Jaynes, Ronda 96
Jobe, Kevin 97
"Johnny Ringo" 34, 102, 103, 105, 167
Johnson, Barry 56, 64, 66, 68
Johnson, Douglas 96
Johnson, Jamey 160
Johnson, Matt 66
Johnson, Mike 60, 86, 177

Photo courtesy of Lynda Warren.

Johnson, Steve 73
Johnston, Steve 61
Jones, George 100, 110, 127, 138, 143, 156
Jones, Lewis 13
Jones, Louis 12, 13, 14, 17, 23, 31, 68, 69
Jones, Paul 17
Jones, Terry 66, 187
Jordan, Amanda 97
Junior Miss 94, 96, 97, 136, 184
Junior Miss Rodeo 94, 96, 97, 136, 184
Justin Boots Firm Footing Award 54
Justin Cowboy Crisis Fund 65

K

Keasler, Mike 95, 96
Keenan, Alan 68, 70, 164
Keenan, Debbie 186
Keith, Toby 146
Keller, Jenny 97
Kelly Schools 65
Kelso, Cory Lee 96
Kendall, Jeannie 115
Kendall, Royce 115
Kendalls, The 115
Kendell, Joseph 97
Kennedy, John F. 40
Kenny Rogers Children's Center 47, 48, 49, 64, 115
Benefit Concerts 45, 48, 49, 115
Charity Walk 48
Telethon 48, 49, 65
Kenny Rogers Day 45
Kentucky Fried Chicken 52
Kerby, Andrew 66
Kershaw, Sammy 138
Kidnapping 21
Kilgore, Mikell 96
Kincade, Geneva 181
Kincade, James 181
King, Don 130
King, Ed 160
King, Martin Luther Jr. 40
Kingshighway 92
Kinney Brothers Rodeo 84
Kinney, Cotton 84
Kinney, Edward 84
Kirby, Butch 84
Kirby, Sandy 62
Kirby, Ted 18
Klein, Jean 16
Klueppel, Dave 66, 170
Kluesner, Samantha 97
Knight, Dustin 66
Knox, Kenny 36
Kobiske, Dawn Baugher 72
Kohlfeld Distributing 169
Kohlfeld, Mike 169
Kordahl, Chester 188
Kragen, Ken 42, 44
Kuehn, Brandon 66

L

LaBrot, Brenda 88
LaBrot, Jim 88
LaBrot, Langston 88
LaBrot, Mike 88
LaBrot, Vikki 97
Lambert, Doug 60
Lambert, Leah 97
Lambert, Steve 71
Lambert, Sydney 97
Landon, Michael 38, 40, 109, 110
Landon, Michael "Little Joe Cartwright" 186
Lane Frost 12, 75
Lape, Dan 51, 57, 61, 65, 68, 70, 164
Lape, Deke 68
Lape, Ken 68, 71, 178
Lape, Sandy 186
Lape, Terry 70, 164
LaPlant, Rik 53, 61, 71, 68
Lasater, Gary 8, 61, 68, 169, 183
Lasater, Larry 175
Lasater, Sarah 8
Lawrence, Charles Wade 97
Lawrence, Tracy 137, 139, 140
Lawson, Andrew 66
Lawson, Marcie 170
Ledbetter, Bryn 66
LeDoux, Chris 74, 142, 143
Lee, Brenda 113, 118
Lee, Johnny 123
Lee, Terry 164
Legion Park 15
Leible, Marc 66
Lenderman, Todd 184
Lester, Laura 96
Lewis, Bill 37, 166
Lewis, Kristi 96
Lewis, Lauri 97
Lewis, Rich 166
Lindsey, Ryan 64, 66, 68
Linzenbee, Robin Denise 96
Lions International 49
Little Big Town 157, 158
Little House on the Prairie 110
Little League Football 65
Little, Lori 97
Little Miss Western 33, 34, 94, 95, 96, 97, 118, 169
Little Mr. Western 33, 94, 95, 96, 97, 169
Littleton, Justin 66, 173
Littleton, Larry 61
Litzelfelner, Wendy 96
Logan, Pete 74
Loggins, Kenny 131
Lomax, Steve 71
Lonestar 149, 150, 161
Long, Jeff 60
Love, Tommie Ray 96
Lowe, Rachel 97, 184
Lowry, Charles 81
Lucy, Jordan Tyler 97
Lund, Larry 15
Lynn, Doo 125
Lynn, Loretta 124, 125
Lynyrd Skynyrd 158, 160

M

Mabury, Shayn 66
Mahan, Larry 74
Make-a-Wish Foundation 46
Malden, Missouri 181
Malone 18, 92, 94
Malone Avenue 18
Malone Park 94
Malone Street 92
Malvern, Arkansas 14
Mamas and the Papas, The 157
Mandrell, Barbara 39, 41, 110
Marshall, John 68
Marshall, Lee Van 96
Marshall, Mike 68, 169
Marsh, Joe 68
Martin, Ross 108
Matt Barnes Memorial Scholarship 65
Matthews, Chris 68
Matthews, Farrah 96
Matthews, Kathy 96
Matthews, Matt 55, 68
McBride, Martina 140
McCall, Elena 97
McCall, Mattie 97
McCann, Alton 13, 14, 68
McClendon, Joshua 97
McDonald, Bradley 96
McDonald, Brittany 97
McDonald, Brooke 97
McDonald, John 62
McGill, Charles 38, 39, 57, 61, 68, 70, 111, 164
McGill, Heath 66, 187
McMahon, Ed 130
McMullin, Patti 96
McNew, Corey 68
McSpadden, Clem 74, 75
McTigue, Marshall 66
Mellons, Ken 142
Melton, Hannah 88
Melton, Jake 88
Melton, Paula 88
Melton, Sherry 94, 97
Memphis Park Commission 15, 16
Menz, Brian 68
Menz, Kaci 97
Menz, Misty 97
Merideth, Ross 6, 66, 68
Merideth, Ryan 56, 66, 68, 170
Merideth, Tim 60, 68
Messina, Jo Dee 148
Miles, Jeff 68
Miller, Carolyn 186
Miller, Devin 88
Miller, Larry 57, 61, 63, 68, 70, 164, 186
Miller, Mark 46
Millhouse, Frog 24
Milsap, Ronnie 116
Mims, Jennifer Denise 96
Miss Jaycee Bootheel Rodeo 96, 184
Missouri Delta Medical Center 31, 48, 64, 65
Regional Dialysis Center 65
Miss Rodeo America 76
Mitchell, Bob 13, 14, 16, 68, 172
Mitchell, Jack 68
Mitchell, Jaycee Charles 103
Mitchell, Rob 68
Mitchell, Todd 96
Mock, Dale 66
Moll Printing 48
Montgomery, Christy 49
Montgomery, Eddie 149
Montgomery Gentry 148, 149
Montgomery, John Michael 147, 148, 149
Montgomery, Richard 49
Moody, Walt 66
Moore, Justin 163
Morehouse, Missouri 20, 94
Morgan, Craig 156
Morgan, Freddie 17
Morgan, George 137
Morgan, Lorrie 137, 138
Morton, J.T. 66
Mountaineers 19, 100
Mountaineers of Memphis 19
Moyers, Jana 96
Mt. Vernon, Illinois 87
Murphey, Michael Martin 126
Murphy, David Lee 146
Murphy, Luther 28
Murray, Ty 75
Myer, Lance 66
Myers, Paul 66, 187
Myrick, John Tyler 97
Myrick, Jordan 97

N

Nabors, Jim 37, 38, 41, 106, 169
Nashville, Tennessee 44, 55, 114, 115, 116, 124, 125, 130, 133, 140, 146, 150, 152, 153, 154, 155, 156, 160, 163
National Finals Rodeo 11, 54, 55, 74, 75, 82, 84
National Guard Armory 17
National Jaycee 65
Neal, Chris 184
Neal, Lad 66
Nelson, Willie 53, 132, 162
Nester, Kim 97
Nettles, Jennifer 157
New Christy Minstrels 42, 113
Newell, Preston 97
Newfield, Heidi 153
New Madrid, Missouri 16
Newton, Avery 97
Newton, Don 68
Newton, Kylyn 97
New Wave Communications 187
Niemann, Jerrod 162
Nixon, Jay 49, 185
None 96
North Ingram Street 30, 101
North, Jay 33, 41, 105
Norton, Dan 68
Norton, Jerry 60
Nowell, Allison 97
Nunnelee, Alice 40
Nunnelee, Tom 15, 35, 40, 41, 42, 43, 44, 45, 57, 65, 70, 97

O

O'Bannon Family Care Center 65
O'Brian, Hugh 34, 72, 103
Old, Shad 13, 14, 15, 16, 17, 92
One Plaza Drive 48
Owen, Randy 151
Ozark Cowboys 100
Ozark Jubilee 24

P

Paisley, Brad 152, 157
Palmer, Katie 97
Paragould, Arkansas 16
Parker, Fess 37, 109
Parma, Missouri 33, 94
Parris, Jessica 97
Parton, Dolly 150, 152
Pasaka, Don 13, 14
Pat Boone Family, The 111
Pate, Deanne 97
Patterson, Katie 97
Patterson, Kelsy 97
Paul, Duncan 90
Paycheck, Johnny 39, 41, 110, 141
Paylor, Bill 13
Payne, Ron 56, 68
Perry, Kimberly 162
Perryman, Jimmie 18
Perry, Neil 162
Perry, Reid 162
Phillips, Sam 100
Pierce, Todd 61, 68
Pike, Carolyn 186
Pike, Ed 50, 61, 68, 70
Pine Street 30
Pobst, Ralphie 66
Polhamus, Boyd 170
Polivick, Lew 68, 71
Polivick, Lisa 179
Porter, Bob 15, 33, 68
Porter, Christopher 97
Porter, Michael 96
Pounds, Jason 66, 68, 170
Powell, Billy 160
Powell, Tony 178
Pratt, Kristen 97
Presson, Catherine 97
Professional Rodeo Cowboys Association (PRCA) 3, 11, 12, 14, 31, 54, 55, 57, 58, 74, 75, 76, 77, 78, 81, 83, 84, 86
Pro Rodeo Hall of Fame 3, 74, 75, 76, 83, 84, 85, 86, 106, 110, 114, 116, 118, 119, 120, 122, 125, 126, 127, 134, 160
Puchbauer, Matt 68
Puckett, Bill 13, 14
Puckett Field 30
Pyle, Artimus 160
Pyle, Gomer 37, 38, 41, 106

R

Rafter H Rodeo Company 51, 60, 84
Rains, Ashtyn 97
Ramada Inn 43
Randy Travis 130
Rascal Flatts 157
Raven, Eddy 126
Rawhide 35, 40, 103, 104, 171
Raye, Collin 149, 150
Ray, Kaitlin 97
Regional Center 48
Reid, Don 119
Reid, Harold 119
REO Speedwagon 158
Restless Heart 131, 132
Rhodes Show, The 90
Rhodes, Slim 19, 24, 100
Rhodes, Speck 90
Richey, Tom 48
Rich, John 161
Ricochet 146
"Rifleman, The" 40
Riley, Lindsey 97, 184
Rimes, LeeAnn 113
Ringo, Johnny 34
Roberts, Bill IV 96
Roberts, Ken 83
Robins, Marty 126
Robison, Jim 81
Rodeo Clowns 8, 18, 46, 52, 72, 73, 75, 83, 85, 86, 94, 108, 171, 176, 182, 183
Rodeo Headquarters 184
Rodeo Pageant 20, 94
Rodeo Queen 20, 41, 94, 95, 96, 97
Rodeo Spirit Award 187
Rodeo Week 12, 17, 55, 57, 58, 87, 94, 171
Rogers, Dusty 41
Rogers, Kenny 42, 43, 44, 45, 47, 48, 49, 53, 64, 65, 88, 113, 114, 115, 129, 150
Rogers, Roy 41, 111, 166, 188
"Rollin" 42, 113
Ross, Ethan 88
Rossington, Gary 160
Ross, Vikki 88
Roundy, Chris 185
Rowland, John 68
Rowland, Linda 94, 96
Roy Rogers Show, The 111
Rucker, Darius 159
Rudy Gatlin 115
Russell, Kitty 31, 102
Rustic Rock Inn 18
Ryan, Dixie 44

S

Saddle Bronc Riding 76, 79, 80, 89
Salcedo Road 90
Sapp, Bill 36
Satterfield, Jamie 97
Saunders, Art 3, 11, 12, 14, 23, 31, 69, 70, 71, 187

Sawyer Brown 46, 130, 156
Schaffer, J.D. 68
Schell, Gail 96
Scherer, Teresa 41, 95, 96
Schlapman, Kimberly 158
Scott County Milling Company 16
Scott County Sheriff's Posse 3, 98
Scott County Young Democrats 17
Self, Ronald 97
SEMO District Fair 37
SEMO Shriners (Mounted Patrol) 3, 22, 98, 128, 188
Shadwick, Nelson 97
Sharp, Harry 18
Shelby, Christopher 97
Shelton, Amanda 97
Shelton, Blake 55, 154
Shelton, Helen 48
Shelton, Patrick 66
Shelton, Ricky Van 131
Shenandoah 134
Sheppard, T. G. 122
Sherman, Audra 96, 97
Shofner, Ben 185
Shoulders, Jim 74, 75
Shriner 128, 166
Shuffit's Nursing Home 94
Shuffitt, Mary 96
Sides, Jack 68
Sides, John 68
Sigmon, Woody 164
Sikes, Bill 13, 30, 168
Sikes, Steve 68
Sikeston Area Youth Baseball 65
Sikeston Bulldogs 36
Sikeston Cotton Oil Mill 92
Sikeston Country Club 13, 15, 32, 33
Sikeston Department of Public Safety 65
Sikeston Eagles 48
Sikeston Freshman Band 93
Sikeston High School Band 90
Sikeston High School Field House 45, 114
Sikeston Jaycee Bootheel Rodeo Corporation 33
Sikeston Jaycee Crawfish Boil 6, 64
Sikeston Little League 16, 30
Sikeston Municipal Airport 30, 33
Sikeston Nutrition Center/ Heritage House 65
Sikeston Oil Cotton Mill 18
Sikeston Police Department 16, 168
Sikeston Red Peppers 15, 18
Sikeston Senior High School 65
Sikeston Stags 16
Sikeston Swim Team 65
Sikeston United Way 65
Siler, Abbigayle 97
Silver Buckle Award 20, 167, 178
Sisk, Jay 68
Skaggs, Ricky 127, 128
Slack Competition 185
Slinkard, Paul 68
Smith, Brooke 97
Smith, Craig 96
Smith, Gary 61
Smith, Jonathan 110
Smith, Sandy 96
Snider, Bryan 180
Snider, Debbie 180
Snider, Dennis 66
Snider, Jayson 66
Snider, Michael 94, 96, 169
Snyder, Jayson 170
Sons of the Pioneers 41, 109, 111, 126
Sons of the Pioneers, The 41
Southeast Missouri State University 65
South Grade School 92
Spitzmiller, Sharon 96
Springfield, Missouri 24
Stafford, Austin 97
Stamp, Charles "Charlie" Jr. 44, 65, 68, 166
Standard-Democrat/Sikeston Standard/Daily Standard 7, 12, 13, 14, 15, 16, 18, 22, 24, 25, 26, 29, 33, 45, 53, 64
Staples, Katie 97
Statler Brothers, The 119
Steer Wrestling 77, 78
Steiner Rodeo Company 83, 84
Steiner, Tommy 22, 51, 74, 83, 84
Stevens, Ray 128
Stinett, Zach 97
St. Louis, Missouri 22, 161
Stock Contractors 3, 83
Stoker, Craig 179
Stokes, Crystal 97
Stone, Doug 135
Stone, Julie 97
Stone, Milburn 30, 31, 99, 102, 108, 172
Stoner, Lloyd F. II 68
Strait, George 125, 126
Strong City, Kansas 25
Stuart, Marty 140
Styx 158
Sugarland 157
Summers, Bob 16
Sutton, Jeff 54, 68, 175, 180
Sweet, Phillip 158
Swift, Taylor 113

T

Taylor, Britt 66
Taylor, Bruce 61
Taylor, Steve 68, 166
Teachout, David 57, 66, 68, 71, 187
Team Roping 55, 75, 78, 80, 82
Templeton, Craig 64, 66
Templeton, Reuben 21
The Band Perry 162
Thomason, Carla 96
Thomas, Sam 56, 64, 66
Thompson, Faye 13, 14
Thompson, Kelsey 97
Thomure, Ryan 66
Thornbrough, Heather 97
Thornbrough, Lindsey 97
Thornton, Linus 78
Three Rivers Community College 64, 65
Throop, Rebecca 97
Throop, Robby 97
Tibbs, Casey 74
Tie-Down Roping 80, 82, 173, 184
Tillis, Mel 42, 45, 48, 50
Tillis, Pam 137
Toby Keith 147
Todd, Stephanie 97
Todt, Courtney 97
Tonight Show, The 45
Top Five Outdoor Rodeo of the Year Award 54
Toton, Bridgett Danielle 97
Tough Enough to Wear Pink 76, 170
Towe, Shawn 66
Travis, Randy 129
Treece, Lloyd 166
Trickey, Patricia 97
Trick Pony 153
Tritt, Travis 134
Truman, Harry 27
Trum, Frannie 97, 136
Tucker, Ike 18
Tucker, Tanya 41, 113
Tull, Frank 13
Turnbow, Greg 68, 73
Tuttle, Randy 68
Twitty, Conway 122

U

Underwood, Carrie 152
"Urban Cowboy" 52, 123

V

Vanover, Sherry 97
Van Zant, Ronnie 160
Vasser, Phil 154
Vaughn, David 61, 68, 71, 73, 178, 183
Vaughn, Spence 97
VFW Memorial Park 12, 13, 14, 15, 16, 17, 19, 20, 25
Vietnam War 40, 120
Vinson, Christopher 96
Vinson, Jack 63
Vinton, Bobby 41, 112
Vowels, Matt 68, 73, 179

W

Wade, Kevin 71
Wade, Mark Adam 97
Wade, Whitney Lyn 97
Wagner, Dan 68
Wagner, Jeff 61
Wagon Train 40
Walker, Blake 66, 187
Walker, Clay 142
Wallace, Conner 97
Wallace, Harold 18, 21
Walls, Charles 68
Walls, Charlie 61
Walters, Ken 15, 68, 81
Ward, Kevin 61, 68, 73
Warf, Jim 15
Warren, Lynda 59, 68, 73, 190
Watkins, Nat 13
Watkins, Nate 14
Watts, Erin 97
Weaver, Dennis 30, 31, 99, 102, 108, 172
Weller, Lawrence 21
Werner, Ben 57
Werner, Bud 68, 164, 178
Werner, N.J. "Bud" 51, 57, 61, 65, 70
Wescoat, Stacey 95, 96
Westbrook, Jimi 158
West, Dottie 45, 47, 48
Western, Little Miss 96
Western, Little Mr. 96
West, James 107
West, Shelly 124
Wethington, Blake 66, 173
Wheeler, Onie 24, 100
Whitfield, Fred 75
Whitley, Keith 138
Whitten, Deene Ann 96
Wibbenmeyer, Bryce 66
Wibbenmeyer, Heather 170
Wibbenmeyer, Justin 56, 66, 68
Wild, Wild West, The 36
Wilkeson, Leon 160
Wilkins, Leigh Ann 97
Williams, Don 117
Williams, Hank Jr 120, 121, 158
Williams, Mamie 97
Williams, Tanner 97
Wills, Bob 126
Wilson, Bill 87
Wilson, Brad 15
Wilson, Dixie 87
Wilson, Gretchen 161
Wilson, Susan 96
Winchester, Joyce 170
Wirth, Beverly Ann 33, 34, 94, 96
Wishbone 35, 103
Wolfenkoehler, Brandy 97
Women's Professional Rodeo Association (WPRA) 3, 54, 75, 82
Wooley, Sheb 35, 103
World Finals Rodeo 82
Worley, Darryl 155, 156
Wrangler Million Dollar Silver Tour 55
Wrangler National Patriot Program 65
Wrather, Rich 68, 70
Wyatt, Al 28
Wyatt Earp 34, 72, 103

Y

Yant, Geary 50, 52, 61, 68, 70, 83
YMCA 64
Yokley, Gene 68
Young, Rick 60, 85, 86, 87, 170, 182
Yount, Amy 96

Z

Zaharopolis, Nick 48
Ziegenhorn, Bart 56, 64, 66, 68
Ziegenhorn, Dennis 41, 68
Ziegenhorn, Keith 68

Ya
Come